Endorsements for *Our God Loves Justice*

"The church today needs to learn from the courageous witness of Helmut Gollwitzer, and Travis McMaken's succinct and profound introduction to his thought is the book we have been waiting for."
David W. Congdon, University Press of Kansas

"There is simply no better introduction to this 'largely forgotten' and 'irregular' theologian's life and work than this very timely book."
Jason Goroncy, Whitley College

"Theology and church have much to learn from Gollwitzer today, and this book is an excellent place to begin."
George Hunsinger, Princeton Theological Seminary

"What makes this book truly distinctive is its broader concern to show the deep, vital, and abiding consonance between theological reflection and socialist politics."
Paul Dafydd Jones, University of Virginia

"This book is both deeply relevant and highly provocative."
Paul T. Nimmo, University of Aberdeen

"McMaken discovers Gollwitzer's contextual theology, and especially his theological criticism of capitalism, as 'an instructive example of how the church might respond to the challenges' of the present situation."
Andreas Pangritz, Rheinische Friedrich-Wilhelms-Universität Bonn

Our God Loves Justice

Our God Loves Justice

An Introduction to Helmut Gollwitzer

W. Travis McMaken

Fortress Press
Minneapolis

OUR GOD LOVES JUSTICE

An Introduction to Helmut Gollwitzer

Reprinted with permission: Helmut Gollwitzer, *Muß ein Christ Sozialist sein?*,
taken from: *Jenseits vom Nullpunkt? Christsein im westlichen*. Hrsg. Von Rudolf
Weckerlig. Stuttgart 1972, S. 151–170. © Kreuz Verlag part of Verlag Herder
GmbH.

Reprinted with permission of Scribner, a division of Simon & Schuster, Inc. from
The Christian Faith and Marxist Criticism of Religion, by Helmut Gollwitzer,
translated from the German by David Cairns. Copyright © 1970 by Saint Andrew
Press. Originally published as *Die marxistiche Religionskritik und der christliche
Glaube*. Tubingen, J. C. B. Mohr (Paul Siebeck), 1962. All Rights reserved.

Reprinted with permission of Westminster John Knox: Helmut Gollwitzer, *The
Existence of God as Confessed by Faith*, trans. James W. Leitch (Philadelphia:
Westminster Press, 1965). Helmut Gollwitzer, *An Introduction to Protestant
Theology*, trans. David Cairns (Philadelphia, PA: Westminster Press, 1982).

Cover image: The old charred cross at Coventry Cathedral ruins, Coventry, West
Midlands, England, UK /David Bagnall / Alamy Stock Photo
Cover design: Laurie Ingram

Print ISBN: 978-1-4514-8274-4
eBook ISBN: 978-1-5064-3852-8

The paper used in this publication meets the minimum requirements of American
National Standard for Information Sciences — Permanence of Paper for Printed
Library Materials, ANSI Z329.48-1984.

Manufactured in the U.S.A.

This book was produced using Pressbooks.com, and PDF rendering was done by
PrinceXML.

To Connor and Ryan,
A better world is both possible and necessary.
May you both work for it and live to see it.

Contents

Acknowledgments

This project has consumed more years than I expected it would. Helmut Gollwitzer proved to be a far richer resource, and a far more demanding taskmaster, than I could have anticipated—and I have only scratched the surface! Karl Barth, Gollwitzer's teacher, once described John Calvin as "a cataract" and "a primeval forest." He continued, "I lack completely the means, the suction cups, even to assimilate this phenomenon, not to speak of presenting it adequately. What I receive is only a thin little stream and what I can then give out again is only a yet thinner extract of this little stream."[1] This is how Gollwitzer has been for me. I could not have captured a small portion of this cataract, or mapped a corner of this primeval forest, without incurring a number of debts that it is my pleasure to repay here in some small way.

George Hunsinger first introduced me to Gollwitzer's theopolitical work, but it was my editor at Fortress Press, Michael Gibson, who first suggested that I write a book on Gollwitzer. I am very grateful that he did. This is my second book with Gibson and Fortress, and the entire Fortress staff remains a pleasure to work with. I am thankful especially for the help rendered by Gibson, Esther Diley, Michael Moore, Marissa Wold Uhrina, and Emily Holm.

Here, at Lindenwood University, I am grateful for the support I have received from my colleagues and administrators. Since Fall 2013, they have granted me reduced teaching loads so that I could dedicate more time to this project. I especially thank both President (emeritus) James Evans and President Michael Shonrock in this regard. Carl Hubenschmidt, master of interlibrary loans at Lindenwood's Butler Library,

---

1. Karl Barth and Eduard Thurneysen, *Revolutionary Theology in the Making: Barth-Thurneysen Correspondence, 1914–1925*, trans. James D. Smart (Richmond, VA: John Knox Press, 1964), 101.

ensured that all the obscure German texts that I needed found their way into my hands.

A number of Lindenwood folks also provided valuable assistance with the translations found in the appendices. Justine Pas, associate professor of English and associate dean of the School of Humanities, helped me to think through important questions of translation theory, one of her areas of specialization. Sydney Larson, an undergraduate student who worked for the School of Humanities during her time at Lindenwood, rendered valuable service working with transcriptions. Lara-Marie Winterhalter and Julia Geigle, both students working with the Lindenwood University Foreign Language lab and native German speakers, worked with me on some draft translations. Matthew Bruce, my colleague from the doctoral program at Princeton Theological Seminary and in the Lindenwood religion department during 2012–2015, graciously suffered frequent requests for aid in working through particularly knotty sentences.

Looking beyond Lindenwood, Andreas Pangritz of Evangelisch-Theologische Fakultät at the Rheinische Friedrich-Wilhelms-Universität Bonn graciously provided assistance through correspondence with questions pertaining to bibliography. He also carefully reviewed the complete manuscript and provided important feedback. I deeply appreciate the interest he took in this project. Benedikt Brunner, also of the Rheinische Friedrich-Wilhelms-Universität, conducted a final translation review and offered suggestions on my account of Gollwitzer's biography in chapter 2. I hold out some hope that he might be convinced to write a truly critical biography on Gollwitzer, which we desperately need. I owe special thanks to the Gollwitzer family, and especially to Christiane Gollwitzer and Jan Bergmann. They welcomed my work and facilitated my every request. Thanks also to Peter Beier and Maxi Schulenburg of the Evangelisches Zentralarchive in Berlin for fielding questions and working with me to secure various copyright permissions, especially for the photograph of Gollwitzer that appears on the book's cover. Francesca Bressan of Verlag Herder GmbH, as well as Reinhard Gaede and Anneke Bochow of the Bund der Religiösen Sozialistinnen und Sozialisten Deutschlands, were instrumental for my securing the necessary copyright permissions to publish the translations of Gollwitzer's works found in the appendices.

Two friends deserve my deepest thanks. Both Scott Jackson and David Congdon read the manuscript and provided insightful comments, which I have done my best to incorporate. David and I have worked as a theological community for many years and there are few aspects of my thought that have not, in some way, been decisively shaped in conversation with him. This volume is no different. If there is anything true, just, pure, commendable, excellent, or worthy of praise in this book, David deserves a share of the credit. Of course, all shortcomings are my own.

Finally, my family has been increasingly subjected to outbursts of amateur Marxist-socialist political analysis around the dinner table. So, I conclude by thanking them for their indulgence. This book is dedicated to my sons.

1

Reading Helmut Gollwitzer in America

Helmut Gollwitzer was a socialist. He was also a Christian. And perhaps the most surprising thing, at least for those of us deeply embedded in white American Christianity, is that Gollwitzer was a socialist precisely because he was a Christian. This book tries to make sense of that "precisely because" in Gollwitzer's life and thought.

Why Gollwitzer Today?

But why should there be such a book? Why write a book on Helmut Gollwitzer—Confessing Church pastor, prisoner of war in Russia, professor of theology, public intellectual, interreligious dialogue practitioner, and socialist critic of capitalism? And even more: why write a book on Helmut Gollwitzer *now*?

The Greek word *kairos* plays an important role in the New Testament. At the most basic lexical level, this term speaks of a moment of time. But it also frequently connotes not merely a moment of time in general, but a moment that is fitting with respect to a particular event. It is not just a moment of time, but the *right* moment in time. So we read in Romans 5:6: "For while we were still weak, at the right time [*kata kairon*] Christ died for the ungodly." Paul Tillich, an important twentieth-century theologian, gets at this dynamic by distinguishing between *chronos* and *kairos*, quantitative time and qualitative time.[1] Quantitative time refers to time that you can divide up and measure in minutes and hours, or even years and centuries. Qualitative time is a bit more elusive. Rather than being measureable, *kairos* must be discerned and experienced. A kairotic moment is "a fertile moment"[2] in which God's transcendent Spirit breaks into the dynamics of history and provides a glimpse of the ultimate relativity of those dynamics. It is a moment in which immanence is opened to transcendence.

My claim is that Christianity in the United States is living through a *kairotic* moment in its history. Furthermore, I contend that this moment is one in which Helmut Gollwitzer's intellectual legacy—and especially his work at the intersection of theology and politics—can provide the valuable service of clarifying and enriching our vision. The Teacher of Ecclesiastes tells us that "for everything there is a season, and a time for every matter under heaven" (Eccl 3:1). My claim is that *now* is the right time for us to encounter Gollwitzer. But to recognize the potency of this claim requires something of a history lesson.

Christianity and Economics in US History since the Civil War

Four recently published books coalesce to outline the important socio-historical, economic, political, and theological dynamics that provide the backdrop for the present *kairotic* moment. The first of these is Heath Carter's *Union Made*, which examines how forces at work in theological and ecclesiastical spheres intersected with economic and political developments in Chicago during the second half of the nineteenth century. To be more precise, Carter tracks the clash of labor and capital in rapidly expanding Chicago by looking at how representatives of Christianity in those communities responded to the conflict. He helpfully frames this response not in terms of middle-class Christianity on one side, and radical socialist atheism on the other. Instead, what played out was an internal conflict within Christianity: "The battle was not between Christianity and secularism, but rather between competing interpretations of the Christian gospel."[3]

Carter charts the development of Christianity in Chicago, beginning

---

1. Paul Tillich, *Systematic Theology*, 3 vols. (Chicago: University of Chicago Press, 1951–63), 3:369. For an in-depth discussion of this concept, see chapter 3 ("Kairos") in Paul Tillich, *The Protestant Era*, trans. James Luther Adams (Chicago: University of Chicago Press, 1948).
2. Tillich, *Systematic Theology*, 3:220.
3. Heath W. Carter, *Union Made: Working People and the Rise of Social Christianity in Chicago* (Oxford: Oxford University Press, 2015), 31. It is important to note that the story I will tell about US history is primarily a white Protestant story. But because it is also a mainstream American story, it involves and has consequences for other communities within the United States.

in the antebellum period. At this stage, the average pastor earned roughly as much each year as the average laborer. As a result, Christianity saw great success among the working class, even achieving what can be described as "mass Christianization."[4] Things changed rapidly after the Civil War, however. Ministerial pay grew quickly, reflecting increased patronage by the city's leading figures. By the time of the general strike in 1867, the clergy were prepared to line up on the side of capital rather than support the demands of labor. At the very least, they engaged in "a kind of rhetorical acrobatics" in hope of "keeping both industrialists and workers in the fold."[5] This strategy failed as the working class saw it for what it was—a failure to support them, and a declaration of allegiance to capital. Chicago's working class watched their leading Christian lights betray the very gospel they claimed to serve. Consequently, and as the decades progressed, "Chicago's working-class communities" became "hotbeds of alternative Christianities"[6] that were increasingly cut off from the "respectable" Christianity institutionalized in the middle- and upper-class churches.

This was an uncomfortable state of affairs for the establishment clergy. They interpreted the absence of the working class from their churches as evidence that this class was leaving Christianity behind. Consequently, much time and effort was spent parsing the causes of this disconnect and looking for solutions. But these solutions did not break the connection between the churches and capital, nor did they reverse the tendency to place the blame for working-class struggles on working-class shoulders. The result was predictable: the working class continued to view the churches "as both corrupted by and complicit in economic injustice."[7] Philanthropic work did little to change this perception for philanthropy fails to address the sources of economic injustice; it is "alleviative rather than preventative,"[8] serving only to treat symptoms while the cancer continues to grow. Besides, charitable giving by capital functions to legitimize what would otherwise be more readily recognized as a fundamentally immoral system.

It should come as no surprise that the working class would look for spiritual sustenance elsewhere. They found it in a fresh encounter with Jesus in the midst of their struggle and the social conditions that pre-

4. Ibid., 10.
5. Ibid., 27.
6. Ibid., 75.
7. Ibid., 104.
8. Ibid., 120.

cipitated it. Socialists and anarchists in Chicago articulated a "radical historical Jesus,"[9] and radical politics became closely associated with Christianity for the working class and its supporters. Interestingly, this close association was perhaps articulated most clearly by Catholics. In the last decade of the nineteenth century, Father Thomas McGrady argued that "a Catholic can be a socialist, for socialism stands for the moral teachings of Christ, and the repudiation of socialism is the repudiation of Christianity."[10]

This connection between socialism and Christianity among the working class undoubtedly provided much of the impetus behind the mainstream churches' acceptance of the Social Gospel in the early twentieth century. For here was a way for the churches to position themselves as being on the side of the working class by effecting real change through voluntary associations and the regulation of capital without fundamentally questioning the capitalist system itself. This version of social Christianity triumphed in the New Deal, enacted while the United States wallowed in the throes of one of capitalism's most significant failures—the Great Depression. And at that crossroads moment in United States history, the nation looked for economic salvation to a social Christianity coopted and defanged by capital, rather than to a more robust working-class Christian socialism. As Carter points out, many saw the New Deal as "the Social Gospel in practical form," noting also that "several members of [Roosevelt's] Cabinet were themselves steeped in the ideals of social Christianity."[11]

There is more of this story to tell, however, which brings us to the second of the four books I mentioned earlier. If Carter offers us a window into the conflict between mainstream Christianity and working-class Christianity in late-nineteenth-century Chicago, Timothy Gloege addresses this dynamic from the standpoint of a more conservative and innovative form of North American Christianity. In his *Guaranteed Pure*, Gloege tells the story of D. L. Moody and Chicago's eponymous Moody Bible Institute with attention to the socioeconomic conditions that

---

9. Ibid., 86. Studying Jesus's life provides ample resources for radical and revolutionary interpretations. One thinks, for instance, of Jesus driving the money changers from the temple (see Matt 21, Mark 11, Luke 19, and John 2) or commanding the rich young man to sell his possessions and give the money to the poor (Matt 19, Mark 10, Luke 18).

10. Ibid., 148; see 143–49. Despite its care to avoid questioning the capitalist system and its frequent denunciation of socialism, the 1891 encyclical *Rerum Novarum*'s insistence that natural justice demands that laborers be paid a living wage may nonetheless have paved the way for such statements.

11. Ibid., 180. For an overview of the Social Gospel and its impact on Christianity in the United States, see chapter 5 ("Christian Socialism and the Social Gospel") in Rosemary Radford Ruether, *The Radical Kingdom: The Western Experience of Messianic Hope* (New York: Harper & Row, 1970), 75–91.

shaped them. The heart of this story is how Moody and his Institute used alignment with capital in an effort to appear socially respectable. Whereas capital stood to gain respectability through its alliance with the more established, mainstream churches, it was Moody and his Institute as representatives of a new and less traditional Christianity who sought to acquire respectability through their alliance with capital.

This dynamic is evident in Moody's own life. Moody was a shoe sales-man and so familiar with the strategies and dynamics of the market, such as its penchant for logistic organization and fundraising. He used that knowledge to good effect in his ministry. As Gloege puts it, the preparations for Moody's revival meetings were "made with a business eye" and can be described as a "mass sales pitch." But more than bringing the market dynamics more explicitly into the planning and execution of his meetings, Moody also seated prominent businessmen on the stage with him, along with more established clergy and prominent politicians, in order to provide "a striking visual reminder to the audience that his message had the blessing of elites." He also dressed in business—rather than clerical—attire to reinforce this image.[12]

Moody was able to gain the support of this broad coalition of elites, and especially of capital, because he promised to succeed where the more established churches had failed: he would reach the working-class masses with a respectable brand of Christianity that would uphold—rather than undermine—the capitalist order. But Moody ultimately failed in this precisely because of his alliance with the elites, which "limited the circulation of his gospel among the oppressed."[13]

<hr/>

12. Timothy E. W. Gloege, *Guaranteed Pure: The Moody Bible Institute, Business, and the Making of Modern Evangelicalism* (Chapel Hill, NC: University of North Carolina Press, 2015), 34–35. For a parallel study that traces how Wesleyan Methodism in the late nineteenth and early twentieth centuries moved away from support of radical social reforms and toward a quietist fundamentalism centered on individual holiness, see Randall J. Stephens, "From Abolitionists to Fundamentalists: The Transformation of the Wesleyan Methodists in the Nineteenth and Twentieth Centuries," *American Nineteenth Century History* 16, no. 2 (2015): 159–91.

Walter Benjamin famously suggested that capitalism is a religion. Given this perspective, what occurs in North American Christianity in the early twentieth century is the syncretistic merger of two religious traditions—Christianity and capitalism. We might even see the role that capitalism played in legitimizing the Moody brand as the moment when capitalism took the upper hand in this merger. This moment thus serves as the transition point in its particular context for the shift that Benjamin describes: "Capitalism has developed as a parasite of Christianity in the West . . . , until it reached the point where Christianity's history is essentially that of its parasite—that is to say, of capitalism"; or, "Christianity . . . did not favor the growth of capitalism; instead it transformed itself into capitalism." Walter Benjamin, "Capitalism as Religion," in *Walter Benjamin: Selected Writings, Volume 1 1913–1926*, ed. Michael W. Jennings (Cambridge, MA: Belknap Press, 1996), 289–90.

13. Gloege, *Guaranteed Pure*, 52; see also 61, where Gloege discusses Moody's "tone-deafness to working-class concerns" after the Haymarket Affair in 1886.

Especially with the ascension of Reuben A. Torrey as the head of Moody's Chicago operation, there was an increasing push to develop "a radically individualistic spirituality that complemented the individualistic political economy of the Gilded Age" by way of "contract ideology."[14] The focus shifted off of structural or systemic concerns and on to the individual's behavior. Philanthropy played a part here as a way to make a difference for certain individuals, who would hopefully develop capitalist virtues such as thrift, a disciplined work ethic, and submissiveness toward their employers, but "it did not fundamentally challenge the power relations that created inequality."[15]

A new phase began after Moody's death, when Henry Parsons Crowell became chairman of the Moody Bible Institute's board. Crowell was an accomplished businessman and innovator in the new brand of corporate capitalism that arose in the late nineteenth and early twentieth centuries, and he applied that background to his work on the board. He brought a number of respected businessmen onto the board, reorganized the Institute according to the best managerial practices of the time, and increasingly treated the name of Moody and the Institute as a trademark. By both creating and exploiting the growing "ideological overlap between modern consumer capitalism and religion," the Institute "found the means to create a faith that was both appealing and safe for middle-class consumption."[16] Gloege even shows how the colossally influential project of publishing *The Fundamentals* was an advertising ploy and served to create a religious constituency—or, better, market—for the Institute to capitalize on where there had been none before.[17]

One important upshot of the story that Gloege tells is the contribution made by Moody and his Institute to naturalizing capitalism for Christians in the United States. In addition to the implicit acceptance of the capitalist system exhibited by their methods and structures, which promoted the fiction that concrete problems such as race and economic injustice have spiritual solutions,[18] *The Fundamentals* also

---

14. Ibid., 67, 77.
15. Ibid., 75.
16. Ibid., 139.
17. See ibid., 176–87, and esp. 181.
18. See ibid., 218. Gloege is helpfully aware of the racial dynamic at play in this story. I regret that issues such as gender and race cannot assume a more prominent place in my retelling. Those with particular interest in the latter should begin by consulting the following: J. Kameron Carter, *Race: A Theological Account* (New York: Oxford University Press, 2008); James H. Cone, *The Cross and the Lynching Tree* (Maryknoll, NY: Orbis Books, 2011); Cornel West, *Prophesy Deliverance! An Afro-American Revolutionary Christianity*, anniversary edition (Louisville, KY: Westminster John Knox Press, 2002). My own position echoes that of Andrew Wilkes: "The chief deception is the notion

included two articles that explicitly promoted capitalism on religious grounds. Accepting capitalism as a natural state of affairs that established the boundaries within which religion rightly functions undoubtedly played a role in ensuring that the New Deal did not fundamentally question the system.[19]

The stage is now set for the third phase of this story and the third of the four books. Kevin Kruse's *One Nation Under God* tracks the union of religious and civic identity in the United States as it emerged in the years following World War II. It was during these years that capital, chastened by and chaffing under the New Deal but certainly not overthrown, once again began to assert itself. As part of this process, social Christianity was eclipsed by the sort of individualistic religious approach advocated by Moody Bible Institute and its confreres—now personified by Billy Graham—all in the name of "liberty." Indeed, Leviticus 25:10 became perhaps the central biblical touchstone for this new Christian libertarianism: "proclaim liberty throughout all the land unto all the inhabitants thereof."[20]

The earliest stages of this shift are typified by the examples of two entertainment industry moguls, Walt Disney and Cecil B. DeMille. Both men began their careers as supporters of the New Deal, but their experiences with the government and with labor strikes in the 1940s led them to believe that their God-given freedom to conduct their businesses had been compromised by invasive government regulations and powers. In this climate, the New Deal and its provisions were increasingly vilified as socialist, and "'socialist laws,' such as ones supporting minimum wages, price controls, Social Security pensions for the elderly, unemployment insurance, veterans' benefits, and the like, as well as a wide range of federal taxation" were characterized as "'tyrannical' in nature." In opposition to this tyranny stands "the natural law" of free enterprise, "which inheres in the nature of the universe and

---

that we can have genuine racial equity and economic dignity without overhauling"—I would say, overthrowing—"capitalism itself." Andrew Wilkes, "Doing Political Theology in an Election Season: Howard Thurman on Deception," *Religion Dispatches* (October 3, 2016), http://religiondispatches.org/doing-political-theology-in-an-election-season-howard-thurman-on-deception/. As Jürgen Moltmann says, "The racism under which the blacks chafe, and the capitalism under which the poor and the people 'who haven't made it' suffer, belong together to this downside of America." Jürgen Moltmann, *A Broad Place: An Autobiography* (Minneapolis, MN: Fortress Press, 2009), 143–44.

19. For a continuation of the story of fundamentalism and the New Deal, see chapter 8 ("Christ's Deal Versus the New Deal") in Matthew Avery Sutton, *American Apocalypse: A History of Modern Evangelicalism* (Cambridge, MA: Belknap Press, 2014), 232–62.

20. KJV. See especially Kevin M. Kruse, *One Nation under God: How Corporate America Invented Christian America* (New York: Basic Books, 2015), 27, 144, 267.

is the will of God."[21] The great achievement of this movement was the extent to which it managed to equate capitalism, Christianity, and patriotism in the minds of a wide segment of the American population. So deep was this resonance that advertisers met little difficulty in illustrating and thereby equating "the American way of life" with consumer goods such as Coca-Cola, attending baseball games and eating popcorn, and with names such as Sears and Roebuck.[22] As one piece of propaganda put it, the critical issue is that "free Americans begin to understand and appreciate the benefits provided by God under the American free enterprise system."[23]

Two pieces of legislation in the 1950s solidified this unholy alliance between capitalism, religion, and patriotism. In 1954, legislation modified the US Pledge of Allegiance to read "one nation under God" rather than simply "one nation." This represented the ratification of Christian libertarianism's assertion that the government's power is subservient to God's divine ordinance of the world, which includes the "natural law" of capitalism. This was followed in 1956 by legislation ordering that the phrase "In God We Trust" appear on US currency. As Kruse notes, "the addition of the religious motto to . . . currency was particularly important, as it formally confirmed a role for capitalism in the larger love of God and country."[24] In other words, capitalist practices of monetary exchange had been "baptized" in direct opposition to the Soviet Union's ostensibly atheist communism.

Both these pieces of legislation were supported and ultimately

21. Ibid., 25. For Disney and DeMille, see respectively pp. 127–30 and pp. 140–48. Of course, capitalism is far from an element of "natural law." It is, instead, a product of social development, like all other aspects of culture. As Ellen Meiksins Wood concludes her study of this subject, capitalism "is a late and localized product of very specific historical conditions." Ellen Meiksins Wood, *The Origin of Capitalism: A Longer View* (New York: Verso, 2002), 193.

22. Kruse, *One Nation under God*, 105. Theologian Paul M. van Buren was a clear-sighted critic of this cultural shift, explaining in his lectures from the late 1950s that "the church in our land is . . . under subtle attack by a powerful cultural religion, known as the 'American Way of Life.'" It is worth noting that he makes this comment immediately after—indeed, within the same paragraph as—recounting the fate of the German church under the Third Reich. Paul M. van Buren, *The Austin Dogmatics: 1957–1958*, ed. Ellen T. Charry (Eugene, OR: Cascade, 2012), 4.

23. Kruse, *One Nation under God*, 150.

24. Ibid., 125. Consider also Greene's reflection on this historical moment: "Religious leaders and corporate leaders together naturalized the alliance between church and state, capital and Christianity. Soon enough, Americans forgot that God had not always been in the pledge and on the dollar." Alison Collis Greene, *No Depression in Heaven: The Great Depression, the New Deal, and the Transformation of Religion in the Delta* (New York: Oxford University Press, 2016), 198. Theodore Roosevelt and Jewish congressman Abraham Multer both opposed this legislation, arguing that placing such a motto on currency was religiously improper. Kruse quotes Roosevelt: "My own firm conviction . . . is that such a motto on coins not only does no good, but positive harm and is in effect, irreverence, which comes close to sacrilege." Kruse, *One Nation under God*, 112. On Multer, see especially p. 119.

signed into law by President Eisenhower, who came into office in part due to the support of Christian libertarian businessmen and their movement's machinery. Even though Eisenhower supported the merger of capitalism, Christianity, and patriotism, "he refused to roll back the welfare state" and "ensured the longevity of the New Deal," even pushing "Congress to extend Social Security coverage to another ten million Americans and increase benefits as well."[25] Despite Eisenhower's reticence to dismantle the New Deal's social safety net, the unholy alliance achieved during his presidency laid the groundwork for the gradual erosion of these programs that began in the last decades of the twentieth century and continues today. While both the Democratic and Republican parties during this period have promoted and enacted policies that have served to further unfetter and empower capital, the latter party has been unabashed in making this a major plank in its platform.[26]

It is impossible to miss a reactionary drift in this story. From something like a working-class Christian socialism, through its cooptation by and transformation into a middle-class social Christianity that left the capitalist system intact, which was, in turn, aided and abetted by a newly emerging conservative Protestantism that looked to capital for legitimation, we arrive at the mutually legitimizing union of capitalism, religion, and patriotism. The effect of this reactionary drift is that by the end of the twentieth century, socialism is seen as un-Christian and unpatriotic precisely because it is anticapitalist. Alison Collis Greene sums up this drift well: "Corporate powers had worked to link the three concepts—Americanism, capitalism, and Christianity—in the Gilded Age, but not without challenges from both radicals and progressives, who deemed such an alliance unholy." By the second half of the twentieth century, however, "challenges to capitalism met with charges of treason."[27]

The fourth book provides a more personal, biographical illustration of this reactionary drift, particularly in the middle-to-latter part of the twentieth century. Thomas C. Oden was a conservative Protestant theologian who taught for many years at Drew University in Madison,

25. Kruse, *One Nation under God*, 87. For further discussion of religion, economics, and the New Deal, this time from a bit further South, see Greene, *No Depression in Heaven*.
26. The most recent GOP platform's preamble castigates the Obama administration for "regulating to death" the "free market economy," and calls for "relieving the burden and expense of punishing government regulations." Republican National Committee, "Republican Platform 2016," ii (https://www.gop.com/the-2016-republican-party-platform/).
27. Greene, *No Depression in Heaven*, 198.

New Jersey, and is best known as a proponent of "paleo-orthodoxy." This movement promotes a return to the theological framework of an idealized early Christian consensus. Less well known perhaps, at least prior to the publication of his biography entitled *A Change of Heart*, is that Oden came out of a very socially engaged and progressive form of Methodism and academically pursued the intersection of Bultmannian theology and psychoanalysis. He came to see this progressive social and theological vision as bankrupt because he thought it lacked the depth of more "traditional" Christianity.

Oden explains his shift in perspective in the individualist religious terms that the previous historical narratives lead us to expect: "While examining the motives of capitalists and warlords, I did not examine my own motives. The biblical words for this are egocentricity, arrogance and moral blindness. I confess now that I became entrapped with the desire for upward mobility in an academic environment that would generate ideas for a regulatory society."[28] Oden here deflects attention from concrete sociopolitical issues and suggests that what is truly problematic is the personal and spiritual, even suggesting that the personal and spiritual dimensions supply the proper solution for sociopolitical problems. This echoes the sentiment seen above in the discussion of Moody and the Moody Bible Institute.

With this shift, Oden began to emphasize what he came to see as sociohistorical continuity in contrast to progressive disruption. He tells the story primarily in a theological key, talking about how his progressive theological approach amounted to "floating on the wave of secularization," and describing the challenge of that earlier period as trying "to learn to sound Christian while undermining traditional Christianity."[29] Everything depends on definitions, however. Throughout his account, Oden assumes that his late twentieth-century conservative Protestant nostalgia for an idealized early Christian consensus adequately encompasses the essence of Christian belief and practice. But this is only an assumption, and the strength of its hold over Oden evinces how thoroughly naturalized capitalism had become in the imaginations of many American Christians. Oden provides a glimpse of this aspect of his intellectual shift, explaining that he moved to engage "the intellectual history of conservative thought," that he associated with emerging neoconservative thinkers, and that he

---

28. Thomas C. Oden, *A Change of Heart: A Personal and Theological Memoir* (Downers Grove, IL: IVP Academic, 2014), 56.
29. Ibid., 80–81.

"viewed the protection of property rights as an intrinsic aspect of human dignity."[30]

Oden supplies a case study in the social and theological consequences of the historical trajectory sketched above in which reflexes about what it means to be a Christian and an American became dominated by capitalism. Rather than understanding the Christian theological tradition as supplying resources to resist this capitalist intellectual and cultural imperialism, Oden turns to that tradition as a means of legitimizing capitalism and delegitimizing its critics.

The View From and For Today

It did not have to be this way. I provide this historical sketch because it helps to explain why one could claim that Protestant Christianity in the United States now finds itself in a *kairotic* moment. As Karl Marx teaches us, all intellectual and cultural endeavors are inextricably bound to material conditions, and this holds for both theology and politics. Material conditions play an important role in setting both the terms and the boundaries in these spheres. And the critical point is that material conditions in the United States increasingly resemble those that obtained in periods that have been more favorable for alliance between Christianity and socialism. Heath Carter well puts his finger on the issue in the final paragraph of his study: "Now, in the early decades of the twenty-first century, American capitalism appears once more poised to overwhelm American democracy. . . . It remains to be seen whether present-day believers will quietly abide this state of affairs, or whether it will at some point call forth a generation of prophets comparable to those that visited Gilded Age Chicago."[31]

It is not difficult to substantiate such claims about the present material conditions in the United States. Allen Wood, for instance, writes that "American society today is by many measures even more unequal than the capitalist order against which Karl Marx wrote in revolutionary protest."[32] Wood documents this inequality. I will relate just two

30. Ibid., 148, 154–55.
31. Carter, *Union Made*, 182. A recent study out of Princeton University argues that the increasing influence of economic elites over policymaking in the United States means that "America's claims to being a democratic society are seriously threatened" despite the persistence of "many features central to democratic governance." Martin Gilens and Benjamin I. Page, "Testing Theories of American Politics: Elites, Interest Groups, and Average Citizens," *Perspectives on Politics* 12, no. 3 (2014): 577.
32. Allen W. Wood, *The Free Development of Each: Studies on Freedom, Right, and Ethics in Classical German Philosophy* (Oxford: Oxford University Press, 2014), 252. As a recent working paper clarifies: "Since 1980, growth in real incomes for the bottom 90% adults has been only about half of the national

of the more striking statistics: first, the richest 1 percent of Americans have increased their income many hundreds of times over while wages for the average worker have remained stagnant since 1980, adjusted for inflation; second, 93 percent of income growth coming out of the Great Recession in 2008 has gone to the top 1 percent. All this has made the United States one of the most economically unequal societies—perhaps even *the most* unequal—among developed countries, and this is to say nothing of the increasing gulf of inequality that exists between the United States and nations of the global South. As Joerg Rieger reminds us, such inequality is not only about financial differentials but is "ultimately about differentials of power and influence. . . . Such power and influence determine who gets to shape the world."[33]

That socialism has once again become a topic of conversation, and even shed some of its stigma, should come as no surprise given these material conditions. For instance, the Pew Research Center on U.S. Politics & Policy released the results of a survey in early 2010 on political rhetoric. They found that negative reactions to capitalism and positive reactions to socialism are on the rise. The shift is especially noticeable among the younger generations, who have been some of the hardest hit by recent economic instability. In the Pew study, respondents who were 18–29 years of age registered almost identical response to socialism and capitalism: socialism was seen positively by 43 percent and negatively by 49 percent, while capitalism was seen positively by 43 percent and negatively by 48 percent.[34] A more recent YouGov survey suggested that this shift has become even more pronounced. When asked whether they have a more favorable or less favorable view of socialism, respondents 18–29 years old returned a 43 percent favorability rating and only a 26 percent unfavorability rating.[35] Perhaps the

average on pre-tax basis and about two-thirds on a post-tax basis. Median pre-tax incomes have hardly grown since 1980." Thomas Piketty, Emmanuel Saez, and Gabriel Zucman, "Distributional National Accounts: Methods and Estimates for the United States" (Washington, DC: Washington Center for Equitable Growth), 32. For more historical background on the radical left and Marxism in United States, see Paul Buhle, *Marxism in the United States: Remapping the History of the American Left*, revised edition, Haymarket Series (New York: Verso, 1991).

33. Joerg Rieger, *No Rising Tide: Theology, Economics, and the Future* (Minneapolis, MN: Fortress Press, 2009), 3. Rieger also presents and documents statistics such as those provided by Wood, as does George Hunsinger, with an eye also to the global situation. See George Hunsinger, *The Beatitudes* (Mahwah, NJ: Paulist Press, 2015), 11–13. For detailed analysis of this growing inequality and its development, see "Part Three" of Thomas Piketty, *Capital in the Twenty-First Century*, trans. Arthur Goldhammer (Cambridge, MA: Belknap Press, 2014).

34. "A Political Rhetoric Test: 'Socialism' Not So Negative, 'Capitalism' Not So Positive" (Washington, DC: The Pew Research Center for The People and The Press, May 4, 2010).

35. William Jordan, "Democrats More Divided on Socialism" (YouGov.com, January 28, 2016): https://today.yougov.com/news/2016/01/28/democrats-remain-divided-socialism/. For one interpretation of these findings, see Julia Mead, "Why Millennials Aren't Afraid of Socialism," *The Nation*

most interesting study, however, was that done on wealth distribution with "a nationally representative . . . sample of respondents."[36] Respondents were shown three unmarked wealth distribution charts—representative of equal distribution, the actual distribution in the United States, and the actual distribution in Sweden—and asked to indicate which distribution they would prefer. Only 10 percent preferred the actual US distribution, while 43 percent preferred equal distribution, and 47 percent preferred the actual Swedish distribution. Many Americans characterize Sweden as a socialist country.

These shifting opinions on socialism have produced new political possibilities. Kshama Sawant is one example. A member of the Socialist Alternative party, she won a seat on the Seattle, Washington, City Council in 2013 and was reelected in 2015. One of the primary issues in her campaign was raising the city's minimum wage to $15 an hour, and this increase subsequently took effect in early 2015. Moving from the local to the national political scene, a few words must be said about Bernie Sanders. Although he does not seem to be a member of any socialist party, campaigned for president as a Democrat, and his positions can perhaps be more accurately described as New Deal-esque social democracy, Sanders is a self-proclaimed socialist. And yet, this self-description did not seem to hinder and may well have aided the amount of traction that he generated, especially among the younger voters who formed the core of his support.[37] Speaking positively about and describing oneself as a socialist may no longer be the great act of American political suicide that it once was.

It is against the backdrop of this shifting sociopolitical scene that Helmut Gollwitzer stands out as an instructive example of how the church might respond to the challenges of the present *kairotic* moment. If Thomas Oden can be seen as a representative Christian thinker in a capitalist and reactionary period, Gollwitzer provides the necessary counterexample for an increasingly radical political climate. Oden understood himself as moving from a socialist and Marxist perspective that lacked grounding in the Christian theological tradition to a redis-

(January 10, 2017): https://www.thenation.com/article/why-millennials-arent-afraid-of-the-s-word/.

36. Michael I. Norton and Dan Ariely, "Building a Better America—One Wealth Quintile at a Time," *Perspectives on Psychological Science* 6, no. 1 (2011): 9.

37. It is interesting to think of what might have been had Sanders received the presidential nomination from the Democratic Party, but dialectical theologians do not engage in counterfactual speculation. Given the political results of 2016, it is important to remember that socialism and fascism are mortal enemies. This is yet another reason why Christianity in the United States needs the example of Gollwitzer's socialism today.

covery of that tradition and its purported support of capitalism. Gollwitzer, on the contrary, moved from a more conservative sociopolitical position to an affirmation of socialism precisely because of his thorough grounding in the Christian theological tradition. He provides an example of rigorously religious and theological commitment that funds progressive rather than conservative political impulses, thereby disproving the regnant American assumption that religion is fundamentally conservative.[38]

To return to my earlier claim, *now* is the right time for Christians in the United States to encounter Gollwitzer. As German theologian Andreas Pangritz has said, "the current world economic crisis shows that Gollwitzer's theological criticism of capitalism and his call to Christians to politically intervene . . . is likely to be more current today than ever before."[39] In hearing Gollwitzer today, Christianity in the United States can take a step toward avoiding what Tillich describes as the condition of being "a-*kairos*": "missing the demand of the historical moment."[40] The purpose of the present work is to facilitate that hearing.

The Shape of What Is to Come

It is always helpful to have a basic roadmap to the terrain ahead. Chapter 2 provides a sketch of Gollwitzer's life. This sketch is necessary because Gollwitzer is so little known in English language theology, which is particularly unfortunate because his was an eventful life. For instance, he was in the thick of the Confessing Church movement in its resistance to Adolf Hitler's National Socialist (Nazi) regime in Germany, was drafted into the German military, was captured on the Eastern Front at war's end, and lived as a prisoner of war in Soviet Russia

---

38. For more on this assumption, see Thomas J. Whitley, "America's Religion Problem," *Marginalia Review of Books* (January 4, 2017): http://marginalia.lareviewofbooks.org/mrblog-americas-religion-problem/.

39. Andreas Pangritz, "Helmut Gollwitzer als Theologe des Dialogs" (Rheinischen Friedrich-Wilhelms-Universität, Bonn; December 3, 2008), 9. Gollwitzer's voice would seem to qualify as a prophetic one according to Jürgen Moltmann's definition: "Protestant theology is prophetic when it asks about the 'right word' at the 'right time' and seeks for the word that binds and looses in a given situation." Moltmann, *Broad Place*, 263.

40. Tillich, *Systematic Theology*, 3:6. It is worth noting that Tillich first developed his concept of *kairos*, at least in part, as a way to conceptualize the importance of supporting democratic socialism in the context of the Weimar Republic. For Tillich on socialism, see chapter 17 ("Marxism and Christian Socialism") in Tillich, *Protestant Era*, 253–60, and Paul Tillich, *The Socialist Decision*, trans. Franklin Sherman (Eugene, OR: Wipf & Stock, 2012). For brief reflections on the Troeltschian context of Tillich's socialism, see the introduction to Dennis P. McCann, "Ernst Troeltsch's Essay on 'Socialism'," *Journal of Religious Ethics* 4, no. 1 (1976): 159–63.

for five years. He quickly became a leading public intellectual in Western Germany after returning from imprisonment, and became involved in a number of interesting domestic policy debates and events. For instance, he was close with the student protesters in Berlin in the late 1960s. Having a background knowledge of Gollwitzer's life is also important because the vast majority of Gollwitzer's work was conducted in deep engagement with the people and events around him. It is impossible to gain a proper perspective on Gollwitzer's theology without an appreciation of how it fits into his biography. His life and work must be considered together, and when seen in that perspective, it is clear that Gollwitzer's story is one of grace upon grace.

Chapter 3 builds on the sketch of Gollwitzer's life by beginning to articulate the intersection of theology and politics in his thought. The task here is to locate Gollwitzer within the dialectical theology movement as represented especially by Karl Barth and Rudolf Bultmann. Gollwitzer received his education in this movement, especially from Barth, and it provided him with a theological baseline from which to work. Dialectical theology is always also political theology, for Gollwitzer, and this chapter traces this logic in his thought. In brief: the consequence of dialectical theology's insistence upon God's nonobjectifiability is that all theology is contextual theology, limited by the horizons of its particular place and time. Those horizons include socioeconomic and political conditions, of course, which means that all theology is necessarily—whether implicitly or explicitly—politically embedded. Consequently, all theology is political theology, and Gollwitzer argues that the sort of political theology demanded by encounter with the nonobjectifiable God is decisively liberative. We will see Gollwitzer's account of theology's liberative character especially through his engagement with black theology.

The logic of Gollwitzer's political theology traced in chapter 3 sets the stage for engagement with Gollwitzer's theological politics in chapter 4. Gollwitzer's democratic socialism plays a central role in his theopolitics. He first became committed to socialism as Karl Barth's student before the war, but he retreated from this commitment as a result of his experience as a prisoner of war in Soviet Russia. Gollwitzer advocated a reformed, humanist capitalism through the 1950s, but finally recognized that as a dead end. By the close of the 1960s, he had returned to his earlier socialist commitment, even arguing that Christians *must* be socialists. Gollwitzer also wrote extensively on war, and especially on how the advent of nuclear weapons imploded the logic that had supported the Christian just war tradition. He was not an absolute pacifist, however, and this comes out clearly in his reflections on revolution and revolutionary violence. Gollwitzer even articulates criteria for a just revolution along the same lines as traditional just war criteria. What governs Gollwitzer's thought on all these issues, however, is his unwavering commitment to subject every socioeconomic and political structure to judgment by the true socialism of the kingdom of God. The bottom line for Gollwitzer is that Christians must take sides on political issues, and they must take the side of those whom society has left out, left behind, or left for dead.

Finally, chapter 5 articulates the unity of Gollwitzer's political theology and theological politics as they coalesce in his doctrine of the church. Unlike those—both in our own day and in Gollwitzer's—who conceptualize the church as a political entity unto itself, with its own culture and language that must be spread through assimilation, Gollwitzer stays true to his dialectical theological core and argues that the church is an *event.* Just as God cannot legitimately be objectified, so also the church cannot legitimately be objectified. The true being of the church occurs as it responds in faithful obedience to its encounter with God's Thou-objectivity, which necessarily includes renunciation of its privilege and political advocacy on behalf of the marginalized and oppressed. But if this is the case, what does it mean that the church in the global North remains apparently unconcerned about its bourgeois class bondage? Is this not a danger to the church's very existence that demands a clear and unambiguous response? The chapter—and book—concludes by addressing these questions through affirming that the church in the global North finds itself today in a *status confessionis,* a moment in which it must unambiguously confess its faith in the face of a threat to its very existence as the church.

Concluding Reflections

I would like to offer four reflections on the character of this project before drawing this introduction to a close. First, I want to be clear that this volume in no way constitutes a comprehensive treatment of the intersection of theology and politics in Gollwitzer's life and thought, much less of his life and thought in general. There remain a great many things for us to learn from Gollwitzer, especially in English-language theological and ecclesial circles. I will consider the labor that went into this volume more than justified if it inspires even one other person to engage deeply with Gollwitzer. Second, and consequently, my intention is not that this volume would be a last word on Gollwitzer in the North American context, but—hopefully—a first word. In the hope of generating further words about Gollwitzer, third, I have tried to balance my reliance on sources available only in German and those also available in English. Those with the necessary linguistic capabilities for work in the original sources will receive direction as to some of the most relevant texts, while those without that facility will also learn where they might best engage with Gollwitzer in translation. The appendices also provide translations of two important essays from Gollwitzer on the subject of Christianity and socialism, which will allow readers to think more deeply alongside Gollwitzer on that subject in the English language than has been possible before. Fourth, Gollwitzer was a white, male theology professor—a person of privilege. He was aware of his privilege, and his work aimed at awakening other privileged Christians to self-awareness as such so that they might use their privilege to serve others as well as to dismantle the social structures that privilege some and oppress others. I am also a white, male theology professor—a person of privilege. The many other privileged members of North American Christianity are my primary audience in this book, and I intend it as an act of solidarity with those who do not share my privilege. Inevitably, the following pages will demonstrate that there remain ways in which I am blind to my privilege. I apologize in advance for any patriarchal, racist, classist, or otherwise patronizing residue that remains.

2

———

Grace upon Grace:
Helmut Gollwitzer's Life and Work

Helmut Gollwitzer (1908–1993) was "one of the most influential Protestant theologians of the twentieth century," according to Andreas Pangritz,[1] but he has attracted little attention. This is especially true in English language theological circles. Despite Gollwitzer's position as one of Karl Barth's most significant students, even those who know a great deal about Barth have only a passing familiarity with Gollwitzer's name. But his life and work have much to offer the church today. Indeed, it is impossible to isolate Gollwitzer's life from his work or his work from his life. Friedrich-Wilhelm Marquardt, one of his students, highlights this when he describes the "existential compass" that guides Gollwitzer's thought and binds it together in a vital "movement of life."[2] Gollwitzer was—to use Barth's terms—an "irregular" rather than a "regular" theologian. He wrote primarily in a topical mode, addressing contemporary issues without concern for articulating a complete and balanced "systematic" theology.[3] Because of this existential com-

---

1. Andreas Pangritz, "Helmut Gollwitzer als Theologe des Dialogs" (Rheinischen Friedrich-Wilhelms-Universität, Bonn; December 3, 2008), 1.
2. Friedrich-Wilhelm Marquardt, "Helmut Gollwitzer: Weg und Werk," in *Bibliographie Helmut Gollwitzer*, ed. Christa Haehn, Ausgewählte Werke (München: Chr. Kaiser, 1988), 11, 18.
3. Ibid., 25. Marquardt makes the same point in his introduction to Helmut Gollwitzer, *Skizzen eines*

pass and irregular character, we need a sense of Gollwitzer's life if we are to understand his relevance today.

This chapter provides a basic orientation to the vital interconnection of Gollwitzer's life and work, thus laying a foundation on which following chapters can build. Reflecting late in life, Gollwitzer divided his adult life into two periods. The first period comprised life in the immediate shadow of the Third Reich and its consequences, while the second encompassed all that came after he returned in 1950 from his time as a prisoner of war.[4] I will follow this basic structure while also prefixing to it an account of Gollwitzer's youth and education. Because this is a book about the intersection of theology and politics modelled by Gollwitzer, this intersection will run like a red thread through my account of his biography. But I will not pursue this thread in a reductionist fashion. Gollwitzer's life makes for a good story, and his thought was forged in the best Christian tradition of a faith confessed in, and challenged by, the fullness of life's suffering and joy.

Theologian in the Making

Youth and Early Influences

Helmut Gollwitzer was born on December 29, 1908, as "the son of an evangelical-Lutheran pastor in Bavaria."[5] One of his earliest memories was of falling asleep listening to the adults talk about World War I in 1914, and having his mother come in to comfort and pray with him until he fell sleep. Gollwitzer's mother, Barbara, had been one of his father's confirmands. She married Wilhelm as soon as she was of marriageable age. The years of the Weimar Republic, stretching from the end of World War I to the ascent of Adolf Hitler and the National Social-

---

Lebens. Aus verstreuten Selbstzeugnissen gefunden und verbunden von Friedrich-Wilhelm Marquardt, Wolfgang Brinkel und Manfred Weber (Gütersloh: Christian Kaiser Verlagshaus, 1998), 9. For Barth's distinction between regular and irregular theology, see Karl Barth, *Church Dogmatics*, trans. and ed. by Geoffrey W. Bromiley and Thomas F. Torrance, 4 volumes in 13 parts (Edinburgh: T&T Clark, 1956–75), 1.1:275–78. It is worth noting that Marquardt does helpfully delineate Gollwitzer's major publications according to traditional dogmatic loci. See Marquardt, "Weg und Werk," 27.

4. Gollwitzer, *Skizzen eines Lebens*, 342. This work is the primary source for Gollwitzer's biography. It was published posthumously and is composed of autobiographical reflections from various sources that have been organized by the editors, who also provide valuable contextual information that aids in bringing the work together as a more coherent narrative. While this is a valuable biographical source, however, the work of composing a truly critical biography of Gollwitzer remains undone. For those interested in consulting a second biographical sketch of Gollwitzer in English, see Paul Oestreicher, "Helmut Gollwitzer in the European Storms," in *The Demands of Freedom: Papers by a Christian in West Germany* (New York: Harper and Row Publishers, 1965), 7–27.

5. Gollwitzer, *Skizzen eines Lebens*, 11.

ists (Nazis), also stood out in Gollwitzer's mind as particularly memorable. Like all middle-class families, the Gollwitzers—and especially, Helmut's mother—struggled to deal with the various economic and material difficulties of those years.[6] Although Gollwitzer would later distance himself from aspects of his upbringing, as we will see shortly, he nonetheless appreciated his parents and the way they had endeavored to form him. He paid tribute to their positive contribution in this way:

> One thing I must highlight as particularly important: both parents conveyed to us, through their lives and the atmosphere of their house, an index of values that was crucial for all our lives. . . . Each person is equally interesting because they are loved by God, whether they are at the bottom of the social ladder or at the top. It is more important whether you can stand with your decisions before God than whether you can stand with them before people, and having a pure conscience is more important than what consequences you have to bear. You could hardly give your children better rules for life.[7]

Wilhelm Gollwitzer was theologically and politically conservative, and his conservatism came to expression especially as nationalism. There is nothing unique about this combination in the Weimar period. His nationalism extended to support for the National Socialists. Indeed, Helmut was involved in many patriotic youth organizations, even serving as a messenger boy for the National Socialist *Sturmabteilung* (SA) during the Beer Hall Putsch in early November, 1923.[8] Things started to change for Helmut during his time in Augsburg at the St. Anna *Gymnasium*. He began attending this well-regarded educational institution in 1925, and it expanded Helmut's horizons by bringing him into close personal contact with a wide variety of people. This led him to question some of his social and political views insofar as it taught him that "pacifists are not necessarily cowards, despicable socialists are not necessarily November-criminals, and Jews are not necessarily damned by God."

6. Ibid., 15–19.
7. Ibid., 26.
8. For Wilhelm's conservatism, see ibid., 21. For Helmut's connection with the SA, see ibid., 28. Marquardt describes Gollwitzer in this period as an "SA propagandist." Marquardt, "Weg und Werk," 17. The Beer Hall Putsch was an attempted coup in Bavaria that, failing to gain the support of the police and military, was dispersed by machine-gun fire. Hitler was arrested in the aftermath. A reflexive, if not overtly vicious, anti-Semitism was part of the conservatism that Helmut inherited from his father and which fed into support of National Socialism. Space does not permit doing this side of the story justice at present, but I have addressed it elsewhere. See W. Travis McMaken, "'Shalom, Shalom, Shalom Israel!' Jews and Judaism in Helmut Gollwitzer's Life and Theology," *Studies in Christian-Jewish Relations* 10, no. 1 (2015): 1–22.

Beyond this initial negative move, however, Gollwitzer took a positive step that would prove decisive for his later life. He continues: "From then on I began reading Marx and engaging in discussion with fellow leftist students." And when Helmut graduated from St. Anna in the spring of 1928, he was commended for the exam he wrote on religion.[9]

Already during Helmut's later years at St. Anna, his older brother Gerhard was studying in Munich and coming under the influence of Georg Merz. It was Merz who, in association with the Christian Kaiser publishing house, oversaw the production of *Zwischen den Zeiten* (*Between the Times*). This journal served as the organ for the dialectical theology movement during 1923–33. It was founded by Merz, Karl Barth, Friedrich Gogarten, and Eduard Thurneysen, and attracted contributions from Emil Brunner, Rudolf Bultmann, Fritz Lieb, and others.[10] Gerhard began to introduce Helmut to this theological world, and consequently, Helmut began his university studies at Munich in the summer of 1928. Furthermore, Helmut began working for Merz on minor *Zwischen den Zeiten* assignments. For instance, he compiled a bibliography of sources by and about Karl Barth. Encountering this new theological movement excited Helmut. He had never resonated with the sort of conservative Lutheran theology advocated by his father, but now dialectical theology was blowing "the dust of boredom" away from theology.[11]

This new theological direction taken by Gerhard and Helmut introduced some tension into the Gollwitzer family between the brothers and their father. Barbara functioned more as a mediator than a partisan, working to maintain the familial ties. The two sides of the family were brought back together as the Gollwitzer parents became increasingly disillusioned with Adolf Hitler and the National Socialists. What Wilhelm saw as Hitler's interference in the church pushed him toward the Confessing Church movement. Wilhelm died in 1939, but Barbara lived for almost forty more years. During the intervening decades, she provided Helmut with both support and constructive criticism. She

---

9. Gollwitzer, *Skizzen eines Lebens*, 40. The stereotypes enumerated in the first quote are connected with the "stab in the back" myths that were popular during the Weimar period and served as propaganda tools for the National Socialists. These myths blame Germany's defeat in World War I on political sabotage ostensibly committed by these marginalized groups. For Helmut's graduation from St. Anna, see ibid., 36.

10. On *Zwischen den Zeiten*, see Eberhard Busch, *Karl Barth: His Life from Letters and Autobiographical Texts*, trans. John Bowden (Philadelphia: Fortress Press, 1976), 144–47. For a study of Merz, see Manacnuc Mathias Lichtenfeld, *Georg Merz—Pastoraltheologe zwischen den Zeiten: Leben und Werk in Weimarer Republik und Kirchenkampf als theologischer Beitrag zur Praxis der Kirche*, Lutherische Kirche, Geschichte und Gestalten (Gütersloh: Gütersloher Verlagshaus, 1997).

11. Gollwitzer, *Skizzen eines Lebens*, 41; see also 51.

studied theology later in life and became interested in thinkers such as Albert Schweitzer, Luther, the Blumhardts, and Barth—especially his doctrine of angels in *Church Dogmatics* 3.3. Gerhard Gollwitzer eventually became disillusioned with Barth's dogmatic turn and walked a more mystical path influenced by Emanuel Swedenborg.[12]

Theological Education

Gollwitzer's university studies began in earnest when he followed his brother to Munich. Helmut pursued his studies in the standard German fashion of the day by spending time in many different institutions to sample the intellectual flavors offered by the different faculties. It is worth briefly sketching his studies during these years to gain some sense of his academic formation and the teachers who shaped him.[13]

Despite the importance that meeting Georg Merz and becoming associated with *Zwischen den Zeiten* had for Gollwitzer's theological trajectory, he only spent the summer semester of 1928 enrolled in Munich. During that time, he interacted with three Jewish thinkers: Paul Joachimsen, who Gollwitzer heard on church history; Otto Salomon, who put Gollwitzer in contact with the theology and eschatology of the Blumhardts; and Fritz Strich, who was a professor of German literature lecturing on lyric poetry. Salomon was especially important for Gollwitzer and they became close. Gollwitzer later reflected that "Otto Salomon was one of the first poets I met with whom I could be friends."[14] Rolf Stieber-Westermann notes in his study on Gollwitzer that "this personal encounter [with Salomon] became an effective vaccine against any anti-Semitism, whether political or theological."[15] Finally, in Munich, Gollwitzer also heard phenomenologist Alexander Pfänder's lectures on an introduction to philosophy. Gollwitzer spent the second half of this academic year (winter semester 1928–29) in Erlangen, now pursuing a specifically theological education. He was drawn there by the prospect of studying Luther, who became one of Gollwitzer's major influences. Both Paul Althaus and Werner Elert then taught at Erlangen, and both were noted Luther scholars. Indeed, Althaus was perhaps the leading interpreter of Luther alive at that time. Althaus and Elert were both sympathetic to Hitler

---

12. Ibid., 12, 20–24.
13. This sketch of Gollwitzer's education draws on ibid., 12, 53–57, except as otherwise noted.
14. Ibid., 48.
15. Rolf Stieber-Westermann, *Die Provokation zum Leben: Gott im theologischen Werk Helmut Gollwitzers*, Europäische Hochschulschriften (Frankfurt am Main: Peter Lang, 1993), 18.

and the National Socialists, and by this time, Gollwitzer had distanced himself from that part of his past, thanks to his experience at St. Anna and the influence of the *Zwischen den Zeiten* circle. Nonetheless, Gollwitzer was grateful to have had the opportunity to study with them despite their divergent theological and political commitments. He also heard Oskar Grether, scholar of the Old Testament and the Hebrew language, while in Erlangen.

Summer semester in 1929 saw Gollwitzer travel to Jena. He went there to study with Friedrich Gogarten, whom he knew and was attracted to as one of *Zwischen den Zeiten*'s editors and contributors. In addition to his professorial responsibilities, Gogarten also served as pastor of a church in the area. Gollwitzer and some friends bicycled on Sundays to hear his sermons. Eberhard Grisebach, a philosopher associated with the dialectical theology movement, also made an impression on Gollwitzer. When time came for the winter semester of 1929–30, Gollwitzer returned to Erlangen. The character of Gollwitzer's studies now changed. He had a reputation for being a friendly and outgoing companion, but now, he entered into a period of personal and spiritual purification during which he lived an almost monastic existence. He gave up casual romantic relationships and burned his poetry, which had been very important to him. Furthermore, he decisively broke with his earlier nationalist connections and burned his correspondence from that period (a move he later regretted). Gollwitzer was preparing for a new life in which he would dedicate himself to the theological task, and he would look to Barth for direction.

Arriving in Bonn for the summer semester in 1930, Gollwitzer presented himself at Barth's door on May 1 and saw him for the first time. Barth met with him and Gollwitzer gave an account of his education up to that point. Then, walking down the stairs from his office, Gollwitzer noticed portraits of Adolf von Harnack and Friedrich Schleiermacher hanging on the wall. "Herr Professor," Gollwitzer commented, "I thought that you are against them!?"[16] Barth's reply was that he would be happy to be counted among them one day, and that theological judgment must be distinguished from God's final judgment. In addition to Barth, Gollwitzer was also influenced in Bonn by Ernst Wolf. Wolf was a church historian with particular interest in Luther who would later be a leader in the Confessing Church. Fritz Lieb, who was an expert in Russian intellectual history and Marxism, was also important

---

16. Gollwitzer, *Skizzen eines Lebens*, 57.

for Gollwitzer.[17] Finally, Gollwitzer benefited from study of the New Testament under Karl Ludwig Schmidt.

Gollwitzer returned to Erlangen for the winter semester of 1931–32, at the end of which he took his theological exams. He performed well, and was rated as "excellent" in the area of systematics. These strong exams meant that Gollwitzer could immediately begin his professional education for ministry (what we in North America refer to as "seminary") at Munich, which Helmut's father regarded as a place of honor and as a signal for future distinction among Bavarian clergy. But Gollwitzer was forced to leave the Munich seminary in November, shortly after beginning the winter semester. A fellow theological student had visited him in his room, which produced a scandal because the student in question was a woman. Karl Barth intervened to bring Gollwitzer back to Bonn to begin work immediately on his doctorate under Barth's supervision. Barth left Germany in the summer of 1935 after being dismissed by Hitler's government, and he immediately took up the post in Basel that he would hold for the remainder of his career. Barth was able to retain a number of his doctoral students—Gollwitzer among them—because the border between Switzerland and Germany remained open for a number of years. Gollwitzer submitted his thesis and passed his doctoral examination in February 1937. He dedicated his thesis to his parents, perhaps in compensation for their disappointment when he left Munich.[18]

Gollwitzer's Primary Theological Influences

It is fitting to pause here to reflect on those figures who had the greatest impact on Gollwitzer's theological orientation and with whom he remained in intellectual dialogue throughout his life. Marquardt observes that "Helmut Gollwitzer *enjoys* learning with fathers and brothers,"[19] where "fathers" are symbolic of one's own tradition and "brothers" refer to those from outside that tradition. For Marquardt, the former category includes especially Barth and Luther, but also the Protestant scholastics. The latter category can be thought of in terms of concentric circles, with scholars from other Christian traditions in

---

17. Stieber-Westermann credits Lieb with leading Gollwitzer to a deeper understanding of the intersection and divergence between theological issues and socialist ideas. See Stieber-Westermann, *Provokation zum Leben*, 21.
18. Gollwitzer, *Skizzen eines Lebens*, 14–15, 75–76, 141. For the context of Barth's departure of Germany, see Busch, *Karl Barth*, 255–71; see esp. 267 for Barth's retention of his German students "Walter Kreck, Helmut Gollwitzer and Hans Heinrich Wolf."
19. Marquardt, "Weg und Werk," 40.

the center, Jewish thinkers in the next sector, and out from there to philosophers and other intellectuals, such as Karl Marx. Stieber-Westermann names figures such as Ernst Bloch, Dietrich Bonhoeffer, Martin Buber, Rudolf Bultmann, Friedrich Gogarten, Kornelius Heiko Miskotte, and Paul Tillich as important interlocutors.[20] Here, I will focus primarily on Gollwitzer's undisputed theological "fathers"—Karl Barth and Martin Luther—while also saying something about Gollwitzer's engagement with Martin Buber because of the light that it shines on the intersection of Barth and Luther in Gollwitzer's thought.

Karl Barth

Gollwitzer acknowledged Barth as his most important theological "father," saying that he "received the most lasting impression of my life from him."[21] Gollwitzer and Barth became close in Bonn. He served as Barth's *famulus*, or teaching assistant, and was often at Barth's house.[22] A number of interesting anecdotes come out of this close association. For instance, when Dietrich Bonhoeffer visited Barth in the summer semester of 1931, he was invited to attend the staging of a play that Barth had written when he was a youth and that was being produced under Gollwitzer's direction![23] During that same summer, Gollwitzer was part of a group of students that Barth convened to review his Münster dogmatics with an eye to revision. After a few meetings, Karl Gerhard Steck replied to Barth's request for a list of all necessary changes by exclaiming: "You can't leave a single line from this stuff!" And so, Barth moved on to his *Church Dogmatics*. When it was time to lay out the first part-volume of *Church Dogmatics* for publication, Barth could not decide upon the best way to include the historical and exegetical digressions. Should they be left in the body of the text or placed in notes? Gollwitzer advocated the use of small print, thinking that placing the material in notes would be too inconvenient for readers.[24] Gollwitzer and Barth remained in touch throughout the years, and perhaps their continued association is best indicated by pointing out that Barth attended Gollwitzer's wedding and Gollwitzer spoke at Barth's memorial service.[25]

20. Stieber-Westermann, *Provokation zum Leben*, 74.
21. Gollwitzer makes the comment in his preface to ibid., 1.
22. Gollwitzer, *Skizzen eines Lebens*, 70. Busch refers to Gollwitzer as "Barth's assistant" during this period. Busch, *Karl Barth*, 262.
23. See ibid., 28; Eberhard Bethge, *Dietrich Bonhoeffer: A Biography*, revised edition (Minneapolis, MN: Fortress Press, 2000), 177.
24. Gollwitzer, *Skizzen eines Lebens*, 60–61.

What of Karl Barth's theological influence on Gollwitzer? Stieber-Westermann identifies the key theological insight that Gollwitzer acquired from Barth as the recognition of God "as inaccessible vis-à-vis humanity," with the consequent affirmation that theology is an interpretation of God's "antecedent reality."[26] This is nothing other than *the* key starting point of Barth's theology, expressed already in the second edition of his landmark work on Paul's epistle to the Romans by the striking phrase, "God is God."[27] The pivotal affirmation here is that God is nonobjectifiable, that is, not a factor in the world that humans can conceptualize independently. We have to do with God and know God only by way of the "concrete address of God" that cuts across all our creaturely doing and knowing. God becomes accessible to us only insofar as God speaks—*Deus dixit!*—and never because of an inherent human possibility. Stieber-Westermann connects the dots between this insight and Barth's rejection of natural theology and apologetics, as well as the intersection of God's love and freedom in Barth's doctrine of universal election.[28]

Association with Barth also involved political consequences for Gollwitzer. While he had already moved far and decisively to the left of his conservative upbringing, Gollwitzer's time in Bonn further nurtured this movement. Anecdotally, Gollwitzer told the story that Barth said to him one day: "Herr Gollwitzer, someone told me you joined in the Internationale at a meeting last night. You're making great progress!" Gollwitzer even chided Barth when the latter finally joined the German social-democratic political party (SPD) because of its stuffy and bourgeois reputation.[29] This continued movement to the left was not the result of Barth's political views alone, as though they could be separated from his theology. These things remained closely connected in

---

25. See ibid., 250; Busch, *Karl Barth*, 499.

26. Stieber-Westermann, *Provokation zum Leben*, 38.

27. Karl Barth, *The Epistle to the Romans*, trans. Edwyn C. Hoskyns (Oxford: Oxford University Press, 1968), 411. "Faith is born in fear and trembling from the knowledge that God is God. All that is not thus born is not faith." For more on this phrase and its importance for Barth's early theology, see Eberhard Busch, *Barth*, Abingdon Pillars of Theology (Nashville, TN: Abingdon Press, 2008), 1–5. For Gollwitzer's own comments on the importance of this phrase, see Helmut Gollwitzer, "Introduction," in *Church Dogmatics: A Selection*, ed. G. W Bromiley (New York: Harper Torchbooks, 1961), 18.

28. Stieber-Westermann, *Provokation zum Leben*, 39. For more on Barth's use of the phrase *"Deus dixit,"* see Bruce L. McCormack, *Karl Barth's Critically Realistic Dialectical Theology: Its Genesis and Development, 1909-1936* (Oxford: Clarendon Press, 1995), 337–46.

29. I have taken Barth's comment to Gollwitzer as translated in Timothy Gorringe, *Karl Barth: Against Hegemony*, Christian Theology in Context (Oxford: Oxford University Press, 1999), 18n69. See also the following, the last of which contains Gollwitzer's remarks about Barth and the SPD: Pangritz, "Helmut Gollwitzer als Theologe des Dialogs," 2; Gollwitzer, *Skizzen eines Lebens*, 64.

Gollwitzer's mind, and he credited Barth for his recognition of "the political relevance of the Christian message." For Barth, "the Gospel had always struck a revolutionary rather than a conservative note. It had always seemed to call for the alteration and amelioration of the *status quo* rather than its legitimation."[30]

Gollwitzer explains that the place of socialism in Barth's theology is as "a predicate of the Gospel" insofar as "God wants socialism." This is not to say that God wants any particular, concrete form that socialism assumes in the world. Rather, God wants "the true socialism of the kingdom of God."[31] At stake here is the importance of maintaining the ability for the gospel—or, the kingdom of God—to function critically vis-à-vis any particular socialist party or policy proposal. But affirming this kind of critical reserve does not relativize the importance of promoting and achieving a shift from the *status quo* to socialist—and ever more truly socialist!—forms of sociopolitical and economic life. What Gollwitzer appreciates in Barth is that he recognizes this as a theological task inextricably linked with the gospel and, thus, as a task that is unavoidable for those who would be faithful to that gospel. Gollwitzer is also critical of Barth, however, with reference to the Marxist insight that theory and praxis (i.e., concrete, embodied life oriented toward sociopolitical change) must be unified. For Gollwitzer, "the entire direction of Barth's thought leads to praxis." Indeed, he explicates Barth's theology as an attempt to develop the theory necessary to fund true socialism's praxis.[32] Nonetheless, Gollwitzer also suggests that there might be "a vestige of idealism" in Barth's tendency to assume that right theory will necessarily lead to right praxis, that is, that right doctrine will produce right ethics.[33] This can be seen in Barth's tendency to emphasize the sermon as the critical moment that calls the church back to faithfulness. A proper approach will not rely only on the sermon, but will also do the hard organizational, structural, and even political work to change society.

Barth's vestigial idealism can perhaps be connected to his "limited study" of the Marxist tradition.[34] These comments on Barth's limits and weaknesses help to clarify how Gollwitzer understood himself in relation to Barth. As mentioned at the beginning of this chapter, Gollwitzer

---

30. Gollwitzer, "Introduction," 20–21.
31. Helmut Gollwitzer, "Kingdom of God and Socialism in the Theology of Karl Barth," in *Karl Barth and Radical Politics*, ed. George Hunsinger (Philadelphia: Westminster Press, 1976), 77–78.
32. Ibid., 97, 88–89.
33. Ibid., 111.
34. Ibid., 103.

was an irregular—rather than a regular—theologian. Rather than starting from theological scratch, as it were, Gollwitzer wanted to fill in the gaps that Barth left while working within Barth's general orientation. Marquardt suggests Gollwitzer believed that Barth's *Church Dogmatics* could not be surpassed—at least for the time being—and so set about the work of translating that theory into praxis.[35] This meant connecting the dots between Barth's theology and concrete sociopolitical issues.

Finally, Barth was Gollwitzer's gateway into the Confessing Church.[36] The Confessing Church was a collection of allied organizations that developed in protest against how certain stakeholders in the German churches, who called themselves "German Christians," sought to apply the policies of Hitler's government within the ecclesiastical sphere. Barth was in the front lines of the Confessing Church movement, providing a visible theological rallying point. For example, in 1934, Barth served as one of the principle authors of the Barmen Declaration. He even went so far as to send a packet of theological materials to Hitler in an attempt to better acquaint him with the issues at stake.[37] Gollwitzer took his cues from Barth during this controversy, especially in the early 1930s, when Barth was still in Germany. And his position as one of Barth's students and assistants gave him access to many of the key players.

Martin Luther

Gollwitzer had contact with Luther through his father's vocation long before he had ever heard of Karl Barth. But it was only by coming into contact with Barth and the dialectical theology of *Zwischen den Zeiten* that Gollwitzer became interested in theology. Georg Merz, who helped to draw Gollwitzer into this new theological movement, published a book on Luther in 1926, and Gollwitzer's theological education featured prominent Luther scholars. Stieber-Westermann suggests that it was

---

35. Marquardt, "Weg und Werk," 27–28.
36. For a good introduction to the Confessing Church and the "church struggle" (*Kirchenkampf*), see Victoria Barnett, *For the Soul of the People: Protestant Protest against Hitler* (New York: Oxford University Press, 1992). Those interested in further study should consult Klaus Scholder, *The Churches and the Third Reich*, 2 vols. (Philadelphia: Fortress Press, 1988); Mary M. Solberg, ed. *A Church Undone: Documents from the German Christian Faith Movement, 1932–1940* (Minneapolis, MN: Fortress Press, 2015).
37. For more on Barth's role in the composition of the Barmen Declaration, see Busch, *Karl Barth*, 235–48. For more on Barth's mailing to Hitler, see Klaus Scholder, *Churches and the Third Reich* (Philadelphia: Fortress Press, 1988), 2:55. For Scholder's comments on the Barmen Declaration, see 2:134–55.

Barth's theology that gave Gollwitzer his basic orientation, including a critical reserve concerning Luther and the Lutheran tradition. For his own part, Gollwitzer treats these two influences in a more egalitarian manner: "Luther is—beside Barth—my decisive theological teacher, and both always basically sounded together for me for all their differences."[38] He goes on to specify how Luther's doctrine of justification intersects, for him, with Barth's understanding of the relation between Gospel and Law to bring out the "sociocritical consequences" of the kingdom of God. It is on this basis that Gollwitzer criticizes not only the Lutheran tradition but also Luther himself when he departs from his best insights.

It is difficult to overestimate the importance of Luther's doctrine of justification for Gollwitzer. Indeed, Gollwitzer tells of having a spiritual awakening while reading Luther's commentary on Romans, when he understood for the first time the deep power and far-reaching implications of Luther's doctrine of justification. This realization enabled him to see the people around him in a new light: no longer did he look down his nose at them from his "high moral idealism," viewing them with distaste as stuffy and bourgeois. "Suddenly the story of justification dawned on me and I realized that all of these people are loveable for God, and that he loves each one."[39]

As we will see later, the logic of justification plays an important role at the intersection of Gollwitzer's theology and politics. It also grounds Gollwitzer's criticism of the Lutheran tradition. As Stieber-Westermann explains, Gollwitzer saw Luther as breaking out of the logic of *quid pro quo* that dominated "the medieval doctrine of grace." However, this logic creeps back in whenever the hidden God (*deus absconditus*) lurks in the background and "radically calls into question" the "gift of grace" given by the revealed God (*deus revelatus*). For Gollwitzer, this occurs in Melanchthon and Lutheran orthodoxy when they betray Luther's best insights by forgetting that salvation occurs in Christ and not in the act of human faith, which is properly understood as reception of this salvation into an individual's life but *not* as that salvation itself. While Luther resisted the temptation to divide humanity into good people on one side and bad people on the other, such a division is later transposed into that between believers and nonbelievers.

38. Helmut Gollwitzer, "Klassenkampf ist keine Illusion. Ein Interview," in *Forderungen der Umkehr: Beiträge zur Theologie der Gesellschaft* (München: Chr. Kaiser Verlag, 1976), 219. See also Stieber-Westermann, *Provokation Zum Leben*, 54. Stieber-Westermann notes Merz's book on Luther: Georg Merz, *Der vorreformatorische Luther* (München: Chr. Kaiser, 1926).
39. Gollwitzer, *Skizzen eines Lebens*, 35.

And this betrays the universal character of God's love and the reconciling work of Jesus Christ.[40] For Gollwitzer, such theological missteps are inextricably linked to mistakes in Christian praxis. His sermons denounce failures to "imitate God's all-embracing love" by substituting "a quite restrictive love, confined to good people, and basically entirely selfish." A love properly tutored in God's love and forgiveness would seek to share God's gifts, both the spiritual and material sort, with others who stand in need of them. Gollwitzer resorts to what was perhaps his favorite quotation from Luther—"What is not service, is robbery"—and he pointedly asserts: "It might thus be that we, who do not consider ourselves as robbers, are exposed as robbers, dishonestly holding on to God's gifts and misappropriating them for our own use."[41]

Another aspect of Gollwitzer's debt to Luther is the concept of "temptation."[42] For Gollwitzer, at stake here is the faith-character of the Christian life as lived or experienced. In other words, and as Stieber-Westermann articulates it, at issue are "concrete experiences of the discrepancy between promise and fulfillment."[43] In the gospel of Jesus Christ, God makes certain promises to humanity—promises to love and care for humanity, to be with humanity, and so on. But the Christian's experience of life belies those promises. In this way, faith in God remains faith, rather than sight—a question of trust in God's promises, rather than their objective demonstration. Christians thus participate in Jesus's experience of Gethsemane and Calvary precisely by believing not because of appearances, but in spite of them. Believers are those who experience God's absence, and yet, still believe.

---

40. Stieber-Westermann, *Provokation zum Leben*, 64–65. Recall that emphasis on the universality of God's electing grace was one of the dogmatic lessons Gollwitzer learned from Barth.

41. Helmut Gollwitzer, *The Way to Life: Sermons in a Time of World Crisis*, trans. David Cairns (Edinburgh: T&T Clark, 1981), 68. Gollwitzer uses this quotation from Luther frequently, and Weinrich testifies to Gollwitzer's penchant for it. See Michael Weinrich, "Gesellschaftliche Herausforderungen der Theologie: Erinnerungen an Helmut Gollwitzer," *Evangelische Theologie* 59, no. 3 (1999): 171. I am grateful to David Congdon's help in tracking this statement to a sermon that Luther preached on March 29, 1523: Martin Luther and Ludwig Enders, *Dr. Martin Luthers vermischte Predigten*, Zwieter Band, Dr. Martin Luther's Sämmtliche Werke (Frankfurt am Main: Heyder & Zimmer, 1878), 38.

42. The German term is *Anfechtung*, and it is a technical one in Luther studies. As translator Martin Lohrmann explains: "Another choice facing a translator is what to do with the German word *Anfechtung* (plural: *Anfechtungen*), a term that has major significance for Luther's theology. . . . *Anfechtung* can mean doubt, distress, assault, affliction, trials, or temptations. Since it has no clear single equivalent in English and is such an important term for understanding Luther, I have left it untranslated so that it can mean all those complicated things at once." Berndt Hamm, *The Early Luther: Stages in a Reformation Reorientation*, trans. Martin J. Lohrmann (Grand Rapids, MI: Eerdmans, 2014), xii–xiv. Since this is not a technical study of Luther, I translate this term as "temptation" since that communicates the main concern of Gollwitzer's use.

43. Stieber-Westermann, *Provokation zum Leben*, 65; for what follows, see also 66–67.

Stieber-Westerman highlights how Gollwitzer understands this aspect of Luther's theology as an attempt to do justice to the biblical book of Job. Luther sounds this theme already in the lectures on Romans that played such an important role for Gollwitzer: "He who believes God makes God truthful and himself a liar. For he discredits his own feelings as false in order that he might trust in the Word of God as true, which, however, is absolutely contrary to his own feelings."[44]

All good theologians also tempt, disrupt, and challenge the church. Luther's thought performed just such a role for Gollwitzer, and Gollwitzer recognized this. So it seems fitting to conclude here with his own words of tribute:

> [Luther's] importance to our time rests in the fact that he has interpreted the Christian message with an originality and forcefulness such as has been granted to hardly any other interpreter during the two thousand years of its existence. And who could deny that we have, so far, not got to the point when we can reject this message as a thing of the past? The truth is that it will never be a thing of the past, but that we shall always have it before us as a challenge.[45]

Martin Buber

Buber's influence on Gollwitzer was not so broad and critically formative as that of Barth and Luther. Nonetheless, Buber's influence helps to tie together Gollwitzer's inheritance from both Barth and Luther in a way that intersects with what we might call Gollwitzer's theological existence or his way of being in the world as a theologian. Pangritz has spoken of Gollwitzer's "genius of friendship,"[46] his ability to live in solidarity with and for others while respecting their otherness. This kind of friendship played an important role in Gollwitzer's life as we saw already with reference to his experience at St. Anna. Buber provides a way of conceptualizing this kind of friendship.

One of Buber's major intellectual contributions is the distinction between conceptualizing the other as an "It" or as a "You." With an "It" conception, one approaches the other as an object to be known and manipulated, whereas the "You" conception recognizes the relationship that exists between the self and the other. This relationship impli-

---

44. Martin Luther, *Luther's Works, 25: Lectures on Romans, Glosses and Scholia*, ed. Jaroslav Pelikan (Saint Louis, MO: Concordia, 1972), 284.

45. Helmut Gollwitzer, "The Real Luther," in *Martinus Luther: 450th Anniversary of the Reformation* (Bad Godesberg: Inter Nationes, 1967), 14.

46. Pangritz, "Helmut Gollwitzer als Theologe des Dialogs," 1.

cates the self in the process of knowledge, thus insisting that the other be engaged in its otherness, rather than in a way that subordinates that otherness to one's self. Thinking in terms of personal categories is superior to thinking in terms of abstract causal categories. One important payoff of this approach for Gollwitzer, as Stieber-Westermann explains, is the insight that "only personal categories can testify to the relationship between God and humanity if the biblical foundation is not to be abandoned."[47] In other words, proper speech concerning God is not *about* God in an abstract sense (i.e., "God is . . ." or "God exists"), but *to* God. Likewise, God's speech does not communicate abstract information but takes the form of direct personal address. This insight further extends, for Gollwitzer, to all human existence, which is best characterized as dialogical.

Gollwitzer understands Buber's significance against the backdrop of early-twentieth-century Protestant theology, and it is here that we can see how Buber functioned for Gollwitzer as a focal lens for insights he found in Barth and Luther. For instance, Gollwitzer suggests that the reason why Protestant theology in this period could be so open to Buber was because of Luther. One finds in Luther a divine word that addresses the sinner in a way that both reveals the sinner's otherness to God and overcomes that otherness. This is an advance on the scholastic tendency to think in terms of abstract causes. Here, Gollwitzer instead finds a "personal logic" that is fundamentally aligned with Buber's insights.[48] Indeed, Gollwitzer notes that Buber developed his thinking in the wake of the early-twentieth-century Luther renaissance that also influenced the primary theological movements of that period. Consequently, Buber's thought is tied up with Luther's in the theological currents that produced thinkers such as Emil Brunner, Rudolf Bultmann, Friedrich Gogarten, Paul Tillich, and Karl Barth. With reference to Barth specifically, Gollwitzer highlights Barth's admission of basic agreement with Buber on the relational character of human existence.[49] Buber responded to this by lamenting that Barth was only

47. Stieber-Westermann, *Provokation zum Leben*, 68; see 67–71.
48. Helmut Gollwitzer, "Martin Bubers Bedeutung für die protestantische Theologie," in *Leben als Begegnung. Ein Jahrhundert Martin Buber (1878–1978), Vorträge und Aufsätze*, ed. Peter von der Osten-Sacken (Berlin: Institut Kirche und Judentum, 1982), 65. In some ways, this essay on Buber represents the high-water mark of Gollwitzer's engagement with Judaism. See McMaken, "'Shalom, Shalom, Shalom Israel!'," 17–21.
49. See Barth, *Church Dogmatics*, 3.2:277–78. David W. Congdon helpfully discusses the influence that the early-twentieth-century Luther renaissance had on the development of dialectical theology, noting especially that the motor of this renaissance was "the young Luther's notion of the 'experience of justification' (*Rechtfertigungserlebnis*), taken from the then-newly discovered 1516 lectures on Romans that were first published in 1908." David W. Congdon, *The Mission of Demythologizing:*

able to access this insight christologically, but Gollwitzer affirms the possibility of rapprochement between Barth and Buber because they both develop their ideas from a "biblical origin," and because of how Barth thinks of the "togetherness of Israel and the church."[50]

In the Shadow of the Third Reich

Karl Barth's telephone call in the middle of the night of January 30, 1933, disturbed Gollwitzer's sleep. Barth called to inform Gollwitzer that Adolf Hitler had become the Chancellor of Germany.[51] This event would dominate the next 17 years of Gollwitzer's life.

The Confessing Church

From his vantage point as Barth's doctoral student, Gollwitzer observed that Barth became more than just one theologian among others in the midst of the church struggle. His authority and stature grew quickly as he provided much needed leadership. It was also during this period that it became clear that Barth's theology was truly a church theology concerned with moving beyond the merely intellectual by bringing its resources to bear on the church's life and practice. Gollwitzer himself played a significant supporting role in this.[52]

One of the difficulties encountered by the Confessing Church movement was confessional diversity among its supporters. Each German region had its established church. Some of these were "union" churches where the Reformed and Lutheran traditions existed together while others were Lutheran alone, and some of the Lutheran

Rudolf Bultmann's Dialectical Theology (Minneapolis, MN: Fortress Press, 2015), 262. Gollwitzer experienced an important spiritual awakening through reading these lectures, as we have seen.

50. Gollwitzer, "Martin Bubers Bedeutung für die protestantische Theologie," 75. Gollwitzer notes that he is unaware of whether Barth read Buber in the preparation of this material, but it is plausible that he did so insofar as Busch documents interactions between Barth and Buber. This includes correspondence during the church struggle. Buber also had contact with Barth's friend and theological fellow traveler, Eduard Thurneysen, already in the 1920s. Such interaction suggests that Barth may well have been aware of Buber's ideas. See respectively, Busch, *Karl Barth*, 272, 144. George Hunsinger briefly discusses Barth's critical appropriation of Buber in Barth's theological anthropology. George Hunsinger, *How to Read Karl Barth: The Shape of His Theology* (New York: Oxford University Press, 1991), 62–63. He also discusses the importance of "personalism" as a motif in Barth's thought. See pp. 5, 40–42.

51. Gollwitzer, *Skizzen eines Lebens*, 65.

52. Ibid., 67–68. For a detailed and extensive account of Gollwitzer's place in the church struggle, from which I draw extensively, if implicitly, in what follows, see Dietrich Braun, "Helmut Gollwitzer in den Jahren des Kirchenkampfs 1934–1938," in *Coena Domini. Die altlutherische Abendmahlslehre in ihrer Auseinandersetzung mit dem Calvinismus, dargestellt an der lutherischen Frühorthodoxie* (München: Chr. Kaiser, 1988).

churches were very traditionalist in their theological orientation. This diversity was exacerbated since the Confessing Church tended to be made up of people within these diverse churches who were more theologically alive, which often involved somewhat inflexible commitment to their different traditions. In a twentieth-century echo of the historical conflict between the Reformed and Lutheran traditions, eucharistic theology became an important point of contention within the movement. There would even be a split within the movement over this point in 1936,[53] enabling Hitler's regime to follow the time-honored imperial strategy—divide and conquer.

Barth saw this threat of fragmentation within the Confessing Church movement and advocated for a common confession in the face of a political situation that relativized these traditional divisions.[54] Gollwitzer helped to advance this agenda through writing.

He began with an essay in 1934, entitled "Lutheran, Reformed, Protestant," in which he assumed a mediating role between the Lutheran and Reformed confessions by emphasizing their common commitment to scripture. Gollwitzer then focused on the crux of the issue in a 1936 essay, entitled "The Lord's Supper as a Task for Church Doctrine." This essay distinguishes between theological differences that arise because of fundamentally different conceptions of the gospel, and those that arise from differing temperaments or conceptual formulations. His emphasis is on the unity that occurs in the celebration of the Supper, which he argues is more important than differences in how this event is conceptualized.[55] Finally, Gollwitzer took the Lord's Supper as the subject of his dissertation, which he completed in 1937. His preface makes the horizon of the work clear. Continuing the theme of relativizing divergent doctrines of the Lord's Supper by emphasizing the church's experience of it, Gollwitzer writes: "In the sacrament the church is hushed. Her Lord alone speaks. No doctrine of the sacrament should have any other purpose than to bring the right silence before the mystery of [God's] condescension. . . . [Such a doctrine] has served its purpose if it provides a little help to the commu-

53. Scholder, *Churches and the Third Reich*, 2:233–34. Some of the more conservative Lutheran supporters of the Confessing Church seem, at times, to have thought that association with German Christians was preferable to association with Reformed supporters of the Confessing Church (see p. 134)!

54. Ibid., 2:55.

55. Helmut Gollwitzer, "Lutherisch, reformiert, evangelisch," *Evangelische Theologie* 1 (1934): 307–25; Helmut Gollwitzer, "Die Abendmahlsfrage als Aufgabe kirchlicher Lehre," in *Theologische Aufsätze: Karl Barth zum 50. Geburtstag*, ed. Ernst Wolf (München: Chr. Kaiser Verlag, 1936), 275–98. Other essays written by Gollwitzer in this period also address these issues indirectly from diverse angles.

nity as it seeks community and life in the mystery of Christ during these times of great distress."[56]

While working on his dissertation, Ernst Wolf helped Gollwitzer secure a job as castle preacher for Heinrich XXXIX, Prince Rueß, for whom he worked from January 1934 until January 1936. In addition to his preaching responsibilities, Gollwitzer also tutored the prince's children, undertook pastoral work in nearby communities, and did organizational work for the Confessing Church. Prince Heinrich held estates in both Austria and the German province of Thuringia, and it was in Thuringia that Gollwitzer first met Martin Niemöller in 1935. The prince gave him a very positive recommendation at the end of this period, describing Gollwitzer as "in the deepest sense a 'preacher of the word'" who had brought life into the "small castle church."[57] Gollwitzer was happy in the Austrian Lutheran church and considered staying there, but he decided to accept ordination and a position in Thuringia where he could continue working in support of the Confessing Church movement. He continued his work for the Confessing Church in the region until he was given the opportunity to become Niemöller's assistant in Dahlem, a suburb of Berlin, which was the center of the more radical wing of the Confessing Church.

Gollwitzer arrived in Dahlem on May 1, 1937. Niemöller was arrested on July 1. Despite his acquittal by the courts in 1938, Hitler personally intervened to send Niemöller to a concentration camp as a "personal prisoner of the Führer."[58] Niemöller remained there until the Reich fell. Gollwitzer took Niemöller's place in the Dahlem pulpit. Paul Oestreicher describes the situation that faced Gollwitzer as follows: "Not only was this one of the wealthiest suburbs of the German capital, but in it lived a high proportion of the most influential and powerful people in Nazi Germany. To preach the Gospel here was to preach it in the open jaws of hell."[59] This tenuous position meant that "Gollwitzer's work was constantly watched by the Gestapo. Informers attended worship and community events." At the same time, Gollwitzer was able to stay well informed because members of the community had ties to the *Wehrmacht*—the German military establishment.[60] Gollwitzer was imprisoned during the summer of 1938 and tensions were raised fur-

---

56. Helmut Gollwitzer, *Coena Domini. Die altlutherische Abendmahlslehre in ihrer Auseinandersetzung mit dem Calvinismus, drgestellt an der lutherischen Frühorthodoxie* (München: Chr. Kaiser, 1988), xi.

57. Gollwitzer, *Skizzen eines Lebens*, 76, 79.

58. Braun, "Helmut Gollwitzer," 95.

59. Oestreicher, "Helmut Gollwitzer," 14.

60. Stieber-Westermann, *Provokation zum Leben*, 21.

ther when he preached on the yearly Day of Repentance, which fell only six days after the pogrom of November 1938. Speaking carefully but nonetheless clearly, Gollwitzer castigated his hearers for having "exchanged God's standard for the standard of current political propaganda," telling them that "God is disgusted at the very sight of you." He concluded with a call to action: "Now just outside this church our neighbor is waiting for us—waiting for us in his need and lack of protection, disgraced, hungry, hunted, and driven by fear for his very existence. That is the one who is waiting to see if today this Christian congregation has really observed this national day of penance."[61]

One intellectual result of his time in Dahlem—as the 1930s drew to a close and the next stage of his life loomed on the horizon—was the production of a remarkable cycle of sermons on the Gospel of Luke. Marquardt writes of these sermons that "the interpretations of St. Luke that Gollwitzer preached and wrote when he was Niemöller's representative in Dahlem . . . have a similarly profound meaning for his theology as work on the *Epistle to the Romans* had for Barth." In these sermons, Marquardt recognizes all the major themes of Gollwitzer's later intellectual life, such as the importance of Israel, Jesus's Jewishness, and the gospel as promise and hope that anticipates fulfilment. One even finds key dogmatic articulations of the christology, doctrine of the Trinity, and understanding of justification that served as Gollwitzer's theological foundation. Indeed, Marquardt is amply justified in his suggestion that it is possible to conceive of "Gollwitzer's theology overall as a Lukan theology."[62] We also see in these sermons the intersection of theology and politics in Gollwitzer's thought, although—like his sermon in response to the November 1938 pogrom—his analysis tends to remain at the level of individual responsibility, which is understandable given the context. Nonetheless, he pronounces challenging state-

---

61. Helmut Gollwitzer, "A Sermon About *Kristallnacht*," in *Preaching in Hitler's Shadow: Sermons of Resistance in the Third Reich*, ed. Dean G. Stroud (Grand Rapids, MI: Eerdmans, 2013), 122, 125. Stroud, the editor of this sermon in its English translation, makes two minor historical mistakes in his introduction to this sermon. First, the pogrom occurred on the night of November 9–10, and not on that of November 8–9. Second, Gollwitzer preached this sermon on Wednesday, November 16, whereas Stroud mistakenly identifies it as a Sunday. Stroud is perhaps unfamiliar with the German Protestant church's *Bußtag* tradition, which may have led him to incorrectly assume that the churches treated the Sunday following the pogrom as an *ad hoc* "day of repentance." For more on this sermon, see Braun, "Helmut Gollwitzer," 98–99; McMaken, "'Shalom, Shalom, Shalom Israel!'," 7–8. The pogrom of November 1938 is often referred to as *Kristallnacht* ("night of glass") because of all the broken glass that littered the streets the following morning. But that somewhat romantic euphemism masks the horror of this brutal state-sponsored act of racially motivated domestic terrorism. Such romanticizing is dangerous in the contemporary United States as threats of violence against Jewish communities and desecrations of Jewish graves are on the rise.
62. Marquardt, "Weg und Werk," 29.

ments: "The one thing that matters for the Church is that she should be both a danger and a help to the world."[63]

There were also important developments in Gollwitzer's personal life toward the end of his time in Dahlem. As Friedrich Künzel and Ruth Pabst introduce the subject: "'she should yodel and be able to cook well.' Helmut Gollwitzer, the 28 year old pastor from Bavaria, had a clear vision for his future wife. Four years later . . . he became engaged to the beautiful Berlin actress Eva Bildt. She could neither cook nor yodel."[64] Eva and Helmut met on August 25, 1940. She was a singer and actress whose dream of a professional career, along with the rest of her life, was derailed because her mother was Jewish. Her father Paul Bildt's status as an Aryan and state-sponsored actor provided some protection to his wife and daughter, but this protection seemed increasingly feeble as the war progressed. They lived with the constant threat of arrest and transfer to a camp. Helmut and Eva rapidly fell in love, and they became engaged in January 1941.

Soldier and Prisoner of War

The period of his courtship with Eva was an uncertain time for Gollwitzer. He had been conscripted into the German army in mid-1940, but some of his friends used their connections to have the order cancelled. Then, when he was issued a gag order and expelled from Berlin on September 3, Gollwitzer moved just outside the city limits and continued with his work as best he could. Gollwitzer was conscripted again on December 5. He and his friends felt that it would not be any more dangerous for him within Germany's armed forces—the *Wehrmacht*—than it already was for him outside of it.[65] Gollwitzer turned down officer training and was placed in a machine-gun company, before transferring to become a medical orderly as quickly as he could. This move would not, in Gollwitzer's mind, make him any less guilty for his complicity in the German war machine, but it would at least enable him to act with a measure of good faith. "I was sure that I would not level my gun at people in earnest, especially not in the service of Hitler, but the wounded and the sick must be provided for in any

---

63. Helmut Gollwitzer, *The Dying and Living Lord* (Philadelphia: Muhlenberg Press, 1960), 95.
64. Helmut Gollwitzer and Eva Bildt, *Ich will Dir schnell sagen, daß ich lebe, Liebster: Brief aus dem Krieg 1940-1945*, ed. Friedrich Künzel and Ruth Pabst (München: C. H. Beck Verlag, 2008), 9. My narration of Helmut and Eva's relationship draws upon this source, as well as Gollwitzer, *Skizzen eines Lebens*, 152–59. The above paragraph is adapted from McMaken, "'Shalom, Shalom, Shalom Israel!'," 9.
65. Gollwitzer, *Skizzen eines Lebens*, 168–69.

case."[66] He was able to make it through the conflict without ever having to shoot someone.

Gollwitzer was first assigned to the occupying force in France, where he stayed well into 1943, and was then transferred to the Eastern Front. His war would end in May 1945, when he was taken into custody by the Soviet army. We get a window into his state of mind in the hours of Germany's final defeat from the memoirs of this period that he later published: "In these days my mind was obsessed with the idea of the German collapse as a gracious divine judgment. . . . Now every opportunist party membership, every perversion of judgment, was having its revenge. . . . Now the Germans were being measured with the measure that they had applied to the Jews. Would they see the connection?"[67]

These memoirs paint a striking picture of Gollwitzer's time as a prisoner of war, which lasted until the very end of 1949. He passed through a number of different camps and describes what life was like for the prisoners as well as for the civilians near the camps. Gollwitzer functioned as a pastor for those around him throughout this period. For instance, he recounts a conversation with Hans, a young lieutenant, about the power of love to differentiate the individual from the mass of humanity and endow the individual with meaning. Hans cannot believe that God would be concerned with individuals, but Gollwitzer pushes him to think about what it would mean if God *was* so concerned. Hans then arrives at a definition of love that Gollwitzer grasps on to: "If someone loves me then I matter to them. I am as important to them as they are to themselves, or as I am to myself." Gollwitzer translates this into a theological register: "The love of God is the meaning of your life, and cannot be destroyed even in the . . . concentration camp. It amounts to just this: I am as important to God as I am to myself, and as He is to Himself."[68] This was also a period of intense engagement with Marxism in its Soviet form, which Gollwitzer conducted through reading and conversations with his jailors.

Gollwitzer kept up a lively and extensive correspondence with his fiancée Eva throughout the war, but communications broke down as Germany fell and Gollwitzer was taken prisoner. Eva became increasingly depressed as the war continued.[69] The Bildt home was destroyed by bombing in early 1944, and both her parents became very ill. Her

---

66. Ibid., 172. On Gollwitzer turning down officer training, see Stieber-Westermann, *Provokation zum Leben*, 23.
67. Helmut Gollwitzer, *Unwilling Journey: A Diary from Russia*, trans. E. M. Delacour and Robert Fenn (London: SCM, 1953), 23.
68. Ibid., 43.

mother died in March 1945, Berlin was occupied on April 26, and on April 27, Eva and her apparently terminally ill father attempted suicide through barbiturate overdose.[70] Eva succeeded, but her father made a full recovery and lived until 1957. Gollwitzer did not learn of his beloved's fate, and the fates of other friends and loved ones lost in the final days of the war, until autumn 1946 when the first correspondence from home caught up with him in Soviet custody. He reacted as one might expect: "I ran howling into the woods."[71] After returning from his time as a prisoner of war, Gollwitzer reconnected with and became close to Eva's father, Paul.

Paul had written the following verse in the front of his Bible in 1935: "From his fullness we have all received, grace upon grace" (see John 1:16). This became Gollwitzer's life-verse. He preached on this text at Paul's funeral in 1957; it was the text of the sermon when he married Brigitte Freudenberg in 1951; and it was the text preached at both Brigitte and Helmut's funerals. Helga Krüger Day says of Gollwitzer's theology that "it was a theology of grace from the beginning and has remained so."[72] What is true of his theology is also true of his life: it was a life of grace throughout, "grace upon grace," given and received.

The Postwar Public Intellectual

Gollwitzer returned from his time as a prisoner of war on New Year's Eve, 1949.[73] He was returning to a very different world. We cannot even say that he returned to Germany, for a united Germany no longer existed. Gollwitzer returned to West Germany, otherwise known as the Federal or Bonn Republic. It would be here—first in Bonn itself and

69. The remainder of this paragraph is adapted from McMaken, "'Shalom, Shalom, Shalom Israel!'," 9–10.
70. Gollwitzer and Bildt, *Ich will Dir schnell sagen*, 317. Eva is described as "witness to rapes" on April 26 (p. 13), which provides some insight into the situation she faced. Rape was widespread as Soviet forces occupied the city. For a particularly poignant story of one Berlin community's experience with this on April 25–26, see Anthony Beevor, *The Fall of Berlin, 1945* (New York: Penguin, 2002), 312–13. See pp. 326–27 for a story from Dahlem and reflections on the phenomenon as it manifested itself in Berlin. Beevor recounts that contemporary estimates of the total number of rape victims in Berlin were from 95,000 to 130,000, including approximately 10,000 deaths—many of which were from suicide (see p. 410).
71. Gollwitzer, *Skizzen eines Lebens*, 228. The correspondence provided here does not explicitly state that Gollwitzer learned of Eva's death in the first delivery of mail, but knowledgeable sources say that he did. See Gollwitzer and Bildt, *Ich will Dir schnell sagen*, 317; Pangritz, "Helmut Gollwitzer als Theologe des Dialogs," 4; Stieber-Westermann, *Provokation zum Leben*, 25.
72. Helga Krüger Day, "Christlicher Glaube und gesellschaftliches Handeln: eine Studie der Entwicklung der Theologie Helmut Gollwitzers" (Doctoral dissertation: Union Theological Seminary, 1973), 333.
73. Gollwitzer, *Unwilling Journey*, 309.

then in West Berlin—that Gollwitzer would distinguish himself as a leading postwar public intellectual.

Bonn

The University of Bonn appointed Gollwitzer as *ordinarius* professor of theology on January 31, 1950. He was called to replace Barth, who had decided not to resume the position in Bonn from which Hitler's government ejected him.[74] Before assuming his position, however, Gollwitzer spent time at home in Bavaria recovering from his ordeal. When the moment came to travel to Bonn and take up his position, he stopped in Frankfurt (am Main) to see Brigitte Freudenberg—an old friend who did children's ministry and church-based relief work there with a Confessing Church pastor.

Brigitte and Helmut knew each other in Dahlem in the 1930s. Her father, Adolf, had worked with the German foreign service. In part because his wife was Jewish, and in part because he and his wife had fallen under the influence of Martin Niemöller, he resigned in 1935, moved his family to Dahlem in 1936, and began studying to become a Confessing Church pastor.[75] Gollwitzer became close with the Freudenbergs, who provided their young and unattached pastor with something of a surrogate family. The Freudenbergs found themselves in Switzerland for the duration of the war. Brigitte completed a certificate program there whereby young women could receive some ministerial training. She was the first member of her family to return to Germany, which she did in October 1945. Helmut and Brigitte's relationship developed rapidly. They already knew each other, shared commitment to and experience in the Confessing Church, and even shared experience of wartime loss since a young man to whom Brigitte had secretly been engaged died serving in Germany's forces. They were married by Martin Niemöller—who had confirmed Brigitte years before—on March 31, 1951, in the bomb-damaged Frankfurt church where Brigitte was working. Brigitte and Helmut were unable to have children and, for a time, they considered adopting. But very quickly Helmut's students became surrogate children. One of his former students, reminiscing

74. Gollwitzer, *Skizzen eines Lebens*, 249. On the Barth connection, see Pangritz, "Helmut Gollwitzer als Theologe des Dialogs," 2–3; Busch, *Karl Barth*, 372.
75. For more on Adolf Freudenberg, see Hartmut Ludwig, "'Christians Cannot Remain Silent About This Crime': On the Centenary of the Birth of Adolf Freudenberg," *Ecumenical Review* 46, no. 4 (1994): 475–85. My narration of Helmut and Brigitte's relationship draws on Gollwitzer, *Skizzen eines Lebens*, 251–60.

about his work in Berlin in the early 1960s, recalled that the students affectionately referred to him as "Golli," that there were always students around him, that his lectures were well-attended, and that he and Brigitte kept their house open to the students.[76]

Gollwitzer's first major postwar publication was the memoir from his time as a Soviet prisoner of war, published in 1951. It became a bestseller, going through numerous printings; it was translated into English (as *Unwilling Journey*), French, and a number of Scandinavian languages. Oestreicher compares the attention this volume attracted in Germany to that received by J. A. T. Robinson's *Honest to God* in the following decade.[77] In these early years, Gollwitzer also published on the intersection of Christianity with Marxism and communism, and he began a program of publishing sermons and short expositions of biblical texts that would continue throughout his life. His sermons on Luke from his time in Dahlem were published in 1941, and he published a second sermon collection in 1954. Another volume of sermons followed in 1968, with further sermon collections appearing in 1972, 1973, and 1980.[78] As an indication of how Gollwitzer's work in the early 1950s was received, and of the high regard in which he was held even internationally, we can point out that he received two of his three honorary degrees during this period. The first was awarded by Heidelberg University in 1954, and the second by the University of Glasgow in 1956.[79]

In 1957, his last year at the University of Bonn, Gollwitzer took a decisive step by publishing for the first time a major work aimed at the overt intersection of theology and a particular political issue facing society. His argument concerned the Christian Just War tradition. While he did not contest the validity of that tradition, he did argue that—if one were to take the stipulations of that tradition seriously—"the same thoughts that previously allowed [Christians] to participate [in war] now make it impossible" in the atomic age.[80] His rejec-

76. Gollwitzer and Bildt, *Ich will Dir schnell sagen*, 318–19. On the couple's inability to have children and consideration of adoption, see Gottfried Orth, *Helmut Gollwitzer: zur Solidarität befreit* (Mainz: Matthias-Grünewald Verlag, 1995), 59. Adoption was a pressing issue at the time. Many women became pregnant as a result of widespread rape during the occupation of Berlin, and while an overwhelming number of the pregnancies were terminated, many children consequently born were abandoned. See Beevor, *Fall of Berlin*, 412.

77. Oestreicher, "Helmut Gollwitzer," 7. See Helmut Gollwitzer, *. . . und führen, wohin du nicht willst. Bericht einer Gefangenschaft* (München: Chr. Kaiser, 1959); Gollwitzer, *Unwilling Journey*.

78. Although I will make comments concerning Gollwitzer's publishing, I will make no attempt to provide a complete bibliography. Such a bibliography is available: Christa Haehn, ed. *Bibliographie Helmut Gollwitzer*, Ausgewählte Werke (München: Chr. Kaiser, 1988). The 1980 sermon collection was translated into English as Gollwitzer, *Way to Life*.

79. Gollwitzer, *Skizzen eines Lebens*, 328. His third and final honorary degree was awarded by the University of Aberdeen in 1966.

tion of Christian participation in atomic war built on his declaration against West German rearmament in 1954. Gollwitzer had been undecided on the question of rearmament prior to 1954, functioning as a mediating figure. This was in opposition to Karl Barth's resistance to rearmament. In all this, however, we see that Gollwitzer was engaged with the political issues of the time, taking part in the shaping of public opinion. Indeed, he was part of a circle of important sociopolitical figures in Bonn who functioned as the Republic's "democratic conscience."[81] Perhaps foremost among this group was Gustav Heinemann, who would later serve as president (1969–74). Gollwitzer knew Heinemann from Confessing Church circles as far back as 1936, and they remained close. When Heinemann rose to prominence in the 1960s, Gollwitzer offered him the option of ending their contact with each other because Gollwitzer recognized that he could be a political liability to Heinemann. Heinemann refused.[82]

Berlin

The Free University of Berlin was founded at the end of 1948. Located in West Berlin, it was meant to offer a "Western" alternative to the Humboldt University of Berlin that had fallen under Soviet control. This new university was organized on more of an American rather than a German model, approved by the American military officials of the occupying Allied forces, and supported by American funds. It is understandable that people such as Karl Barth would see the Free University as a place of ideological bondage. Indeed, Barth counseled Gollwitzer not to accept a position there. Furthermore, and unlike traditional German universities, the Free University had no theology faculty. Leaders within the German Protestant Church wanted a theological presence in this new university, especially one that could engage in interdisciplinary conversation as well as participate in the dialogue with Marxism that was such a pressing issue in Berlin. Gollwitzer fit the bill, and he embraced the opportunity for interdisciplinary work and the task of demonstrating theology's relevance to other fields and conversations. Besides, Berlin was home for Brigitte, and Gollwitzer himself had fond

---

80. Helmut Gollwitzer, *Die Christen und die Atomwaffen*, Theologische Existenz Heute, ed. K. G. Steck; G. Eichholz (München: Chr. Kaiser Verlag, 1957), 48. For later works on the theme of Christianity and war, see Helmut Gollwitzer, *Militär, Staat und Kirche*, Berliner Reden (Berlin: Lettner-Verlag, 1965); Helmut Gollwitzer, *Vietnam, Israel und die Christenheit* (München: Chr. Kaiser Verlag, 1967).

81. Pangritz, "Helmut Gollwitzer als Theologe des Dialogs," 3. On the rearmament issue, see Gollwitzer, *Skizzen eines Lebens*, 250–51; Busch, *Karl Barth*, 386.

82. Stieber-Westermann, *Provokation zum Leben*, 26, 33; see also Gollwitzer, *Skizzen eines Lebens*, 332–35.

memories of the city from before the war. So Gollwitzer assumed his position there for the winter semester of 1957–58, with a joint appointment to teach in the Berlin seminary as well.[83]

Shortly after assuming his position in Berlin, Gollwitzer went on a trip that would prove decisive for much of his work. He and Brigitte, along with Brigitte's parents, visited the state of Israel. This experience made a deep impression. Returning to Berlin, Gollwitzer gave a speech on May 10, 1958, to commemorate the founding of the state of Israel a decade earlier. His speech drew extensively on his experiences in Israel and presents an overwhelmingly positive picture, although he is not entirely uncritical.[84] The issue of Jewish–Christian dialogue became a pressing one for Gollwitzer from this point forward. In 1961, he helped to establish a working group as part of the German Protestant church's *Kirchentag*—a biannual church gathering that is equal parts conference and festival—for discussion between Christians and Jews. He was joined in this by Friedrich-Wilhelm Marquardt, Rabbi Robert Raphael Geis, and others. This group's work experienced "a life-threatening crisis"[85] that came to be known as the "Purim controversy" (*Purimstreit*). Gollwitzer had acted unilaterally to arrange a meeting between the working group and a conservative Lutheran group interested in proselytizing Jews, and Geis reacted very strongly against this. For Geis, Christians missed the "chance to confess Christ to the Jews—in the Third Reich" by standing up to the Reich on their behalf, and, perhaps, sharing their fate.[86] Gollwitzer and Geis were able to repair the damage to their relationship, however, and the working group continued.

83. See ibid., 268–71; Marquardt, "Weg und Werk," 23–24; Pangritz, "Helmut Gollwitzer als Theologe des Dialogs," 7. This seminary began its life as a Confessing Church seminary, and it operated illegally during much of the Nazi regime. Martin Niemöller was instrumental in its creation, and Gollwitzer was involved with its operation during his time as pastor in Dahlem as well as upon his return to Berlin.

84. For more on Gollwitzer's trip and speech, see McMaken, "'Shalom, Shalom, Shalom Israel!'," 11–15. For the speech itself, see Helmut Gollwitzer, "Israel - und Wir," in *Auch das Denken darf dienen: Aufsätze zu Theologie und Geistesgeschichte*, band 2, Ausgewählte Werke (München: Chr. Kaiser, 1988). For an early edition that includes photographs, see Helmut Gollwitzer, *Israel - und Wir* (Berlin: Lettner Verlag, 1958). See also Gollwitzer, *Skizzen eines Lebens*, 282; Orth, *Helmut Gollwitzer*, 60; Pangritz, "Helmut Gollwitzer als Theologe des Dialogs," 5.

85. Andreas Pangritz, "Helmut Gollwitzers Theologie des christlich-jüdischen Verhältnisses. Versuch eine kritischen Bilanz," *Evangelische Theologie* 56, no. 4 (1996): 365.

86. Robert Raphael Geis, *Leiden an der Unerlöstheit der Welt: Briefe, Reden, Aufsätze* (München: Chr. Kaiser Verlag, 1984), 253. The correspondence relating to this controversy can be found on pp. 227–75. For more on this controversy, see McMaken, "'Shalom, Shalom, Shalom Israel!'," 16–17; Friedrich-Wilhelm Marquardt, "Hermeneutik des christlichen-jüdischen Verhältnisses. Über Helmut Gollwitzers Arbeit an der 'Judenfrage'," in *Richte unsere Füße auf den Weg des Friedens: Helmut Gollwitzer zum 70. Geburtstag*, ed. Andreas Baudis, Dieter Clausert, Volkhard Schliski and Bernhard Wegener (München: Chr. Kaiser Verlag, 1979), 144; Pangritz, "Helmut Gollwitzer als Theologe des Dialogs," 5–6.

Many of Gollwitzer's essays on Jewish–Christian dialogue were published in his 1962 collection of essays, entitled *The Demands of Freedom*, although they were unfortunately left out of the English translation.[87]

This collection also includes many essays addressing more political issues, including the relation of Christianity and politics in general, the relation between Christianity and Marxism in particular, and the Christian response to war in an atomic age. Gollwitzer's engagement with Marxism continued in the early years of his work in Berlin and bore fruit beyond these essays in his *The Christian Faith and Marxist Criticism of Religion*, which also appeared in 1962.[88] I will discuss Gollwitzer's socialism and his engagement with Marxism in greater detail later, but his continued interest and participation in these conversations play a role in another important event in Gollwitzer's life that occurred in 1962. Karl Barth retired, giving his farewell lecture on March 1.[89] Gollwitzer was one of the final candidates to replace Barth. Indeed, he was elected to the position by the Basel faculty, but the Swiss ministry of education blocked his appointment. It was precisely Gollwitzer's progressive politics that gave the Swiss authorities pause. As an editorial from the period described matters: "The Basel authorities would have liked to appoint Gollwitzer, the distinguished scholar and persuasive preacher, to the university chair, but not Gollwitzer the representative of the so-called 'Movement for World Peace' and the spokesman of every anti-nuclear congress."[90]

The miscarriage of Gollwitzer's call to Basel as Barth's replacement meant that Gollwitzer was present in Berlin when, as the 1960s progressed, the Berlin student movement gathered steam. Gollwitzer was involved with this movement as a "critical mentor" and a "spiritual adviser."[91] He demonstrated his commitment to dialogue and solidarity

---

87. Helmut Gollwitzer, *Forderungen der Freiheit: Aufsätze und Reden zur politischen Ethik* (München: Chr. Kaiser Verlag, 1962); Helmut Gollwitzer, *The Demands of Freedom: Papers by a Christian in West Germany*, trans. Robert W. Fenn (New York: Harper and Row Publishers, 1965).

88. Helmut Gollwitzer, "Die marxistiche Religionskritik und der christliche Glaube," *Marxismusstudien* 4 (1962); Helmut Gollwitzer, *The Christian Faith and the Marxist Criticism of Religion*, trans. David Cairns (New York: Charles Scribner's Sons, 1970). This work was reissued in 1965, and is an expansion of papers given in 1958 and 1959. For further discussion of this text, see W. Travis McMaken, "The Blame Lies with the Christians: Helmut Gollwitzer's Engagement with Marxist Criticism of Religion," *The Other Journal* 22 (2013): 13–20. For latter works in a similar vein, see Helmut Gollwitzer, *The Rich Christians and Poor Lazarus*, trans. David Cairns (New York: Macmillan, 1970); Helmut Gollwitzer, *Die kapitalistische Revolution* (München: Chr. Kaiser Verlag, 1974).

89. Busch, *Karl Barth*, 457. Barth would continue to teach *ad hoc* colloquia and small seminars.

90. As reprinted in Gollwitzer, *Demands of Freedom*, 149. For more on this controversy, see Busch, *Karl Barth*, 454; Oestreicher, "Helmut Gollwitzer," 27; Eduard Thurneysen, "Warum nicht Gollwitzer?," *Evangelische Theologie* 22, no. 5 (1962): 271–77.

91. Gollwitzer, *Skizzen eines Lebens*, 297.

by making his house available to the student activists. One of the leaders of the student movement, Rudi Dutschke, even lived with the Gollwitzers from time to time, and Helmut introduced Rudi to Gustav Heinemann. Dutschke married an American woman who had been Gollwitzer's student, but they left Germany after Rudi was severely injured in an assassination attempt against him in 1968.[92] Other acts of violence against the students occurred as well, such as one being shot in a protest against the Shah of Persia in June 1967. Perhaps even more striking is the story of student protestors who were beaten bloody by a churchgoer with a cane when they occupied a church. Gollwitzer remarked concerning the student protestors: "In contrast with many of my contemporaries and colleagues, who regard them with deep antipathy or at least shake their heads over them in bewilderment, I have come to love them for their sincerity, their courage, their feeling for freedom, their sense of responsibility for the future, and their dream of a more humane society."[93] His involvement with the student movement also changed the style of Gollwitzer's academic work. One of the changes that the student movement sought was a reimagination of higher education as a cooperative enterprise, where the professor functioned as student-in-chief leading a team of younger scholars. Gollwitzer embraced this new model: "Instead of teaching by means of contiguous lectures, he now taught in the form of sets of theses which, after brief explanation, the students were asked to discuss as soon as possible."[94]

His close contact with the Berlin student movement was a major factor that lead Gollwitzer to a shift in his approach, which manifested itself in 1970 with the publication of a major work entitled *Crooked Wood—Upright Walk*. It can be thought of as a "hinge" between the earlier and latter portions of Gollwitzer's time in Berlin, and Helga Day—writing shortly thereafter—emphasizes the development in Gollwitzer's thinking. At issue is how best to secure Christianity from Feuerbachian and Marxist criticisms of religion. In the early 1960s, as demonstrated in *The Existence of God as Confessed by Faith* (1963), Gollwitzer sought a hermeneutical solution. Now, however, Gollwitzer "knows that understanding Christian statements of faith does not

92. Ibid., 300. See also Claudia Lepp, "Helmut Gollwitzer als Dialogpartner der sozialen Bewegungen," in *Umbrüche: der Deutsche Protestantismus und die sozialen Bewegungen in der 1960er und 70er Jahren*, ed. Siegfried Hermle, Claudia Lepp, and Harry Oelke (Göttingen: Vandenhoeck & Ruprecht, 2007), 227.
93. Gollwitzer, *Rich Christians*, x. For the aforementioned stories of violence, see Gollwitzer, *Skizzen eines Lebens*, 292, 296–97.
94. Gollwitzer, *Skizzen eines Lebens*, 299; see also 293.

depend on hermeneutical reflection but rather on new praxis." Consequently, "preaching alone is not enough; and preaching as dogmatic statement functions only as a passageway to praxis."[95] This development in Gollwitzer's sensibilities, this clear-sightedness about the necessity of true socialism's praxis as the end of theology and theology as the theory that supports such praxis, comes to expression further in 1976 with Gollwitzer's second major essay collection, *Demands of Conversion*.[96]

Gollwitzer concluded his professorial career in the summer semester of 1975 with introductory lectures on Protestant theology. He published these under the provocative title, *Liberation for Solidarity*.[97] He also stayed busy publishing on various issues in a variety of media, attending and speaking at protests and conferences, and preaching. The last time that Gollwitzer gathered a large crowd was in the summer semester of 1987 when he lectured on Luther's *Small Catechism*. Marquardt provides some insight into Gollwitzer's interests in this twilight of his career. He recalls Gollwitzer once saying that if he were going to live for another thirty years, he would study the social sciences. Gollwitzer was increasingly disinterested in *purely* theological work that sought to disconnect itself from other disciplines and modes of analysis. At the end of his career, Gollwitzer was more interested in thinking further about materialist analyses and criticisms of theology.[98]

Brigitte died on January 10, 1986. The loss hit Helmut hard, and it was a number of months before he was able to see a way forward into his remaining years. Stieber-Westermann testifies to her importance for Helmut's life and work by describing their marriage of 35 years as a "community without which his work would not have been possible."[99] For his own part, Helmut testified of Brigitte that "she was always my

---

95. Day, "Christlicher Glaube," 341, 339. For Gollwitzer's texts, see Helmut Gollwitzer, *Die Existenz Gottes im Bekenntnis des Glaubens*, Beiträge zur Evangelischen Theologie (München: Chr. Kaiser Verlag, 1963); Helmut Gollwitzer, *The Existence of God as Confessed by Faith*, trans. James W. Leitch (Philadelphia: Westminster Press, 1965); Helmut Gollwitzer, *Krummes Holz - aufrechter Gang: zur Frage nach dem Sinn des Lebens* (München: Chr. Kaiser Verlag, 1970). For the "hinge" comment, see Gollwitzer, *Skizzen eines Lebens*, 277. Recall Gollwitzer's criticisms of Barth's vestigial idealism. Given that these remarks were written in 1972, relatively shortly after this shift, they are undoubtedly an exercise in Gollwitzer criticizing himself as well as Barth.

96. Helmut Gollwitzer, *Forderungen der Umkehr: Beiträge zur Theologie der Gesellschaft* (München: Chr. Kaiser Verlag, 1976).

97. Helmut Gollwitzer, *Befreiung zur Solidarität: Einführung in die evangelische Theologie* (München: Chr. Kaiser Verlag, 1978). Unfortunately, the title under which the English translation was issued leaves something to be desired: Helmut Gollwitzer, *An Introduction to Protestant Theology*, trans. David Cairns (Philadelphia: The Westminster Press, 1982).

98. Marquardt, "Weg und Werk," 35–36.

99. Stieber-Westermann, *Provokation zum Leben*, 34.

conscience."[100] Helmut lived for another seven years and more, until October 17, 1993. He died when he fell down the stairs of his house. This may seem like an odd detail to include here. I must admit that when I first learned how Gollwitzer died, it struck me as an unjustly ignoble death for one who had lived the life and survived the circumstances that he did. From another perspective, however, that Gollwitzer survived what he did only to die in such a mundane way is perhaps the greatest possible testament not only to his strength and character, but also to the grace of God that characterized his life—grace upon grace. Reflecting on his own life toward its end, Gollwitzer said: "the gospel has made me to constantly be a critical and admonitory voice against the severe injustices in our contemporary society," and "I am particularly thankful that I was allowed to be at the service of the gospel." Helmut Gollwitzer was buried next to Brigitte in the small cemetery at St. Anne's church in the Dahlem parish where he worked during the Confessing Church struggle.[101]

Gollwitzer's Influence

Something must briefly be said about Gollwitzer's legacy by way of conclusion. This chapter began with a quote from Pangritz that identified Gollwitzer as "one of the most influential Protestant theologians of the twentieth century." But that is not the whole quote. Pangritz continues: "nevertheless [Gollwitzer] seems to be largely forgotten now."[102] While Gollwitzer was a leading public intellectual in his own day, his visibility dramatically decreased as his retirement lengthened, and especially after his death. It became difficult to find Gollwitzer's works in bookstores even shortly after his death, which Marquardt attributes both to the unrelenting character of the contemporary news cycle and to the contextual character of Gollwitzer's thought. As he puts it, Gollwitzer "linked his theological work so closely with the course of time that it can, with the time, pass quickly."[103] Of course, this contextual quality is one of the things that makes Gollwitzer's thought so helpful in the contemporary North American context, not only in addressing perennial issues such as economic justice, war, and revolutionary violence, but also in providing a paradigm for thinking through

100. As quoted in Orth, *Helmut Gollwitzer*, 60.
101. Gollwitzer, *Skizzen eines Lebens*, 342; see also 341.
102. Pangritz, "Helmut Gollwitzer als Theologe des Dialogs," 1.
103. Friedrich-Wilhelm Marquardt, "'Was nicht im Dienst steht, steht im Raub': zum ersten Versuch einer Gollwitzer-Biografie von Gottfried Orth," *Evangelische Theologie* 57, no. 2 (1997): 162.

the connection between Christian faith and a progressive sociopolitical vision.

While Gollwitzer's work does not receive the attention that it once did, that is not to say that his legacy has no champions. Friedrich-Wilhelm Marquardt proved to be a faithful student to Gollwitzer, working to extend the conversation on issues close to Gollwitzer's heart—such as Karl Barth's doctrine of Israel (Marquardt's dissertation) and the importance of socialism for Barth's thought (his habilitation). This latter work was rejected by the Berlin seminary where Marquardt submitted the work, and Gollwitzer resigned from his position on the faculty in protest. Marquardt would eventually succeed Gollwitzer in his position at the Free University when Gollwitzer retired.[104] In North America, George Hunsinger represents the adaptation and continuation of the sort of theological engagement with progressive politics that Gollwitzer inherited from Barth and extended. Hunsinger's early edited volume, *Karl Barth and Radical Politics*, made available in English essays on Barth's socialism from both Marquardt and Gollwitzer. Commenting on this volume, Hunsinger notes: "It is no accident that it includes an essay by Gollwitzer. I have always seen him as representing the very best in Barthian theology as it relates to social and political ethics. I have been trying to do something in my particular context, in my own small way, similar to what he did in his."[105] The work to which Hunsinger refers is his founding of the National Religious Campaign Against Torture and the publication of an edited volume that brings together voices from the Abrahamic religious traditions in protesting torture.[106]

Finally, this volume is an attempt to revitalize Gollwitzer's legacy in the North American context. We still have much to learn from Gollwitzer's theological way of being in the world: his ability to identify the key sociopolitical issues and frame them in compelling ways as some-

104. For an overview of Marquardt's life and thought, see Andreas Pangritz, "Friedrich-Wilhelm Marquardt—a Theological-Biographical Sketch," *European Judaism* 38, no. 1 (2005): 17–47; see esp. 27–32 for discussion of his dissertation and habilitation. For more on the controversy surrounding the rejection of Marquardt's habilitation, see Markus Barth, "Current Discussions on the Political Character of Karl Barth's Theology," in *Footnotes to a Theology: The Karl Barth Colloquium of 1972*, ed. Martin Rumscheidt (Waterloo, ON: Corporation for the Publication of Academic Studies in Religion in Canada, 1974), 77–94. To begin with Marquardt first-hand, see Friedrich-Wilhelm Marquardt, "Socialism in the Theology of Karl Barth," in *Karl Barth and Radical Politics*, ed. George Hunsinger (Philadelphia: Westminster Press, 1976), 47–76; Friedrich-Wilhelm Marquardt, *Theological Audacities: Selected Essays*, ed. Andreas Pangritz and Paul S. Chung (Eugene, OR: Pickwick, 2010).

105. From correspondence between the author and George Hunsinger on June 3, 2015. See George Hunsinger, ed. *Karl Barth and Radical Politics* (Philadelphia: Westminster Press, 1976).

106. George Hunsinger, ed. *Torture Is a Moral Issue: Christians, Jews, Muslims and People of Conscience Speak Out* (Grand Rapids, MI: Eerdmans, 2008).

one—to rely once again on Marquardt—always "starving for the Word of God" and "thirsting for the fulfillment of His righteousness."[107] And to this, we might add: longing for the true socialism of the kingdom of God.

107. Marquardt, "Weg und Werk," 14.

3

———

Gollwitzer's Political Theology

From Gollwitzer's biography, we now turn to his political theology. Our task is to understand how the logic of Gollwitzer's theology pushed him inexorably toward political engagement, particularly with socialism. In other words, this chapter is about Gollwitzer's *theology* as *political* theology because its logic is always already on the way to the political. There are three major steps in this logic.

First, the whole enterprise depends on the affirmation of God's nonobjectifiability. To objectify God means to treat God like any object that is generally accessible to us in the world. So, for instance, a hockey puck, quarks, and the speed of light are all things that are generally accessible—albeit in very different ways! Objectifying God in this manner treats God like a fixture of the world that Christians confess to be God's creation. The dialectical theology advocated by people such as Karl Barth, Rudolf Bultmann, and others in the early twentieth century—and in which Gollwitzer was educated—was committed to rejecting such objectification and reaffirming that God is "wholly other."

Second, if God cannot be objectified, cannot be treated like a generally accessible feature of our world, then it necessarily follows that no single instance of "God-talk"—theology—is sufficient for all times and places. In other words, all theology is contextual theology. It is an attempt to speak of God from within a particular sociohistorical location, and it therefore shares in the limitations of that location. This brings dialectical theology to within hailing distance of the various liberation theologies that developed in the second half of the twentieth century. Indeed, Gollwitzer engaged deeply with those theologies, and we will examine his support of black theology as an example of this engagement.

Third, because all theology occurs under the limitations of its particular context and is therefore inextricably bound up with the concerns of that context, and because every theology inevitably speaks to those concerns, it follows that all theology is political theology. Indeed, it is impossible for theology—or any other form of human thought and culture—to be nonpolitical. All theology is political theology, either implicitly or explicitly, depending on whether theologians recognize and embrace theology's contextual nature. Political theology is simply theology that is honest with itself and others about the sort of thing that it is and about how it fits into its particular context. Gollwitzer rejects a number of common distinctions made in the theological tradition that attempt to insulate theology from its political character and gives guidance to Christians as they exercise political responsibility in their sociohistorical contexts. It is here that we see the logic of Gollwitzer's theology produce political consequences, thereby demonstrating that it is a truly political theology.

God Cannot be Objectified

The conviction that God cannot be objectified was part of the heritage that Gollwitzer received from the dialectical theology movement that coalesced around Karl Barth and others in the 1920s. The institutional and intellectual center of this movement was *Zwischen den Zeiten (Between the Times)*, a journal produced by the movement and managed by Georg Merz. As we saw when discussing Gollwitzer's biography, he came to Barth in the late 1920s by way of Merz and this journal. And it was an issue related to God's nonobjectifiability that finally brought this journal and the dialectical theology movement to an end, while also providing the basis for continued debate between the movement's two most significant luminaries—Karl Barth and Rudolf Bultmann. It is important to have some sense of this background before turning to Gollwitzer's contribution because that contribution is best understood as an intervention in these ongoing debates within dialectical theology.

Natural Theology and Hermeneutics in Dialectical Theology

Dialectical theology emphasizes God's nonobjectifiability by affirming that God is "wholly other," which is perhaps the phrase that is most commonly associated with this theological movement. Looking back on this period from the mid-1950s, Barth also highlights this language and associates it with other similar modes of expression. "What expressions we used," Barth wrote, "above all, the famous 'wholly other' breaking in upon us 'perpendicularly from above,' the not less famous 'infinite qualitative distinction' between God and man, the vacuum, the mathematical point, and the tangent in which alone they must meet."[1] This language attempts, in various ways, to safeguard the nonobjectifiability of God, to emphasize a divine transcendence that does not become a generally accessible feature in the world even when God interacts with God's creation. Consequently, one must speak of God's presence as eventful and disruptive, rather than as persistent and reinforcing. Dialectical theology is a destabilizing theology that views God's action as calling radically into question both the theological and sociocultural status quo.

This approach emerged in Karl Barth's thought while he was a pastor in the Swiss village of Safenwil. Barth became very active during this time in the local socialist party, working on behalf of the laborers in his congregation, which alienated the congregation's wealthy factory owners. Furthermore, he did this on the basis of his understanding of Jesus. This socialist engagement helped Barth look past the appearance of things, both in terms of social conditions and the ideologies that legitimate those conditions. Consequently, he was well-prepared to perceive and reject the gospel's ideological captivity when twenty-nine leading theologians and church leaders published a document mounting a Christian theological defense of German involvement in World War I. This document argued that the war was necessary to advance Christian mission, which was understood as an extension of German culture. The war was, in other words, a deeply colonialist enterprise and it was justified by the church and its theologians precisely as such. Barth's famous commentary on Paul's epistle to the Romans, which provided the foundation and impetus for the dialectical theology movement, was an indictment of all ways of thinking about God that would make possible such a confusion of culture and gospel. In

---

1. Karl Barth, "The Humanity of God," *The Humanity of God* (Louisville, KY: Westminster John Knox Press, 1960), 42.

other words, any conflation of culture and gospel is impossible as an implication of Barth's view that God cannot be objectified.[2]

Another complementary way to describe the beginning of dialectical theology, with its affirmation that God cannot be objectified, is as the commencement of Barth's ongoing theological battle against natural theology. Dialectical theology's missionary character binds these aspects together. This missionary connection appears especially in Barth's conflict with Emil Brunner, which occurred shortly after dialectical theology disintegrated with the shuttering of *Zwischen den Zeiten* in 1933. Brunner affirmed a "point of connection" (*Anknüpfungspunkt*) within the structures of human being that could serve as a starting point for the task of evangelization. Barth denied this and affirmed on the contrary that the Holy Spirit creates its own point of contact, rather than making use of a preexisting and generally accessible structure within created being.[3] Because "point of connection" language was already bound up with German missionary approaches, Barth saw Brunner's position as advancing once more the sort of misidentification of gospel and culture that Barth had rejected already in the context of World War I. Barth and Brunner's essays on this subject

---

2. For an example of Barth's early thinking about Jesus, see Karl Barth, "Jesus Christ and the Movement for Social Justice," in *Karl Barth and Radical Politics*, ed. George Hunsinger (Philadelphia: Westminster Press, 1976), 19–45. My description of the emergence of dialectical theology draws freely on the best and most recent work done on the subject in David W. Congdon, *The Mission of Demythologizing: Rudolf Bultmann's Dialectical Theology* (Minneapolis, MN: Fortress Press, 2015), esp. ch. 3 ("The Missionary Essence of Dialectical Theology"), 237–303. Congdon brings these threads together nicely when he writes both that "we must acknowledge the special significance of socialism as an indispensable factor in the formation of dialectical theology," and that "a certain missionary logic or missionary orientation is essential to dialectical theology" because it is "theology without worldviews" as the correlate to "mission without colonialism." Ibid., 287. I am also indebted to the field's standard account of Barth's early development in Bruce L. McCormack, *Karl Barth's Critically Realistic Dialectical Theology: Its Genesis and Development, 1909–1936* (Oxford: Clarendon Press, 1995). Socialism's importance for Barth's development can be overemphasized, but it nonetheless remains important. Gollwitzer argued that Barth's rejection of liberal theology and development of dialectical theology was motivated, at least in part, by the desire to supply the church with the theological theory necessary to ground revolutionary praxis, to arm the church for its mission as "the agent of the necessary revolution." Helmut Gollwitzer, "Kingdom of God and Socialism in the Theology of Karl Barth," in *Karl Barth and Radical Politics*, ed. George Hunsinger (Philadelphia: Westminster Press, 1976), 89. See also Gollwitzer's discussion of Barth in Helmut Gollwitzer, "Must a Christian be a Socialist?," Appendix 1, 177–78, 181–85. McCormack describes how Barth's break with liberal theology was bound up with the travails of German religious socialism. McCormack, *Karl Barth's Critically Realistic Dialectical Theology*, 117–25.
3. My discussion here is indebted to John G. Flett, *The Witness of God: The Trinity, Missio Dei, Karl Barth, and the Nature of Christian Community* (Grand Rapids, MI: Eerdmans, 2010), 89–92, 166–79; McCormack, *Karl Barth's Critically Realistic Dialectical Theology*, 391–411. McCormack rightly highlights the importance of the distance developing between Barth and Friedrich Gogarten. See also Congdon's discussion of Barth's engagement with Bruno Gutmann: Congdon, *Mission of Demythologizing*, 297–303.

appeared in 1934 against the backdrop of the early years of Adolf Hitler's consolidation of power in Germany.

Barth and Brunner's exchange had the positive effect of clarifying dialectical theology's systematic task—namely, bringing Protestant theology's account of how humans know God (theological epistemology) into alignment with its account of how God saves sinners (soteriology). As Barth writes in response to Brunner: the reformers "saw and attacked the possibility of an intellectual work-righteousness in the basis of theological thought. But they did not do so as widely, as clearly and as fundamentally as they did with respect to the possibility of a moral works-righteousness in the basis of Christian life."[4] Dialectical theology's enduring contribution, then, is affirming that Protestant theological epistemology must be decisively shaped by Protestant soteriology so that just as Christians can in no way merit saving grace, theologians can in no way merit revelation by finding it already embedded in the structures of human intellect or creation as a whole. Such a procedure improperly objectifies God. Just as saving grace is an alien grace that comes to sinners from outside of themselves, knowledge of God is likewise an alien knowledge that comes to sinners from outside of themselves. Salvation and revelation thereby become two sides of the same event of God's gracious activity.

Rejecting natural theology is central to dialectical theology's legacy in affirming that God cannot be objectified, but there is another important aspect of this legacy. Since revelation involves an alien knowledge of God just as salvation involves an alien grace, we must critically evaluate all attempts to use human language and concepts to speak about God and God's action. This includes the language and concepts that we find in scripture. It was this critical hermeneutical task to which Bultmann devoted his attention.[5] Much of Barth's rejection of natural

---

4. Emil Brunner and Karl Barth, *Natural Theology: Comprising "Nature and Grace" by Professor Dr. Emil Brunner and the Reply "No!" By Dr. Karl Barth*, trans. Peter Fraenkel (Eugene, OR: Wipf & Stock, 2002), 102. For more on the relationship between Barth and Brunner, see John W. Hart, *Karl Barth Vs. Emil Brunner: The Formation and Dissolution of a Theological Alliance, 1916-1936*, Issues in Systematic Theology, ed. Paul D. Molnar (New York: Peter Lang, 2001), ch. 5 ("Breaking Up (1933–35): The 'German-Christians' and Natural Theology"), 141–75. Also at play here is dialectical theology's purification of Protestant soteriology from its lingering sacramental soteriological framework. Sacramental soteriology views salvation as a transfer of grace from Jesus to the individual Christian by way of the sacraments. Protestant soteriology complicates but does not wholly break with this picture by understanding faith as the mechanism of transfer. Barth's soteriology "demythologize[s] . . . the entirety of traditional sacramental soteriology." W. Travis McMaken, *The Sign of the Gospel: Toward an Evangelical Doctrine of Infant Baptism after Karl Barth*, Emerging Scholars (Minneapolis, MN: Fortress Press, 2013), 72; see 59–88.
5. Congdon highlights the importance of *Sachkritik* in the dialectical theology project and its efforts to defend against natural theology. *Sachkritik* is "the criticism of the [biblical] text *qua* myth in

OUR GOD LOVES JUSTICE

theology as an affirmation of God's nonobjectifiability was spurred, in part, by World War I, and his rejection of Emil Brunner's position occurred in the midst of National Socialism's triumph in Germany. Bultmann's program was spurred in part by World War II and came to clear expression as demythologizing, beginning in 1941.

As Bultmann's biographer Konrad Hammann puts it, "in Bultmann's view, National Socialism required and had dedicated itself to the suppression of the Christian proclamation."[6] What the Nazi regime required, and the German Christians worked to supply, was a mythology that treated German culture—and even, at its most extreme, the person of the Führer—as an expression of God's will and site of revelation. This mythological objectification of God stood in direct opposition to dialectical theology's key insight, and so Bultmann developed his program of demythologizing in an effort to short-circuit such thinking. In short, Bultmann's demythologizing program affirms that God cannot be objectified in any human culture—worldview, concepts, language, ideology, mythology, theology, philosophy, political system, and so on—and therefore, the gospel calls all such attempts at objectification into question. This holds true not only for the ancient cultures, such as those of the biblical authors, but also for any and all contemporary cultures. As David Congdon says, "demythologizing is more than just a way of dealing with ancient myths; it is equally about the myth of National Socialism, along with any other myth that would claim to identify a cultural-historical ideology with the eternal will of God."[7] Just as Barth's discomfort with natural theology was tied to the question of mission, Bultmann's demythologizing program is an intercultural missionary hermeneutic aimed at freeing the gospel for translation into and expression from within any and all sociocultural and historical contexts.

Unfortunately, Barth did not see Bultmann's hermeneutical program as a further extension of dialectical theology's mission-oriented rejec-

---

light of the text *qua* kerygma." Congdon, *Mission of Demythologizing*, 723. In other words, it uses an understanding of the gospel proclaimed by the biblical texts in order to critically evaluate the language and concepts used by those texts to proclaim that gospel. Barth and Bultmann had a disagreement in 1922 about precisely how such criticism should be conducted. As Congdon summarizes the exchange, "Bultmann simply wants in theory what Barth already embraces in practice." Ibid., 735.

6. Konrad Hammann, *Rudolf Bultmann: A Biography*, trans. Philip E. Davenish (Salem, OR: Polebridge Press, 2013), 286; see 267–310 for more on Bultmann's struggle with National Socialism, and 323–36 for more on his 1941 demythologization lecture and its reception.

7. Congdon, *Mission of Demythologizing*, 580; see 576–86. To be clear, the concept of "myth" in this context refers to objectifying thinking. See David W. Congdon, *Rudolf Bultmann: A Companion to His Theology*, Cascade Companions (Eugene, OR: Cascade, 2015), 108–11.

tion of natural theology and affirmation of God's nonobjectifiability. Instead, Bultmann's talk of "preunderstanding," and Brunner's appropriation of this language in his discussion of a "point of connection," led Barth to suspect that demythologizing masked a renewed and even more subtle natural theology objectifying God's being. This deeply unfortunate mischaracterization resulted from Barth's basic misunderstanding of Bultmann's thought, which has obscured the legacy of dialectical theology and divine nonobjectifiability.[8]

Gollwitzer's Intervention

It is precisely into these arguments between Barth and Bultmann that Gollwitzer stepped with his 1964 book, *The Existence of God as Confessed by Faith*.[9] Gollwitzer wanted to parse the deep instability within dialectical theology that resulted from this tension between Barth and Bultmann. Neither side is without its dangers. The first part of Gollwitzer's book articulates these dangers in order to prepare the ground for his own approach.

With regard to Barth, he "must defend himself against the suspicion that he is indulging in a speculative metaphysic of God."[10] Barth's hesitance to engage in the sort of hermeneutical reflection undertaken by Bultmann, and his penchant for discussing the Trinitarian being and attributes of God, suggest that Barth has not fully internalized the danger of objectifying God in human speech. From Bultmann's side of the dialectical theology movement, it is hard to see how Barth is entitled to make such statements. If knowledge of God arises from the event in which one encounters God's saving grace in Jesus Christ, then that soteriological event must control all Christian speaking and thinking of God. General reflections about God's being or even existence are illegitimate exercises in natural theology when detached from that control.

With regard to Bultmann, Gollwitzer argues that the Marburg the-

---

8. On preunderstanding, see Congdon, *Mission of Demythologizing*, 702–14, and esp. 708. On the relation between Barth and Bultmann, see ibid., "Part 1: The Myth of the Whale and the Elephant." Barth's deep and persistent misunderstanding of Bultmann no doubt contributed to the scathing judgment rendered against him by Gerhard Ebeling: "'A significant part of Barth's theology' appeared to [Ebeling] as 'journalism' and Barth himself appeared as a 'political thinker from the beginning and through and through,' from which stem 'all the problematic aspects of his theology and activity': 'the cliques of his school, the despotic style of his thinking, the unwillingness to do justice to something.'" Albrecht Beutel, *Gerhard Ebeling—Eine Biographie* (Tübingen: Mohr Siebeck, 2012), 505. David Congdon supplied this translation in personal correspondence.

9. Helmut Gollwitzer, *The Existence of God as Confessed by Faith*, trans. James W. Leitch (Philadelphia: Westminster Press, 1965); Helmut Gollwitzer, *Die Existenz Gottes im Bekenntnis des Glaubens*, Beiträge zur evangelischen Theologie (München: Chr. Kaiser Verlag, 1963).

10. Gollwitzer, *Existence of God*, 28.

ologian "must defend himself against the suspicion that he uses 'God' to designate merely a state of man."[11] The danger that Gollwitzer detects here is that by submitting speech and thought of God to this rigorous soteriological control, Bultmann loses the ability to distinguish God from human subjectivity. If one cannot affirm that God exists—that is, that God has reality prior to and independent of this event of human encounter with God—then how can one be sure that one is speaking of God, and not just of humanity in a loud voice?[12] To Gollwitzer's credit, he does not think that Bultmann intends this consequence. Nor does Gollwitzer believe that this is a necessary consequence of Bultmann's position. Rather, he thinks that Bultmann holds "an indecisive intermediary position which allows him neither to speak plainly of God in his independent reality nor to regard talk of God as improper."[13] The question then becomes how one might properly resolve this intermediary position.

Herbert Braun exemplifies one way of resolving it. We must remember that, as far as Gollwitzer was concerned, Braun—rather than Bultmann—was the "'main enemy' in the confrontation with existentialist interpretation of the biblical message."[14] On Gollwitzer's reading, Braun turns demythologizing into a question of "whether

---

11. Ibid. Rolf Stieber-Westermann enumerates three worries that Gollwitzer had vis-à-vis Bultmann. See Rolf Stieber-Westermann, *Die Provokation zum Leben: Gott im theologischen Werk Helmut Gollwitzers*, Europäische Hochschulschriften (Frankfurt am Main: Peter Lang, 1993), 182–83.

12. Karl Barth describes late-nineteenth-century Protestant theology, and Schleiermacher in particular, in these terms and rejects them. To do theology properly means "that one can *not* speak of God simply by speaking of man in a loud voice." Karl Barth, "The Word of God and the Task of the Ministry," in *The Word of God and the Word of Man* (New York: Harper & Brothers, 1957), 196. The idea that one might speak about God by speaking about humanity in a loud voice is reminiscent of Ludwig Feuerbach who, for example, asserts that "God is the mirror of man." Ludwig Feuerbach, *The Essence of Christianity*, trans. George Eliot (New York: Harper & Brothers, 1957), 63. See Kevin W. Hector, *Theology without Metaphysics: God, Language, and the Spirit of Recognition*, Current Issues in Theology (New York: Cambridge University Press, 2011), 13. Feuerbach seems to be always in the back of Gollwitzer's mind throughout *Existence of God*.

13. Gollwitzer, *Existence of God*, 30. It is an altogether different question to ascertain whether Bultmann's position is inherently unstable in this way, or whether Gollwitzer's understanding of Bultmann had been prejudiced both by Barth and by encounter with other members of Bultmann's school—such as Herbert Braun—who developed Bultmann's project in what Gollwtizer thought were much more clearly problematic ways. I am inclined to the latter interpretation. As Otto Schnübbe says, "the one who believes that Bultmann reduces faith to a mental consciousness, without taking seriously the objective counterpart of God [*objektiven Gegenübers Gottes*] . . . has not understood him." Otto Schnübbe, *Die Existenzbegriff in der Theologie Rudolf Bultmanns. Ein Beitrag zur Interpretation der theologischen Systematik Bultmanns* (Göttingen: Vandenhoeck & Ruprecht, 1959), 139, as cited in Congdon, *Mission of Demythologizing*, 203n420. Congdon helpfully elaborates Bultmann's position: "in opposing objectifying thinking Bultmann is actually opposing the inappropriate control and manipulation of the biblical text by the human subject. Paradoxically, by exegeting the meaning of the text in relation to the human subject Bultmann is bringing the genuinely *objective* reality of God's revelation to speech." Ibid., 203.

14. Stieber-Westermann, *Provokation zum Leben*, 185.

[Christianity's] meaning can be translated into atheistic language."[15] But this apologetic approach assumes too much. For instance, it assumes that when modern science and philosophy disregard—and atheists openly reject—theistic metaphysics, they thereby reject Christianity. Gollwitzer was intensely interested in the question of Christian engagement with atheists and he engaged deeply in dialogue with Marxist atheists. His approach accepts atheistic arguments against Christianity as indicative of a problematic status quo, in political and socioeconomic terms as well as in ideological and metaphysical terms, emphasizing that these failings "are a catalogue of actual Christian degenerations."[16] In other words, they are ways that Christianity has betrayed its Lord. Braun's approach is, consequently, misguided insofar as it assumes that at stake is a simple opposition between Christianity "as a special case of theism" on one side and atheism on the other: "merely to take up the antithesis of theism and atheism . . . results just as much in distortion of the Christian faith as does denying its theistic outward form as allegedly separable from it. Thus a-theism hits the target of Christian faith and yet misses it after all."[17]

What is this outward form of theism that Gollwitzer thinks is inseparable from Christian faith even while Christianity cannot be treated simply as an instance of the theistic type? That outward form is the affirmation of the reality of God, or of the existence of God, as it is confessed by faith (to borrow from Gollwitzer's title). In Gollwitzer's reading, Braun rejects Christianity as an instance of the theistic type and develops an atheistic form of Christianity that rejects God's reality. The event of encounter with Jesus Christ, which dialectical theology understands as the event of reconciliation and revelation, becomes the moment in which one learns a general truth concerning human existence by way of a certain kind of experience. In more christological terms, Jesus becomes "the 'cipher' for an event that is not identical with his person."[18] Why, then, persist in using theological language to describe this event? Why continue to engage in God-talk if it is no "more than a difference in the way of speaking"? Braun's position hamstrings not only theology but Christianity in general by preventing it

---

15. Gollwitzer, *Existence of God*, 40.
16. Helmut Gollwitzer, *The Christian Faith and the Marxist Criticism of Religion*, trans. David Cairns (New York: Charles Scribner's Sons, 1970), 151; see 150–73. This section in many ways constitutes an advance précis of his *Existence of God*. Their original publication dates are 1962 and 1963, respectively.
17. Gollwitzer, *Existence of God*, 45.
18. Ibid., 90.

from offering anything beyond what is already immanently available in the world and human existence: "With the introduction of the term 'God' there is of course nothing new added in the way of knowledge; it is only an 'expression' for a phenomenon which can also be expressed without it."[19]

Far from enabling a fruitful encounter between atheism and Christianity, however, Gollwitzer argues that this move concedes the match before it has even properly begun. For Braun's position is indistinguishable from that of Ludwig Feuerbach, who famously argued that "the true sense of Theology is Anthropology," that "the knowledge of God is nothing else than a knowledge of man."[20] That is, speech about God is ultimately a mechanism for humanity to objectify—and thereby, come to know—itself. Gollwitzer recognizes that Feuerbach is an important interlocutor for dialectical theology precisely because dialectical theology is finally weaponless in the face of Feuerbach's argument. Dialectical theology's commitment to "the nonobjectifiability of the knowledge of God in the encounter with God" means that "faith is defenseless."[21] There is no way to demonstrate the existence of God in a generally accessible way. To do so would be the quintessential case of abandoning God's nonobjectifiability. It is therefore impossible to prove Feuerbach wrong when he says that God is ultimately a function of human self-understanding. This admission does not, however, require that Christian theology take Braun's approach of accommodating a Feuerbachian interpretation of God. On the contrary: "If Christian talk of God is defenseless against such depth-interpretation in the sense that it is incapable of refuting it by producing its object, yet it will still have to be persistent in its protest."[22]

Christian protest against arguments such as Feuerbach's must include the central affirmation that far from being knockout punches, these arguments do not land at all. This is a facet of Gollwitzer's unwillingness to concede that Christianity is a species within the theistic genus. Christians confess the existence of God in a manner that differs from how theists locate God within metaphysics—as first cause, unmoved mover, condition for the possibility of morality, and so on. Because this is the case, atheist arguments against theistic metaphysics do not constitute arguments against Christianity. The task of Christian

---

19. Ibid., 94. See also Stieber-Westermann, *Provokation zum Leben*, 189.
20. Feuerbach, *Essence of Christianity*, xxxvii, 207.
21. Gollwitzer, *Existence of God*, 102.
22. Ibid., 105. In other words, "God is more an object of hope and faith than of certainty." Jung Mo Sung, *Desire, Market and Religion*, Reclaiming Liberation Theology (London: SCM Press, 2007), 8.

theology is to show "the atheist how his theoretic denial of God cannot even touch what faith confesses."[23] In a critically important sense, Gollwitzer's approach concedes the truth of Feuerbach's argument. It admits that what Christians confess concerning God does not contradict the understanding of the world advanced by such arguments. While Gollwitzer affirms that Christian confession does, in fact, have to do with the reality of God, that reality is transcendent and therefore nonobjectifiable. God can no sooner become a datum of history than an identifiable piece in a metaphysical puzzle. This is what Protestant theology affirms by *concursus dei* in the doctrine of providence—and Gollwitzer appeals here to Barth's treatment of that doctrine. Christian faith's proper response to Feuerbach, then, takes the form of: Yes, but nevertheless![24]

Gollwitzer affirms the shared heritage of dialectical theology represented by Barth and Bultmann. He identifies three aspects of common ground. First, theological statements that objectify God are illegitimate. Second, theological statements that purport to be neutral with reference to God are also illegitimate. And as the positive corollary of this negative point, third, all legitimate theological statements involve Christians in "a confession about themselves"—they are "statements of faith." Furthermore, such statements of faith cannot reduce to expressions of general truths about human existence. If they were expressions of general truths, then they would not be properly theological statements. Statements about God that express general truths about human existence are simply another form of objectification, and as such, they are exercises in natural theology. As Gollwitzer puts it, "the decisive thing" is where theological statements have their ground: "whether in a variation of natural theology ... or in the self-manifestation of God to which Christian faith refers."[25]

His rejection of the hermeneutical form of natural theology is heightened later when Gollwitzer makes an important clarification. People often assume that God's self-manifestation—that is, revelation—occurs in a particular sociohistorical context and then becomes

---

23. Gollwitzer, *Existence of God*, 74.
24. For Gollwitzer's deployment of *concursus dei*, see ibid., 56. Karl Barth's treatment of this subject can be found in Karl Barth, *Church Dogmatics*, trans. and edited by Geoffrey W. Bromiley and Thomas F. Torrance, 4 volumes in 13 parts (Edinburgh: T&T Clark, 1956–75), 3.3:94–107. In brief, *concursus dei* describes God's providential care of the world, which—according to Barth's schema—precedes, accompanies, and follows creaturely action without entering into a competitive relationship with it. Gollwitzer's response to Feuerbach bears a family resemblance to Barth's response to Feuerbach. See Barth's introduction to Feuerbach, *Essence of Christianity*, xxvii–xxx.
25. Gollwitzer, *Existence of God*, 78, rev; Gollwitzer, *Die Existenz Gottes*, 62.

generally accessible as it passes through history. Scripture tends to function as such an artifact in some corners of Protestant theology, for instance. This approach imagines an eternally valid core of God's self-manifestation that persists through perpetual rearticulation in different sociohistorical contexts. The image often used to capture this dynamic is that of the kernel and the husk: the transcultural kernel of divine self-manifestation that, as a secondary step, can be communicated through various cultural husks. At first glance, it may seem as though this analogy prevents the objectification of God's revelation by distinguishing sharply between the essential kernel and the cultural husks. However, it also assumes that the kernel is accessible in order to distinguish between it and the cultural husks. This objectifies the kernel and requires that one distinguish between cultural factors that are part of the kernel—an ostensibly biblical worldview, for instance—and therefore, inviolable, and those that are not and therefore changeable. A subtle form of natural theology thus reasserts itself. Gollwitzer decisively rejects this way of thinking: "How are faith and its ideas connected? The picture of shell and kernel can hardly suffice here." Why? He continues in a footnote: "for the simple reason that in it the relationship is thought of unhistorically (time-conditioned form and timeless content)."[26] Once again, the affirmation that God cannot be objectified rules out all forms of natural theology.

After negatively clarifying his position in this way, Gollwitzer pivots to a positive account of how it is possible to speak of the reality of God—that is, what it means for Christian faith to confess the existence of God. He articulates this account by making four points.[27] First, confession of God must arise out of an event in which one encounters God as one who places demands upon you. Confession of God's existence, therefore, can only take the form of testimony to this encounter. Second, it is impossible to pass neutral or objective judgment on the reality of this event, or to offer arguments for or against the reality of the God encountered therein. This reality can only be acknowledged, and any attempt to dispute that reality is a betrayal of it. Third, acknowledgement of and testimony to the reality of the God encountered in this event becomes an exercise in objectification if these two points are not observed. Christian faith "does not take the step to an ontology

26. Gollwitzer, *Existence of God*, 110. Gollwitzer shows himself close to Bultmann in this. See Congdon, *Mission of Demythologizing*, 516–22. Furthermore, Gollwitzer sees this issue more clearly than did Barth. See ibid., 519n36.
27. Gollwitzer, *Existence of God*, 124–41.

of God. And thus none must be imputed to it either."[28] As we have repeatedly seen, it is theologically illegitimate to objectify God by mapping God into a preexisting or independently grounded account of the world. The goal of Christian God-talk is not to objectify in these ways the reality of God that they encounter in this event, but to testify to and thereby hear that God anew. Fourth, and consequently, "outside this event and apart from it," any talk about God "cannot be at any rate talk of *this* Caller," of the God encountered in this event.[29] All Christian talk of God must be determined by this event of encounter. Any other uses of the term "God" do not refer to the Christian God. Gollwitzer returns to Feuerbach here: the God whom Feuerbach would reduce to an objectification of human self-understanding is not the God whom Christians confess on the basis of this encounter.

Congdon helpfully defines dialectical theology as "a thoroughly destabilizing understanding of the gospel."[30] Gollwitzer's position on Christian faith's confession of God's reality in the event of encounter is such dialectical theology in action. It is thoroughly destabilizing in that it rules out every form of natural theology and perpetually refers Christian faith back to the event from which it springs. Christian faith—in terms of both a life of obedient response to God and of faithful God-talk—is thereby permanently destabilized. It must hear God anew in every moment. Gollwitzer differs from Braun in that he articulates this destabilization as a function of the gospel. What Gollwitzer finds in Braun is an account of how the Christian encounters in the event of faith not the reality of God, but an objectification of human existence and potential. Rather than functioning as a transcendent yet objective "Other" that truly encounters human subjectivity, Braun's position collapses God into that subjectivity.[31] For Gollwitzer, on the contrary, affirming that God cannot be objectified does not mean that God has no objectivity whatsoever. On the basis of this event wherein the Christian encounters God's self-manifestation, it is possible to affirm simultaneously that God cannot be objectified and that what one encounters in this event is God's true "'Thou-objectivity.'" Gollwitzer explains: "In the event in which [God] encounters humanity in judgment and forgiveness, it is true that he cannot be represented in the sense of the idea of a 'piece of world', but it *is* possible to look to him; it is true

28. Ibid., 128.
29. Ibid., 140.
30. David W. Congdon, "Afterword: The Future of Conversing with Barth," in *Karl Barth in Conversation*, ed. W. Travis McMaken and David W. Congdon (Eugene, OR: Pickwick, 2014), 262.
31. Gollwitzer, *Existence of God*, 50.

that he cannot be turned to as an It, but he certainly *can* be turned to as a Thou."[32] For Gollwitzer, God's nonobjectifiability means that God always comes to us from *outside of ourselves*, and God's Thou-objectivity means that *God* always comes to us from outside of ourselves.

Responses to Gollwitzer

Gollwitzer's intervention in the ongoing development of dialectical theology was not without critical response, even if it has not received much attention to date in English-speaking theology. Given that a not insignificant portion of English-language theology since the middle of the twentieth century has been content to valorize Barth and vilify Bultmann, it is perhaps not surprising that Gollwitzer's attempt to present a unified position between them should receive little attention. Responses to Gollwitzer from two theologians in particular—Herbert Braun, who was the target of Gollwitzer's criticism, and Eberhard Jüngel—help shed further light on his position, however, and provide the opportunity to elucidate that position in greater depth.

Herbert Braun

Gollwitzer's *Existence of God* was originally published in 1963. It was a response to a number of articles that Braun wrote over the course of the late 1950s and early 1960s, collected and published as a book in 1962. In February 1964, Gollwitzer and Braun participated in a public conversation at the University of Mainz, where Braun was professor of New Testament. Braun also published an article in response to Goll-

---

32. Ibid., 178, rev; Gollwitzer, *Die Existenz Gottes*, 142–43. For "Thou-objectivity," see Gollwitzer, *Existence of God*, 179. Buber's influence on Gollwitzer is evident here, and Gollwitzer cites Buber a number of times in his discussion. See especially ibid., 189. Gollwitzer is also influenced by Luther. He explicates the epistemological consequences of Luther's doctrine of justification as follows: "For whenever something is heard, somebody must have spoken, and the speaker cannot be identical with the hearer. . . . This, then, is the ground on which Luther's faith is built, a ground at once positive and negative: there is a place where God himself appears, real, unmistakable and actually God and where He allows himself to be heard; anywhere but in this place man hears only himself." Helmut Gollwitzer, "The Real Luther," in *Martinus Luther: 450th Anniversary of the Reformation* (Bad Godesberg: Inter Nationes, 1967), 10–11. Finally, this affirmation of God as "Thou" and rejection of God as "It" is a hallmark of dialectical theology, and Jüngel identifies it as a fundamental point of unity between Barth and Bultmann. Eberhard Jüngel, *God's Being Is in Becoming: The Trinitarian Being of God in the Theology of Karl Barth. A Paraphrase*, trans. John Webster (Grand Rapids, MI: Eerdmans, 2001), 34. Consequently, it also remains a fundamental point of unity between Jüngel and Gollwitzer despite the former's criticisms of the latter.

witzer in the same year.[33] In both settings, Braun pushes Gollwitzer on two related points.

First, Braun takes issue with Gollwitzer's argument that the biblical texts speak of God by way of analogy rather than by way of objectifying modes of thought similar to other ancient texts. Gollwitzer addresses the related issues of anthropomorphism and analogy. While he admits that "all our talk [of God] is anthropomorphic," it is nonetheless the case that "human ways of speaking can correspond to [God]."[34] This is because biblical God-talk ultimately refers to and is controlled by the relationship established between God and humanity "in the special approach to Israel and the appearance of Jesus Christ."[35] For Gollwitzer, these two affirmations—that all God-talk is anthropomorphic, and that biblical God-talk nonetheless corresponds to God—satisfy the conditions for properly analogical God-talk insofar as it recognizes that language used with reference to God simultaneously does and does not succeed in referring to God. In this regard, Gollwitzer affirms that there is an "indirect identity of God's Word and man's word."[36] Braun disputes this, comparing biblical talk of God to mythological or "representational thinking" about God that one encounters in Homer or in other ancient Greek myths. For Braun, this manner of thinking was the default setting of the ancient "world-perspective" (*Weltsicht*), and the biblical authors give no indication of operating differently.[37]

Gollwitzer is unwilling to accept that the biblical texts operate simply within this ancient and mythological point of view. He focusses on the New Testament discussions of Jesus's ascension as an example of this, noting that the heaven to which Jesus returns is not the same sort of heaven that one finds in—for instance—the Hercules myths. The God of the biblical texts is not simply an instance of a generalized or abstract deity: the properly biblical name of God, Gollwitzer insists, is

---

33. Helmut Gollwitzer and Herbert Braun, "Post Bultmann Locutum. Eine Diskussion zwischen Professor D. Helmut Gollwitzer - Berlin und Professor D. Herbert Braun - Mainz Am 13. Februar 1964," in *Mensch, du bist gefragt: Reflexionen Zur Gotteslehre*, ed. Peter Winzeler, Ausgewählte Werke (München: Chr. Kaiser, 1988), 42–85; Herbert Braun, "Gottes Existenz und meine Geschichtlichkeit im Neuen Testament. Eine Antwort an Helmut Gollwitzer," in *Zeit und Geschichte: Dankesgabe an Rudolf Bultmann zum 80. Geburtstag*, ed. Erich Dinkler (Tübingen: J. C. B. Mohr [Paul Siebeck], 1964), 399–421.
34. Gollwitzer, *Existence of God*, 149, 151.
35. Ibid., 152.
36. Ibid., 172. In a recent work on the issue of analogy in Christian theology, Archie Spencer discusses analogy as the attempt to articulate "both the adequacy of language to convey the knowledge of God and yet the incapacity of language to be 'freighted' with the being of God." Archie J. Spencer, *The Analogy of Faith: The Quest for God's Speakability*, Strategic Initiatives in Evangelical Theology (Downers Grove, IL: IVP Academic, 2015), 21.
37. Braun, "Gottes Existenz," 400, 421.

OUR GOD LOVES JUSTICE

"Yahweh," which does not fall under the more general categories of Hebrew "elim" or Greek "theoi."[38] Consequently, the biblical conception of God has to be read as critical of ancient mythological thinking. In all of this, Gollwitzer calls for an understanding of proper God-talk as involving an element of judgment. If Christian God-talk refers to God by way of Jesus Christ, it must involve the judgment of the cross. And although the resurrection transcends this judgment with an ever greater affirmation, the judgment is never eradicated. When used to speak of God, "the concepts shatter and are formed anew, they experience death and resurrection in this new and unique reference."[39]

On what basis can Gollwitzer say that the biblical texts are critical of the ancient mythological mode of thinking and speaking about deity? Braun's second point of criticism against Gollwitzer is that Gollwitzer's reading of the biblical text on these issues is prejudiced by assumptions about the "objective pregivenness"[40] of the biblical message. For Braun, there is a definite element of judgment in the biblical text. It is clear that the dynamic of faith at the heart of the biblical text involves hearing the proclamation of Jesus or Paul and encountering a word of judgment. But this does not mean that the biblical texts step outside the ancient objectifying ways of speaking about God. Instead, it means that this word of judgment is encountered precisely by way of these objectifying modes of speech.[41] Gollwitzer's mistake is to insist on approaching the text with preconceived notions about how it does and does not speak of God, with the assumption that "here something special speaks a special word to me" as a precondition for the hearing of that word.[42]

In response, Gollwitzer resolutely denies that Braun has accurately represented him. He describes the position that Braun attributes to him as a form of natural theology, and responds further by suggesting that such a position compromises Protestant commitment to salvation by grace alone: "I must not bring anything. Nor can I bring anything at all. Nor can I accomplish anything at all."[43] Instead, it is precisely the

---

38. Gollwitzer and Braun, "Post Bultmann Locutum," 51–53.
39. Gollwitzer, *Existence of God*, 164. Stieber-Westermann discusses the incarnation as touchstone for Gollwitzer's hermeneutics. See Stieber-Westermann, *Provokation zum Leben*, 92.
40. Gollwitzer, *Existence of God*, 58, rev; Gollwitzer, *Die Existenz Gottes*, 45. The German phrase in question is *"eine objektive Vorgegebenheit."* The English translates this as: "an objectively given fact." For Braun and Gollwitzer's dialogue on this point, see Gollwitzer and Braun, "Post Bultmann Locutum," 65–66.
41. Braun, "Gottes Existenz," 420.
42. Gollwitzer and Braun, "Post Bultmann Locutum," 66. For discussion of this criticism of Gollwitzer by Braun, see Stieber-Westermann, *Provokation zum Leben*, 186.
43. Gollwitzer and Braun, "Post Bultmann Locutum," 66. For reference to natural theology, see ibid., 65.

encounter with God by way of the text that authorizes a reading of the biblical text that cuts against ancient modes of objectification. In this sense, Gollwitzer's statement about the biblical message's "objective pregivenness" refers to how one must approach the text subsequent to the event of faith. As far as Gollwitzer is concerned, he and Braun have a "shared theological basis" in affirming that faith can occur "only through the content that encounters us." Braun's response to this is an affirmative: "Good." He elaborates by saying that this shows Gollwitzer and himself to be in concert over the third thesis that Braun selected to structure their conversation: "God is within this occurrence" of faith.[44]

The conversation continues on the basis of this common ground. Now the question becomes, "Who is within this occurrence?" Both theologians are able to say that the one encountered in the event of faith is "the one that the New Testament calls God." In an effort to load this abstract definition with some content, they agree on defining God in terms of 1 John 4: "God is the one who loves us."[45] Now Gollwitzer goes on the attack by asking Braun if the statement can be reversed: is it the same to say that God is love and that love is God? Braun affirms this. Gollwitzer presses the point, arguing that the subject "God" must control what the predicate "love" means. For Braun, this move is an exercise in improper conceptual objectification. Braun argues that "where love [agapan] occurs, there is God [theos]." Gollwitzer affirms this, but with reservation. Appealing to Matthew 25, he argues that God is there "where love really occurs," and that "love cannot really happen without the Holy Spirit." In this way, the subject that one encounters in the event of faith provides a critical distance from our normal modes of thought. It is different, Gollwitzer argues, to say "this occurrence is itself God" and "God is the one who is love itself and who gives this occurrence where it occurs." Braun answers: "your latter formulation objectifies and mythologizes in an ancient manner."[46]

Braun and Gollwitzer's exchange clarifies that they share a concern to understand scripture's significance from the event of faith in which one encounters God. Braun's criticisms of Gollwitzer show that they approach the issue from different sides at times, but the resolution of those criticisms signifies an important unity. Real difference remains, however, on the question of what can be said of God on the basis of the event of encounter. In more technical terms, Braun rejects Gollwitzer's

44. Ibid., 67.
45. Ibid., 68–69.
46. Ibid., 71–72.

concept of Thou-objectivity insofar as he is unwilling to speak of God as a real counterpart that humanity encounters in the event of faith.[47]

Eberhard Jüngel

Where Gollwitzer's name is known in contemporary English language theology, it is mainly because of the stinging criticisms leveled against him by Eberhard Jüngel in his highly regarded book on Barth's doctrine of God, *God's Being Is in Becoming*. I will address Jüngel's criticisms of Gollwitzer under two headings—his tendency to misread Gollwitzer, and his criticism of Gollwitzer's distinction between God's will and nature.

First, Jüngel criticizes Gollwitzer at a number of points in ways that are hard to avoid characterizing as uncharitable. These criticisms primarily pertain to Gollwitzer's reading of Bultmann. Jüngel thinks Gollwitzer's interpretation of Bultmann is too indebted to that of Gerhard Noller, who reads Bultmann in a manner that tends to reduce God's transcendence to earthly-historical factors. Jüngel finds this problematic. Although he credits Gollwitzer with trying to interpret Bultmann favorably, dependence on Noller prevents Gollwitzer from succeeding. Consequently, Jüngel faults Gollwitzer for not familiarizing himself with the best available interpretation, and even cites his own review of Noller published in *Evangelische Theologie* in 1963—the same year in which Gollwitzer's book was published.[48] Jüngel later quotes Gollwitzer as an example of someone who worried about Bultmann falling victim to the dangers of natural theology, and defends Bultmann against that accusation.[49] Gollwitzer does not claim that Bultmann is guilty of natural theology, however. He everywhere gives Bultmann the benefit of the doubt, even while urging caution or discussing the ambiguity of Bultmann's position. It is difficult to fault Gollwitzer for such hesitancy, given the picture of Bultmann painted by Braun and Noller.

Second, Jüngel criticizes Gollwitzer's distinction between God's will and nature. Gollwitzer's concern in making this distinction is to guard

---

47. Braun departs from Bultmann here. See the quotes from Otto Schnübbe and David Congdon in note 13 above. Bruce McCormack summarizes the persistent divide between Braun and Gollwitzer with the following question: "Is the word 'God' simply a name we give to the event in which 'faith' takes its rise in the human (Braun's view) or is the name rightly given to an objectively real Reality (Gollwitzer's position)?" Bruce L. McCormack, "God *Is* His Decision: The Jüngel-Gollwitzer 'Debate' Revisited," in *Theology as Conversation: The Significance of Dialogue in Historical and Contemporary Theology, a Festschrift for Daniel L. Migliore*, ed. Bruce L. McCormack and Kimlyn J. Bender (Grand Rapids, MI: Eerdmans, 2009), 52.
48. Jüngel, *God's Being Is in Becoming*, 41n118.
49. Ibid., 118n57.

the true otherness of God so that God does not simply become another way of describing a facet of human experience, as discussed previously. Furthermore, Gollwitzer also wants to ensure that God's otherness remains something inaccessible to or hidden from humanity, apart from the event of encounter with God's Thou-objectivity. The analogy between God and humanity enacted by this encounter "has its ground not in the nature of God [Wesen Gottes], but in the will of God [Willen Gottes], i.e., it is not possible to argue back from it to the nature of God in the sense of how God is constituted, but only to the nature of his will, i.e., from his will as made known in history."[50] Jüngel worries that this sort of hard distinction between God's being and will ultimately undermines the encounter. Does one encounter God's own self, or merely a projection of God's will? And how can one ever be sure that the will of God with which one has to do is not subject to revision? Jüngel puts it in terms of mercy: "if God's unfathomable mercy does not have its ground in God's being, then the concept of mercy is no longer a concept of God." Jüngel is certainly correct that this "is very far from Gollwitzer's intention."[51]

John Webster explains that Jüngel thinks "Gollwitzer's account succumbs" to an "abstract notion of divine aseity," that Gollwitzer errs in advancing too "pure" an account of divine objectivity insofar as he conceives of God's independence "in a non-relational way."[52] Jüngel makes this point by saying that Gollwitzer does not think God's being through in a sufficiently historical way, which is what enables Gollwitzer to make a distinction that so insulates God's being from "historical acts of revelation." It would have been better had Gollwitzer defined "God's being from the beginning in trinitarian terms."[53] Matters are not so simple, however. For instance, Gollwitzer affirms that

50. Gollwitzer, *Existence of God*, 186; Gollwitzer, *Die Existenz Gottes*, 149.
51. Jüngel, *God's Being Is in Becoming*, 107. Jüngel makes this criticism as part of an effort to position himself as Barth's heir. We must remember, however, that Gollwitzer takes his distinction between God's nature and will from Barth. He reflects on this distinction while also emphasizing that God's will and nature are identical in the act of the Father begetting the Son. See Barth, *Church Dogmatics*, 1.1:434. In using this conceptual tool, Gollwitzer simply drew on what he had been taught by Barth. Gollwitzer was in Bonn studying with Barth at the time Barth was preparing this material. By the time Barth began rethinking this distinction in the second volume of his *Church Dogmatics*, the very material whose consequences Jüngel's book endeavors to elucidate, Gollwitzer was preoccupied with pastoring in Dahlem and was then conscripted by the German army. Marquardt rightly notes that Gollwitzer was by then less interested in constructive doctrinal development and more interested in deploying the theological tradition—including Barth's theology—for the sociopolitical struggle. Friedrich-Wilhelm Marquardt, "Helmut Gollwitzer: Weg und Werk," in *Bibliographie Helmut Gollwitzer*, ed. Christa Haehn, Ausgewählte Werke (München: Chr. Kaiser, 1988), 27.
52. Jüngel, *God's Being Is in Becoming*, xiv, xvii–xviii.
53. Ibid., 6–7.

the Christian "must speak of God in inseparable relation to historical phenomena . . . as acts and words of God himself in which he himself comes to men and confronts all men."[54]

It is perhaps true that Gollwitzer made a tactical error when he reached for the distinction between God's will and nature, but the problematic character of this distinction does not fundamentally cripple Gollwitzer's position. In response to Jüngel's criticisms, we must highlight Gollwitzer's insistence on "the identity [Identität] between the revelation and the Revealer, between 'God for us' and 'God in himself,'" in the encounter with God's Thou-objectivity.[55] Given Gollwitzer's affirmation of identity, it is clear that his distinction between God's will and nature is a provisional one that exists only to be overcome in the event of faith. For Gollwitzer, the concept of "God in himself" does the same work as the concept of Thou-objectivity—namely, it affirms that God's being cannot be reduced to a state or characteristic of human consciousness. In other words, he does not intend for his use of this language to carry the ontological connotations and implications that it has had elsewhere in the theological tradition.

This is perhaps the key point of contention between Jüngel and Gollwitzer. In his brief treatment of their exchange, Congdon summarizes the former's criticism by saying that "Gollwitzer backs away . . . from the work of theological ontology."[56] Both Jüngel and Congdon think that such backing away is undesirable. Gollwitzer disagrees. In a set of theses published a decade or so after Jüngel's criticism, Gollwitzer affirms that "an 'ontology of God' is not possible. We can only make statements about this voice" of God that speaks to us in each historical moment and proclaims to us that the transcendent ground of our existence is the friend of human beings. But there is a dialectic at work here: "God remains hidden in mystery, and . . . abandons himself entirely to us. God remains hidden in mystery, that is, his being remains incomprehensible for us. The voice imparts to us the being-for-us of his will. The Word of God is promissio (promise), not . . . theoretical information about the ultimate ground of being; it is promise and acceptance coming out of the dark."[57]

54. Gollwitzer, Existence of God, 199.
55. Ibid., 195; Gollwitzer, Die Existenz Gottes, 157.
56. Congdon, Mission of Demythologizing, 15n19.
57. Helmut Gollwitzer, "Theses for Understanding Biblical Speech About God," in God, Secularization, and History: Essays in Memory of Ronald Gregor Smith, ed. Eugene Thomas Long (Columbia, SC: University of South Carolina Press, 1974), 133. While Gollwitzer would perhaps have conflated the ideas of "theological ontology" and "ontology of God," they are not necessarily identical. It is at least arguably possible, even within Gollwitzer's framework, to engage in the work of theological

This sheds important light on how the distinction between God's nature and will functions for Gollwitzer. God's nature represents God's transcendent beyond that comes to humanity in the event of encounter, giving birth to faith without being possessed by faith. In this event, God makes promises to humanity as the expression of God's will, and faith hopes in these promises. Luther's influence on Gollwitzer is pronounced here. The matrix of promise, faith, and hope is central to Luther's commentary on Romans, which had a major impact on Gollwitzer's thought. As Luther says, "faith ratifies the promise, and the promise demands faith," such that "when the promise ceases, faith ceases; and when the promise is done away, faith is made void, and vice versa."[58] Gollwitzer worries that the construction of a theological ontology will necessarily abstract from proclamation and faith, thereby undermining the mystery of God and the promise-character of the gospel. Understood in this manner, Gollwitzer approximates Bultmann and Gerhard Ebeling.[59]

Gollwitzer's aim is not to construct a doctrine of God's being-in-itself prior to discussing God's being-for-us,[60] thereby setting up too pure

ontology: developing conceptual descriptions of God's being that arise from and are controlled by God's Thou-objectivity in the event of encounter. Gollwitzer is, after all, perfectly willing to make claims about who God is, such as his affirmation that "God is love" in conversation with Braun. Gollwitzer and Braun, "Post Bultmann Locutum," 69. Congdon theorizes such work in connection with Bultmann as "eschatological theontology." See Congdon, *Mission of Demythologizing*, 339–45.

58. Martin Luther, *Luther's Works, 25: Lectures on Romans, Glosses and Scholia*, ed. Hilton C. Oswald (Saint Louis, MO: Concordia Publishing House, 1972), 39–40. There are connections here to what Gollwitzer learned from Jewish-Christian dialogue: "Jewish existence shows us that truth, justice, and love are not identical to our being, but rather lie in front of us and above us, calling us out of what we are to an ever new beginning, to what we can be." Helmut Gollwitzer, "Die Weltbedeutung des Judentums," in *Forderungen der Freiheit: Aufsätze und Reden zur politischen Ethik* (München: Chr. Kaiser Verlag, 1964), 274.

59. Stieber-Westermann discusses the eschatological character of Gollwitzer's understanding of the truth of God-talk. See Stieber-Westermann, *Provokation zum Leben*, 97–98. This resonates with Jüngel's "analogy of advent," and Congdon describes Bultmann as a theologian of perpetual advent. On Jüngel and Bultmann respectively, see Spencer, *The Analogy of Faith*, 279–87; Congdon, *Rudolf Bultmann*, 146–59. Congdon also notes that Jüngel was heavily influenced by Gerhard Ebeling on these matters, tracing the influence specifically to an article that Ebeling published in 1965. See David W. Congdon, *The God Who Saves: A Dogmatic Sketch* (Eugene, OR: Cascade, 2016), 126 n. 79. Gollwitzer interacts with Ebeling frequently in *Existence of God*, both appreciatively and critically, but this important article had not yet been published.

60. Bultmann lodges this criticism against Gollwitzer in a letter on July 26, 1963. "Bultmann . . . rejected Gollwitzer's postulate that theology must first of all postulate God's being-in-and-for-itself and only later take up the meaning of God's being-for-us." Hammann, *Rudolf Bultmann*, 469. Akke van der Kooi summarizes Jüngel's criticism of Gollwitzer in similar terms: "Gollwitzer fails to think the relation between God's being-for-us and the freedom of God's being-for-himself." Akke van der Kooi, "Election and the Lived Life. Considerations on Gollwitzer's Reading of Karl Barth in CD II/2 as a Contribution to Actual Discussions on Trinity and Election," *Zeitschrift für dialektische Theologie* Supplement Series, no. 4 (2010): 73. Gollwitzer does not posit a being of God for Godself prior to and independent of God's being for humanity as Bultmann claims because Gollwitzer is not interested in theological ontology. While Gollwitzer admits a conceptual priority for the former over the latter, they are encountered simultaneously in the event of faith and cannot be sep-

or abstract or nonhistorical a doctrine of God. His distinction between God's being and God's will secures God's transcendence precisely in the moment when God transcends God's own transcendence by encountering us in the event of faith. It couples with Gollwitzer's concept of Thou-objectivity to emphasize that the Thou one encounters in the event of faith is a true Other, and not simply the Feuerbachian projection of some aspect of human experience. As Gollwitzer puts it: "On this beyondness, on the real non-identity of God and man, on God's being over against man, the whole Gospel depends."[61] Might he have found a less problematic conceptual tool to make the necessary distinction? Perhaps. Indeed, the language of "mystery" and "promise" that he employed later is preferable because that language carries less metaphysical baggage than does speaking about God's nature and will. But the use to which he put this questionable distinction falls well within the bounds of dialectical theology, whether in the first generation or the second.

Therefore, All Theology is Contextual

To objectify God is to treat God as a fixture of the world that Christians confess to be God's creation. Like his teacher Karl Barth, and dialectical theology as a whole, Gollwitzer argues that such objectification is improper. God has God's own reality, but God only becomes the object of human knowledge in the event of faith. Gollwitzer understands this event analogically as a personal encounter, such that one really has to do with a God who is other than simply a name given to a particular kind of generally available human experience. This is God's "Thou-objectivity," wherein God remains transcendent even as truly encountered in the event of faith. All faithful God-talk must, therefore, arise from and be critically controlled by this encounter. Explicating all this was the task of the previous section. Now, we must turn our attention to a major consequence of this position: theology's irreducibly contextual character.

---

arated from one another: "we must say at one and the same time both that God is what it, faith, receives him as in his Word and that he is more than it, faith, understands of him, that before his self-bestowal he exists for himself and in his self-bestowal he remains himself—this specific God in his continuity and identity." Gollwitzer, *Existence of God*, 232.

61. Gollwitzer, *Existence of God*, 219. Of course, this statement cannot be abstracted from the affirmation that "there is no way to the event, to the act of God which is called Jesus, that circumvents the word of proclamation with its corresponding answer of faith." The kerygma "points beyond itself to the living God who encounters us in the proclamation but is more than a title for the word-event itself." Ibid., 224–25.

Dialectical Theology and Contextual Theology

If God cannot be objectified, cannot be treated as a generally accessible feature of the world, then it necessarily follows that no single attempt to speak of God is sufficient for all times and places. Indeed, we saw that Gollwitzer rejects the idea that there is an eternal and unchanging "kernel" of revelation wrapped in a contingent, historical "shell."[62] In other words, all theology is contextual theology—God-talk that arises in the midst of, and speaks to, specific sociohistorical locations. As Gollwitzer puts it, "Christian theology is reflection on the Gospel and its consequences for life, and—indeed—reflection on the service of these consequences for life. . . . Theology actually arises only through the collision of the gospel with concrete situations."[63] Rolf Stieber-Westerman comments on Gollwitzer: "the bringing-to-speech of God can never be divorced . . . from the questions of life, namely, the specific questions of real people here and now, not the supposedly timeless, eternal questions of human existence."[64]

It is only through this collision, through the encounter of particular human beings in their particular contextual locations with God's Thou-objectivity in the event of faith, that human beings not only can, but *must* engage in God-talk. God's nonobjectifiability means that revelation always occurs as an event of encounter, and thus, positive theological reflection on the God met in that encounter only takes place in particular places and times—in particular contexts.[65] Encounter with God's Thou-objectivity in the event of faith frees theology *from* the

---

62. Ibid., 110.

63. Helmut Gollwitzer, "Zum Problem der Gewalt in der christlichen Ethik," in *. . . daß Gerechtigkeit und Friede sich Küssen: Aufsätze zur politischen Ethik*, Band 1, ed. Andreas Pangritz, Ausgewählte Werke (München: Chr. Kaiser, 1988), 100.

64. Stieber-Westermann, *Provokation zum Leben*, 5–6. As Dannemann and Weissinger note, "Gollwitzer assumes that theology is always time-bound." Consequently, it is necessary to examine the "workshop" in which a piece of theology developed. Ulrich Dannemann and Matthias Weissinger, "Helmut Gollwitzers Beitrag zur Theologie der Gesellschaft," in *Richte unsere Füße auf den Weg des Friedens: Helmut Gollwitzer zum 70. Geburtstag*, ed. Andreas Baudis, Dieter Clausert, Volkhard Schliski and Bernhard Wegener (Munich: Chr. Kaiser, 1979), 580. Jung Mo Sung makes this point more generally: "There is no other way to God but the one that leads to human beings with the problems, challenges and possibilities resulting from their personal and social contexts." Sung, *Desire, Market and Religion*, 6.

65. Gollwitzer, *Existence of God*, 131. "The negative definition of non-objectivity is . . . a necessary, but not an adequate definition of our talk of God! Only in conjunction with the other definitions, only as a safeguard for the *positive* definitions of God's self-bestowal, does it hold good." The term "non-objectivity" here translates *"Nicht-Gegenständlichkeit."* Gollwitzer, *Die Existenz Gottes*, 104. It is possible to make a technical distinction between *Gegenstand* and *Objectiv*, but Gollwitzer seems uninterested in doing so. For instance, he uses *"Nichtobjektivierbarkeit"* (translated as "non-objectifiability") as well, and indicates their functional equivalence in his study. Ibid., 93; Gollwitzer, *Existence of God*, 117.

idolatry of all false objectifications and frees it *for* radical particularity. The logic of dialectical theology demands contextual theology.

That dialectical theology demands contextual theology contradicts a longstanding but misguided criticism of dialectical theology. Jürgen Moltmann is perhaps the figure most responsible for disseminating the notion that a conflict, or at least a fundamental divergence, exists between dialectical theology and contextual theology. In *Theology of Hope*, Moltmann criticizes both Barth and Bultmann for the different ways they—as he sees it—drive a wedge between theology and historical situatedness: Barth's mistake is to conceptualize God's self-revelation in terms of an eternal present, while Bultmann's error is to construct "God" and the "world" as "radical alternatives."[66] James Cone levels similar criticisms against Barth's theology. For Cone, Barth's theology depends on an "'abstract' revelation" that is "independent of human experiences, [and] to which theologians can appeal for evidence." Cone argues that the opposite is true: "God meets us in the human situation, not as an idea or concept." That Barth abstracts in this way is a critical mistake in Cone's judgment because it functions to separate "what we say about the cross . . . from the real crosses in our midst."[67]

Moltmann and Cone want not only contextual theology, but liberation theology. It is possible to produce contextual theology that attends to the situatedness of God-talk without recognizing how God-talk based in encounter with God disrupts us not only at the personal level, but at the societal level as well. Liberation theology goes beyond contextual theology insofar as it identifies "context as that which needs to be overcome and subverted rather than affirmed."[68] According to criticisms such as those from Moltmann and Cone, dialectical theology fails not only as a truly contextual theology, but also and derivatively as a truly liberating theology.

66. Jürgen Moltmann, *Theology of Hope: On the Ground and the Implications of a Christian Eschatology*, trans. James W. Leitch (Minneapolis, MN: Fortress Press, 1993), 58, 65. These echo Dietrich Bonhoeffer's criticism of Barth and Paul Tillich's criticism of "kerygmatic theology." Dietrich Bonhoeffer, *Letters and Papers from Prison*, trans. Reinhard Krauss, Nancy Lukens, Lisa E. Dahill and Isabel Best, Dietrich Bonhoeffer's Works, vol. 8 (Minneapolis, MN: Fortress Press, 2010), 404; Paul Tillich, *Systematic Theology*, 3 vols. (Chicago: University of Chicago Press, 1951–63), 1:4–5.
67. James H. Cone, *A Black Theology of Liberation*, twentieth anniversary edition (Maryknoll, NY: Orbis Books, 2004), xviii–xix; James H. Cone, *The Cross and the Lynching Tree* (Maryknoll, NY: Orbis Books, 2011), 63. For more on Cone and Barth, see Raymond Carr, "Barth and Cone in Dialogue on Revelation and Freedom: An Analysis of James Cone's Critical Appropriation of 'Barthian' Theology" (PhD dissertation: Graduate Theological Union, 2011); J. Kameron Carter, *Race: A Theological Account* (New York: Oxford University Press, 2008), 160–81.
68. Joerg Rieger, *Christ & Empire: From Paul to Postcolonial Times* (Minneapolis, MN: Fortress Press, 2007), 8.

We need not accept this characterization at face value, however. At the very least, these criticisms ignore Gollwitzer's creative rearticulation of Barth and Bultmann's shared legacy.[69] Dorothee Sölle lends credence to the idea of a contextual, liberationist dialectical theology—while initially criticizing Bultmann's dialectical theology because it "understands itself as essentially apolitical," she nonetheless describes the liberationist form of contextual theology as "a kind of continuation of what Bultmann did."[70] Furthermore, the criticisms that Sölle leveled against Gollwitzer as Barth's heir were misguided. As James Bentley puts it, "her own theological inheritance obscured the fact that she and Gollwitzer were essentially on the same side."[71] Just as Sölle connects liberation theology to Bultmann, Gollwitzer connects it to Barth. In an essay entitled "Karl Barth's Theology of Freedom and Liberation Theology," Gollwitzer undertakes to show how some of the fundamental concepts of Barth's theology establish a trajectory toward liberation theology. Perhaps the most important point for Gollwitzer is how Barth understands human freedom on analogy to divine freedom, which is a freedom for the sake of humanity. Consequently, true human freedom puts itself at the service of others and their freedom.[72] Gollwitzer admits that Barth—as a creature of his own context—remained improperly Eurocentric and blind to widespread oppression in the global South, but his final word is this: "It is indisputable that a direct line goes from [Barth] to the liberation movements and to liberation theology."[73]

---

69. This raises questions about the accuracy of these interpretations of dialectical theology. Specifically with reference to Moltmann's criticisms, see the following: McMaken, *Sign of the Gospel*, 165–68; Congdon, *Mission of Demythologizing*, 789–800; James F. Kay, *Christus Praesens: A Reconsideration of Rudolf Bultmann's Christology* (Grand Rapids, MI: Eerdmans, 1994), 157–72.

70. Dorothee Soelle, *Political Theology*, trans. John Shelley (Philadelphia: Fortress Press, 1974), xix; Dorothee Soelle, *The Window of Vulnerability: A Political Spirituality*, trans. Linda M. Maloney (Minneapolis, MN: Fortress Press, 1990), 122. For more on Sölle's engagement with Bultmann, see Kay, *Christus Praesens*, 142–57.

71. James Bentley, *Between Marx and Christ: The Dialogue in German-Speaking Europe, 1870-1970* (London: Verso Books, 1982), 133; see 131–35. Bentley has this to say about Sölle's criticisms of Barth: "it is not clear that [Sölle's] assessment of the political consequences of Barthianism was either fair or correct." Ibid., 132.

72. Helmut Gollwitzer, "Karl Barths Theologie der Freiheit und die Theologie der Befreiung. Für Wolfgang Schweitzer zum 70. Geburtstag," in *Wer ist unser Gott? Beiträge zu einer Befreiungstheologie im Kontext der »ersten« Welt*, ed. Luise Schottroff and Willy Schottroff (Munich: Chr. Kaiser, 1986), 28–29.

73. Ibid., 42. Gollwitzer also notes that Barth would no doubt have critical questions for the liberation movement and its theology, but that these would come from a position of sympathy rather than antagonism. George Hunsinger follows up on this suggestion in an essay on the subject. See George Hunsinger, "Karl Barth and Liberation Theology," *Journal of Religion* 63, no. 3 (1983): 247–63. By taking this approach, Hunsinger tacitly acknowledges the veracity of Gollwitzer's affirmation of deep sympathy between Barth's theology and liberation theology. For a more recent engagement between Barthian and liberation theology, conducted under Hunsinger's supervision, see

This direct line becomes more clearly visible in Gollwitzer's own thought when he theologically engages with the concept of liberation and concretizes that engagement with reference to black theology.

Gollwitzer, Liberation, and Black Theology

Helga Day notes that Gollwitzer demonstrated a "resolute partiality for the hungry and oppressed," and recognized that different forms of praxis require different theologies. The kinship between his thought and Latin American liberation theology on these points promises that a more detailed look at this aspect of Gollwitzer's thought will bear fruit.[74]

Gollwitzer approaches the subject of liberation by reflecting on history and transcendence. History is "the world in which we live," and transcendence is "whatever power decides the meaning of our existence in this world." Defining these terms is easy enough, but understanding their proper relationship is difficult. Gollwitzer outlines three possibilities: that of nihilism, which denies meaning; that of agnosticism, which is skeptical of meaning; and that of religion, which tends to describe meaning in terms of morality and "socially desirable conduct," evaluating (or judging) one's conduct against that standard.[75] This religious approach deserves the criticism levelled against it by Marxism, namely, that it all too often serves to legitimize and, thereby, reinforce social—and especially class—hierarchies.

Even though the religious approach is prevalent within the Christian tradition, Gollwitzer finds the core of the Christian message in "liberation from final judgment." Consequently, the transcendent no longer imposes itself upon history as an eternal and unchangeable judgment; rather, the transcendent itself is liberated and transformed. The Christian now has to do with a transcendence that affirms and embraces history instead of a transcendence that evaluates and judges it. This was Luther's insight, namely, understanding "the gospel as liberation expe-

74. Helga Krüger Day, "Christlicher Glaube und gesellschaftliches Handeln: eine Studie der Entwicklung der Theologie Helmut Gollwitzers" (Doctoral dissertation: Union Theological Seminary, 1973), 335–36. For a recent survey on the preferential option for the poor and how that notion has developed, see Rohan M. Curnow, "Which Preferential Option for the Poor? A History of the Doctrine's Bifurcation," *Modern Theology* 31, no. 1 (2015): 27–59.

75. Helmut Gollwitzer, "Liberation in History," *Interpretation* 28, no. 4 (1974): 406–7. Unfortunately, Gollwitzer makes some improperly reductionist comments about "the world religions" and "most religions" in this material. We must remember that he is making a theological point, rather than engaging in the sort of descriptive and analytic task pursued by contemporary religious studies.

rience."[76] Gollwitzer wants to push beyond the reformational tendency to emphasize the psychopersonal experience of liberation, however, to speak also of the sociohistorical experience of liberation. He looks to the New Testament to make this important connection:

> [I]n Jesus' cross and resurrection the great transformation of the transcendent is taking place. It consists in God's reconciling the world to himself. . . . And this vertical change of the transcendent causes the horizontal change in history which is a *transformation of community*. This implies that a group which lives together in terms of the Kingdom of God comes into harsh conflict with the way of life of its surroundings, its principles and social rules.[77]

Gollwitzer develops this implication by discussing the New Testament notions of "brotherhood" and "sonship." He points out that members of the Jesus-following movement referred to themselves as "brothers" rather than as "Christians," which was a designation originally employed by those outside the community. Brotherhood designates a new Spirit-empowered sociality that "transcend[s] race and class."[78] And this transcending cannot be limited to the realm of personal feeling, for that only serves to insulate the powers that be from the transformative power of the gospel. Rather, "brotherhood transcending race and class in the New Testament means: actual life together in actual equality, that is, in a new classless society. A system of injustice legitimated as a system of justice is being abolished."[79] The abolition of this illegitimate system of injustice depends on a further theological point: followers of Jesus are sisters and brothers because they are, first and foremost, children—God's children. As such, they are characterized by freedom and love: freedom *from* all external subjugation and *for* the love of God and neighbor. Oppression contradicts this basic truth of human being and existence as proclaimed by the gospel. Gollwitzer puts it this way: "This is the *pneuma*, the Kingdom of God: restoration of God's image, restoration of humanity, as God the creator meant it to be: the family of man free of domination, living in freedom, equality, and brotherhood, man as responsible subject in brotherly communion.

---

76. Ibid., 408.
77. Ibid., 411–12, Gollwitzer's emphasis.
78. Ibid., 412. The masculine language employed in this discussion is true to Gollwitzer's linguistic context and reflects the existing English translation, but the gendered character of the discussion is not materially essential to it. Each reference to "brother" or "son" might just as well be "sister" or "daughter."
79. Ibid., 413.

This vision and its realization belong to the very center of the Christian faith."[80]

This is a theological vision that opposes all subjugations—that is to say, it is a liberationist theological vision. Indeed, Gollwitzer would have heartily affirmed Terry Eagleton's dictum: "all authentic theology is liberation theology."[81] Our examination of Gollwitzer's liberation theology has thus far remained at a general level, however. We must examine how it becomes concrete by focusing on his engagement with a particular liberationist theological movement. Gollwitzer's writings present us with a number of engagements with different liberationist movements, but the one most relevant for a North American context is that of black theology.[82] To understand how Gollwitzer conceptualized this engagement, we must turn to his essay, "Why Black Theology?"

At the very start of his essay, Gollwitzer affirms the radical criticism levied by black theology against white European and American theology, arguing that not only were the church and the theological tradition complicit with the oppressive systems of "colonialism and the slave trade," but also that black theology correctly "falsifies not merely isolated theological statements, but church and theology as a whole." The only way for white theologians to properly address this falsification, in Gollwitzer's view, is by "giving up [their] hitherto uncritical solidarity with the other world and trying to 'become black,'" which Gollwitzer characterizes as a concrete and radical *metanoia*—repentance and conversion.[83]

Gollwitzer then dives into an extended discussion of the history of Christian complicity in colonialism and slavery. He pulls no punches here, identifying two seminal events in Christianity's early history that set the stage for the litany of failings that followed. First, there was the parting of the Jewish and Gentile Jesus movements, and the subsequent "liquidation of Jewish Christianity."[84] This established Jews as

---

80. Ibid., 414. Note Gollwitzer's allusion to the clarion call of the French Revolution: *Liberté, égalité, fraternité!*

81. Terry Eagleton, *Reason, Faith, & Revolution: Reflections on the God Debate*, The Terry Lectures (New Haven: Yale University Press, 2009), 32.

82. This engagement was more than merely literary: Gollwitzer was in the United States in the spring of 1968, attending and participating in Martin Luther King Jr.'s funeral. See Helmut Gollwitzer, *Skizzen eines Lebens. Aus verstreuten Selbstzeugnissen gefunden und verbunden von Friedrich-Wilhelm Marquardt, Wolfgang Brinkel und Manfred Weber* (Gütersloh: Christian Kaiser Verlagshaus, 1998), 319; Stieber-Westermann, *Provokation zum Leben*, 31.

83. Helmut Gollwitzer, "Why Black Theology?," *Union Seminary Quarterly Review* 31, no. 1 (1975): 38. The basic insight here is that the various European theological traditions constitute *white* theology and are just as contextual as black theology. Black theology's existence highlights this contextuality.

84. Ibid., 39.

an "other," as the counterpoint to Christian identity. Second, there was "the Constantinian takeover," which inextricably linked Christianity with a particular cultural-political entity that served to produce and reinforce a sense of superiority among the European or "white" nations vis-à-vis the rest of the world's peoples. Such superiority underwrote colonialism's plunder of the global South in the early modern period, as well as the slavery that accompanied it.

Gollwitzer mentions Bartholomé Las Casas as one of the few Christian voices raised in protest against these developments.[85] Originally, a slave-owner in what is now the Dominican Republic, he became disgusted with slavery's inhumanity and took Dominican orders. Eventually, he became a bishop. Las Casas protested against the subjugation of non-European peoples throughout his ecclesiastical career. Unfortunately, he was a significant exception to the rule.

The situation was little better in Europe, as Gollwitzer makes clear, and he does not spare his own Protestant forebears from criticism. Instead of contesting slavery and colonialism, "Protestant" nations eagerly elbowed their way into the mix. For Gollwitzer, these crimes are also ineluctably linked with the advent of capitalism. Gollwitzer summarizes in words that resonate still today: "The capitalist revolution as the revolution of the white, christianized, Protestant peoples began its worldwide victory and opened up a new age of slavery that even today—although in changed forms of enslavement—has not as yet been terminated." And "the whole development of the wealth of white nations" derives from the twofold exploitation of "surplus" poor Europeans on the one hand, and the natural and human resources of the global South on the other. Any sense that we possess today of having overcome colonialism and slavery is, Gollwitzer tells us, "no more than an apologetic illusion promulgated for our peace of mind."[86]

Black theology protests all this, and Gollwitzer agrees with James Cone: "in white theology, . . . the black person does not appear"[87] despite being one of the major concerns for white political and economic reflection. Gollwitzer refers to the situation of the black person as that of being and "remaining an 'invisible man,'" a clear allusion to the powerful novel by Ralph Ellison.[88] Again, Gollwitzer understands this as a failure of the church and theological tradition, which should

---

85. Ibid. "In contrast to colonial discourse, Las Casas advocated for a God who invariably sides with the otherness of the victim." Paul S. Chung, *Church and Ethical Responsibility in the Midst of World Economy* (Eugene, OR: Cascade, 2013), 25; see 19–27.
86. Gollwitzer, "Why Black Theology?," 42.
87. Ibid., 44.

have spoken and acted otherwise. In a comment thick with sarcasm, he writes: "the Gospel which proclaims liberation to the captives and good news to the poor apparently did not remind them of the colonial misery. And it apparently had no practical consequences that in the body of Christ, Jews, Greeks, barbarians, and masters and slaves are one."[89]

Christianity's history is one of complicity in oppression, in reinforcing a harmful sociopolitical, economic, and theological status quo. What does this history mean for those who have benefited from this status quo? At the most fundamental level, it means entering the realm of political debate and action. There can be no retreat to the merely "spiritual" or personal, although those aspects are important as well. For Gollwitzer, there is an "inevitable relationship between the message of reconciliation and the political battle."[90] But more than just entering the political realm, they must enter the political realm on the side of the oppressed. "Practical solidarity" means taking sides. The call to take sides can often be uncomfortable for those who have benefited from the status quo, which is as true today with reference to the Black Lives Matter movement as it was at the time of the Civil Rights Movement. This discomfort often expresses itself in the facile objection that Christians should love all people, and therefore, not take sides. Gollwitzer has this to say: "this challenge of taking sides, which appears because of black theology, sounds terrifying only to him who is blind to the fact that the empirical church has actually always taken sides. Its ethics of the state and its social ethics meant taking sides for the status quo, insofar as the church tried to improve it while not wanting to recognize a Christian mandate fundamentally to change it or even—with different theological arguments—basically to deny it."[91] In other words, the church and theological tradition has always taken sides. Furthermore, it has taken the wrong side. This must change, even though it means acting "against our own interests" and undertaking a "redistribution of power."[92]

Gollwitzer discusses black theology in his "Liberation in History" essay as well. He affirms Visser 't Hooft's claim that those Christians and congregations who refuse to take the side of the oppressed mark

88. Ibid., 45. See Ralph Ellison, *Invisible Man* (New York: Vintage Books, 1995), originally published in 1952.
89. Gollwitzer, "Why Black Theology?," 44. Note the allusions to Isaiah 61:1–2, echoed in Luke 4:18–19, and Galatians 3:28.
90. Ibid., 54.
91. Ibid., 50.
92. Ibid., 53, 56.

themselves as heretics. Gollwitzer agrees: "all our churches, while accusing each other of heresy and consequently separating from each other, are heretical on account of accommodating the gospel to the ruling class and the systems of exploitation."[93] If taken seriously, this would decisively reshape ecumenical dialogue. Liberation theology movements such as black theology force those of us who have benefited from these systems of exploitation to acknowledge and repent of our self-serving complicity. Because of this, Gollwitzer situates himself as a student of this movement and affirms that "the discipleship of Jesus' community can today only consist in 'becoming black.'"[94] I will therefore give the last word to James Cone, whom Gollwitzer echoes here: "Knowing God means being on the side of the oppressed, becoming *one* with them, and participating in the goal of liberation. *We must become black with God!*"[95]

Therefore, All Theology is Political

The preceding discussion began to broach this next step in our elucidation of dialectical theology's logic, but it is important to make it explicit. Since God cannot be objectified, it necessarily follows that no single theological articulation is sufficient for all times and places. In other words, all theology is contextual theology—particular attempts to speak of God in the midst of particular sociohistorical contexts. Furthermore, because all theology is contextual, it cannot avoid being political. To paraphrase a quote from the poet Charles Baudelaire, popularized by the film *The Usual Suspects*: the greatest trick the devil ever pulled was convincing people that there are aspects of their lives that are not political.[96] Human beings are irreducibly social. It is not good for us to be alone (Gen 2:18)! And since politics is, at the end of the day, nothing more than an exercise in negotiating human life together, this means that human beings are political animals.[97] Any attempt to

93. Gollwitzer, "Liberation in History," 420. Gollwitzer traces Visser 't Hooft's comment to his "opening address at the Ecumenical Assembly at Uppsala (1968)."
94. Ibid., 421.
95. Cone, *A Black Theology of Liberation*, 65.
96. See Charles Baudelaire, *Paris Spleen: Little Poems in Prose*, trans. Keith Waldrop (Middletown, CT: Wesleyan University Press, 2009), 60. "Never, my brethren, forget, when you hear enlightenment vaunted, that the neatest trick of the devil is to persuade you that he does not exist."
97. Describing human beings as "political animals" is, of course, to echo The Philosopher in his *Politics*. See Aristotle, *The Basic Works of Aristotle*, ed. Richard McKeon (New York: The Modern Library, 2001), 1129. John Calvin emphasizes human sociality in his commentary on Genesis 2:18: "Moses now explains the design of God in creating the woman; namely, that there should be human beings on the earth who might cultivate mutual society between themselves. . . . [This] involves a general principle, that man was formed to be a social animal." John Calvin, *Commentaries on*

avoid this and produce a nonpolitical theological statement ultimately devolves into implicit support of the political status quo. It is one of the commendable strengths of dialectical theology in general, and Gollwitzer's theology in particular, that it not only recognizes this truth but embraces it: "a Church and a piety succumbs . . . precisely when it believes that it can be unpolitical," which "is absolutely impossible."[98]

Gollwitzer's theology embraces this absolute impossibility. He writes self-consciously political theology because scripture itself engages— and insists that we engage—political issues.[99] In the following two sections, I will first highlight Gollwitzer's analysis of some ways that the theological tradition has attempted to isolate itself from proper political responsibility before turning to Gollwitzer's own account of that responsibility.

Against the Church's Spirituality

Among Protestants, and especially in the United States, there are four common responses to the affirmation of the church's political responsibility. All of these responses represent facets of what might be called —as Jack Rogers has—"the doctrine of the Spirituality of the Church," which "mandated a complete separation between church and state such that the church was never to speak on what it believed to be social issues."[100] The context that gave rise to this position was the nineteenth-century division within American Christianity over the question of slavery's legitimacy. Rogers documents how even churches in

---

the *Book of Genesis*, trans. John King, Calvin's Commentaries (Grand Rapids, MI: Baker Book House, 2003), 128.

98. Helmut Gollwitzer, *The Rich Christians and Poor Lazarus*, trans. David Cairns (New York: Macmillan, 1970), 26. See also Barth in a passage that Gollwitzer cites on pp. 2–3 of his text: "It is a bad sign when Christians are frightened by 'political' sermons—as if Christian preaching could be anything but political. . . . The Christian Church that is aware of its political responsibility will demand political preaching; and will interpret it politically even if it contains no direct reference to politics." Karl Barth, "The Christian Community and the Civil Community," in *Community, State, and Church: Three Essays* (Gloucester, MA: Peter Smith, 1968), thesis 31, p. 185.

99. Marquardt, "Weg und Werk," 39–43. Philip Ziegler remarked at the 2014 national meeting of the American Academy of Religion that "Christians do politics indirectly. They don't try to do something political, but something Christian. And that inevitably *is* political because it is an expression of freedom and therefore an act of love." Note well the decisive difference between this line of thinking and the following, which incorrectly assumes a sharp distinction between the theological and the political: "I suggest we tweet thinking more about Jesus and less about politics. That's just basic Christian prioritization." Ed Stetzer, "Politics, Social Media, and More Important Things" (ChristianityToday.com, October 10, 2013), http://www.christianitytoday.com/edstetzer/2013/october/politics-social-media-and-more-important-things.html. We will see in the next chapter, however, that Gollwitzer advocates direct political engagement as well.

100. Jack Rogers, *Reading the Bible & the Confessions: The Presbyterian Way* (Louisville, KY: Geneva Press, 1999), 74.

the Reformed tradition fell under this false teaching, despite that tradition's well-known and longstanding emphasis on ethics and living out one's faith in society. If Jim Wallis is right that racism—institutionalized for so long in the legal, constitutional tradition that upheld slavery—is America's original sin, and I think he is, then <u>the false doctrine of the church's spirituality</u> is American Christianity's original heresy.[101]

The first response that one might hear when emphasizing the church's political responsibility is that nowhere in scripture is there a commandment that people of faith involve themselves in politics. This objection has a certain self-evident truth about it. After all, nowhere in the Ten Commandments does one find: "thou shalt engage in politics." But as noted above, it is <u>impossible to avoid</u> political action. Furthermore, Gollwitzer directly disputes the claim that such a commandment is lacking: "through his mission in the world and through his commandment of love, Jesus Christ obliged the church to participate in public life."[102] Gollwitzer finds support from the commandment found in Mark 12:31, which, in turn, derives from Leviticus 19:18: "you shall love your neighbor as yourself." Failure to understand this as a political commandment stems from our loss of what Eagleton calls "the concept of political love," that is, the idea that love must come to structural expression in our negotiation of life together.[103]

Political love is difficult to conceive under the conditions of liberalism, which is the political philosophy on which modern Western culture is built. Domenico Losurdo gives a standard definition of liberalism as "the tradition of thought whose central concern is the liberty of the individual,"[104] but this individual liberty is also restrained by a commitment to equality. The task of government is to balance these two considerations, providing the greatest possible liberty as well as the greatest possible equality. This balancing act presupposes bonds of love among citizens that ensure widespread long-term investment in the state. But as Paul Kahn notes, "liberalism cannot explain

---

101. Jim Wallis, *America's Original Sin: Racism, White Privilege, and the Bridge to a New America* (Grand Rapids, MI: Brazos Press, 2016).

102. Helmut Gollwitzer, "Einige Leitsätze zur christlichen Beteiligung am politischen Leben," in *Forderungen der Umkehr: Beiträge zur Theologie der Gesellschaft* (Munich: Chr. Kaiser, 1976), thesis 1, p. 15.

103. Eagleton, *Reason, Faith, & Revolution*, 32. Helga Day describes Gollwitzer's rejection of the church's spirituality as a bringing together of the Reformed emphasis on God's sovereignty with what Gollwitzer identified as the positive elements in traditional Lutheran two-kingdoms doctrine. See Day, "Christlicher Glaube," 336.

104. Domenico Losurdo, *Liberalism: A Counter-History*, trans. Gregory Elliott (London: Verso, 2011), 1. Losurdo goes on to complicate this definition, however, to show that the history of liberalism betrays a tendency to only begrudgingly extend that liberty to those outside of the elite.

the normative conditions of the political"—these fundamental social bonds—"which do not lie in reason but in love."[105] Should these bonds of love fray so that the pursuit of liberty becomes more important than the pursuit of equality, liberalism will fail. Precisely this imbalance is displayed in neoliberalism, which has displaced liberalism as the dominant political philosophy in the global North in the second half of the twentieth century. While liberalism employed capitalist economic structures, part of the government's role was to ensure that the economic liberty of these structures did not produce too much economic inequality. Neoliberalism discarded the government's regulatory function, instead trusting those economic structures to regulate themselves.[106] Consequently, economic inequality has grown precipitously, as the statistics offered in chapter 1 indicate. In a system that presupposes but could not explain political love, and therefore could not produce it, neoliberalism has all but destroyed the "normative conditions for the political." Of course, we are not restricted to pairing either liberalism or neoliberalism with capitalism. In the next chapter, we will see Gollwitzer argue that socialism can achieve the balance sought by liberalism, and thereby, achieve true democracy. It does so by producing economic structures that promote equality, which establish the material conditions for political love. As Eagleton notes, political love "is the ethical basis for socialism."[107]

---

105. Paul W. Kahn, *Putting Liberalism in Its Place* (Princeton, NJ: Princeton University Press, 2005), 227.

106. "State projects and their associated conceptions of citizenship are today permeated by a powerful neoliberal sensibility that glorifies the convergence of a minimalist state with a deregulated economy and insists implacably that the rate of profit be maximized at every turn." Kenneth Surin, "Rewriting the Ontological Script of Liberation: On the Question of Finding a New Kind of Political Subject," in *Theology and the Political: The New Debate*, ed. Creston Davis, John Milbank, and Slavoj Žižek (Durham, NC: Duke University Press, 2005), 248. Liberalism employed capitalist economic structures but recognized the need to regulate them in pursuit of a common good. Liberalism's weakness, however, is its inability to articulate a common good, that is to say, to produce love. It must depend on other cultural, and especially, religious institutions to articulate the common good that liberalism assumes. The best that liberalism can supply on its own is a practical argument for a government that negotiates the conflicting interests of its various constituents, à la Thomas Hobbes. As the United States and Europe became increasingly multicultural and religiously diverse over the course of the twentieth century, it became more difficult to articulate a vision of the common good that could be shared across these religious and cultural boundaries. In the absence of an overwhelming religious and cultural metanarrative, liberalism was thrown back upon its practical argument. Capitalism, now entrenched in Western societies, transposed this practical argument into economic terms so that the common good became optimization of every aspect of society for the production of surplus value. Thus was neoliberalism born. Under capitalism, however, surplus value is not shared; rather, it is appropriated by those who own capital—the means of producing surplus value. This zero-sum vision of the economic good has become the only conceivable political good under the conditions of neoliberalism, which has increasingly produced a zero-sum politics as various constituencies compete to achieve political monopoly.

107. Eagleton, *Reason, Faith, & Revolution*, 32. Gollwitzer notes that "love today . . . must be love in structures," that is, love embodied in a society's political and economic institutions. Gollwitzer, *Rich Christians*, 16. For discussion of "Equal Right and the Political State" in Marx's thought, see Allen

Another reason why the political character of the commandment to love one's neighbor remains misunderstood is because of the second response to emphasis on the church's political responsibility, namely, the claim that Christianity is mainly a private, individual affair—about one's personal relationship with Jesus, or about the salvation of one's soul, rather than changing society. This response overlooks the first factor in Gollwitzer's statement above that it is "through his mission in the world" that "Jesus Christ obliged the church to participate in public life."[108] In other words, Jesus's significance is not only about the internal or psychological dimension, but also about the external or bodily dimension. The centrality of the sacraments in Christian faith and practice underscore the point that Christianity is something we do with our bodies as well as something that we do with our minds or hearts. Furthermore, Paul emphasizes this when he advises the church at Rome not only to attend to the renewal of their minds, but also to presenting their bodies as an act of worship (Rom 12:1–2). Because Christianity is irreducibly bodily, it is necessary social, and therefore, political. As Gollwitzer says, God is not concerned with the "isolated individual," but with "humanity as a whole" because "humans are essentially social beings," and this means "Christian faith cannot exist without the affirmation and confirmation of social and political responsibility."[109] We do well to recall here how Paul describes this mission: "in Christ God was reconciling the world to himself" (2 Cor 5:19). Then, of course, there is the famous John 3:16: "for God so loved the world. . . ." The Christian theological tradition has always recognized that Jesus Christ's significance extends beyond the boundaries of the communities who confess him as Lord. As Gollwitzer says, "the church does not distance itself from Christ's kingdom in entering the world."[110]

A third response to emphasis on the church's political responsibility admits that the demands of political love hold true within the Christian community, but denies that the Christian community ought to concern itself with structurally embedding these demands in society at large. Gollwitzer counters that such a separation between what holds within the church and what holds outside of it is impossible at both the theoretical and practical levels. He asks this pointed rhetorical question that convicts us still today: "can someone stay in accord with the Chris-

---

W. Wood, *The Free Development of Each: Studies on Freedom, Right, and Ethics in Classical German Philosophy* (Oxford: Oxford University Press, 2014), 260–62.
108. Gollwitzer, "Einige Leitsätze zur christlichen Beteiligung," thesis 1, p. 15.
109. Ibid., thesis 7.g, p. 17.
110. Ibid., thesis 2, p. 15.

tian faith and at the same time wish—and politically sustain—that his brother, with whom he lives 'in the church' on the basis of equal rights, receives outside of the church inferior health care and inferior educational opportunities, appears at a disadvantage in a court of law, and gets less pay for equal work?" It should be clear by now that Gollwitzer's answer to this question is an absolute and unqualified "No!" Gollwitzer lays out the clear alternative that faces the church in a manner that also describes the church's historical failing on this question: "Either the church with its new life takes the offensive in society, or its new life, understood as inner-church idiosyncrasy, is undermined within the church also by the power of inequality in society and reduced to an edifying claim which is constantly contradicted by reality."[111]

Finally, the fourth common response to emphasizing the church's political responsibility concedes further that individual Christians must exercise political responsibility, but denies that the church should either corporately exercise political responsibility or place demands upon how individuals exercise their political responsibility. In other words, the realm of political responsibility is a matter of individual conscience, and the Christian community is forbidden to bind that conscience. Gollwitzer's response to the second objection holds here, too, in an ecclesiological key. The basic mistake in this objection is thinking that the church is something other than the people of faith who comprise it. Cutting through this confusion with alacrity, Gollwitzer writes: "if we as Christians are concerned with politics, then the church is also concerned with politics."[112] The next section delineates Gollwitzer's understanding of the parameters that the gospel sets for this political concern.

Christian Political Responsibility

When thinking through Gollwitzer's emphasis on the church's political responsibility, we must keep in mind that his conviction on this score was forged in the crucible of the Third Reich and the Confessing Church movement. For him, one of the primary "insights gained" from that period was the "recognition that the Christian congregation has

111. Gollwitzer, "Liberation in History," 415–16.
112. Helmut Gollwitzer, "Was geht den Christen die Politik an?," in *Forderungen der Freiheit: Aufsätze und Reden zur politischen Ethik* (München: Chr. Kaiser Verlag, 1962), 60; translated as "What Has the Christian to Do with Politics?," in *The Demands of Freedom: Papers by a Christian in West Germany* (New York: Harper & Row, 1965), 62–73.

political responsibility." He thinks this insight was verified by the experience of the German church. Whereas Protestant Christianity in Germany prior to the church struggle was overwhelmingly "conservative, antidemocratic, . . . sympathetic to the monarchy, the Army and national strength," there was no relapse to this position after the war.[113] Instead, the church's political complexion evinced a great diversity that included elements on the far left of the political spectrum. This not only confirmed the insight about the church's political responsibility, but also demonstrated that—at least for the moment—the church's understanding of that political responsibility was moving in the right direction.

Gollwitzer reflects on the shape of that responsibility as it pertains to Christian communities. As he says, the Word of God "gives us clear and practical instruction for political life."[114] But what guidance does it give? We must begin by speaking about what it does *not* give—namely, a political program. God's Word does not supply political solutions on demand, as if it were some kind of "automatic machine." Nor does it supply something like a definitive "battle plan" to which all Christians are bound by demands of obedience.[115] Gollwitzer admits that there are innumerable questions and decisions that arise as Christians engage in political responsibility that must be arbitrated by "human reason guided by love," and that "there is a freedom of choice depending on the force of the argument" so that "reasonable debate has its place" even—and especially!—inside the church. The guidance provided by the Word of God for Christian political responsibility, then, is *not* a hegemonic, totalizing political worldview or ideology that leaves no room for flexibility, adaptation, and individual conscience. Instead, the Word of God guides by providing what Gollwitzer calls, borrowing a phrase from Karl Barth, a "direction and orientation."[116] Insofar as it listens to its Lord, the Christian community is pointed in the right

---

113. Helmut Gollwitzer, "The Christian in the Search for World Order and Peace," in *Responsible Government in a Revolutionary Age*, ed. Z. K. Matthews (New York: Association Press, 1966), 65–66.
114. Gollwitzer, "Was geht den Christen die Politik an?," 62.
115. Gollwitzer, "Liberation in History," 418. This is in direct contrast to conservative Christian "culture warriors," who believe that the Bible *does* provide a monolithic political program.
116. Ibid. This formulation occurs frequently in Gollwitzer's writings. See Gollwitzer, "Must a Christian be a Socialist?," Appendix 1, 178, 182; Helmut Gollwitzer, "Why Am I, as a Christian, a Socialist? Theses," Appendix 2, theses 4.7–8 (p. 194), and 4.10 (p. 195). See also Gollwitzer, "Kingdom of God and Socialism," 98; Helmut Gollwitzer, *Reich Gottes und Sozialismus bei Karl Barth*, Theologische Existenz Heute, ed. Karl Gerhard Steck (Munich: Chr. Kaiser, 1972), 41. Perhaps the most relevant occurrence in Barth's writings is Karl Barth, *Christengemeneinde und Bürgergemeinde*, Theologische Studien (Zollikon-Zürich: Evangelischer Verlag, 1946), 22. Unfortunately, the English translation truncates the phrase *"Richtung und Linie"* simply as "direction." Barth, "Community, State, and Church," 168.

direction even if it must still feel its way forward step-by-step in faith and reasonable debate, guided by the Holy Spirit. Or as Gollwitzer puts it, the Word of God "speaks to us clearly concerning those things about which we must not disagree, which we have to advocate together."[117] The Word of God provides principles even if it does not provide a program. And when it comes to those principles, "at this point there is only loyalty or disloyalty" to Jesus Christ.[118]

What then are those principles to which Christian political responsibility is bound by loyalty to its Lord? Gollwitzer sketches three such principles in his essay, "What has the Christian to do with Politics?," which began as a lecture delivered in 1952. Although Gollwitzer would fill in this sketch with much greater detail in the following decades, its broad strokes remain a reliable guide to the shape of his thought. The form that Gollwitzer gives to these principles is also important: they are all statements describing God. For Gollwitzer, Christian political responsibility is guided by faithfulness to the God that believers find in Jesus Christ. Who this God is determines what it is that Christians must pursue in their political responsibility.

First, "In Jesus Christ God reveals himself as a *God of Peace.*"[119] Consequently, Christian political responsibility includes the pursuit of peace. This principle has a number of corollaries, which cut to the quick still in our own time. To begin, Christians "have to keep free of the toxic cloud of hate." Hate can be nothing other than a decisive betrayal of the God who loved the world by sending his Son to die for it, to use the traditional language. Also, Christians must resist the desire to use war and military power as a "political tool." This means, in turn, that Christians must "openly and bravely confront any tendencies in the people that are hostile to peace." Gollwitzer does not hesitate to follow this line of thinking to its conclusion: the church "must urge its own members in the parties, parliaments and governments to understand their political work as a service to earthly peace and to question each political decision in terms of whether it will contribute to the work of war or to the work of peace."[120] This commitment to peace should reinforce a predisposition to emphasize Christian unity across the boundaries of nation-states, and this emphasis on international Christian unity will, in turn, reinforce the commitment to peace. Fur-

117. Gollwitzer, "Was geht den Christen die Politik an?," 62.
118. Gollwitzer, "Liberation in History," 418.
119. Gollwitzer, "What Has the Christian to Do with Politics?," 64.
120. Gollwitzer, "Was geht den Christen die Politik an?," 63.

thermore, the Christian community should unite those who pursue peace, regardless of their membership in different political parties, and "should relentlessly remind . . . politicians of their responsibility concerning peace."[121]

Second, in the statement from which this volume derives its title, Gollwitzer confesses that "God is a God who loves justice." This statement requires some disambiguation since it has become far too easy in our own time to assume that "justice" is a function of legality such that an action counts as just if it is judged to have been performed legally. Today's language of the "criminal justice system" reveals and reinforces this reduction of justice to legality. But this reduction is improper. Justice depends not upon the all too human laws enacted by any particular state. It refers, rather, to "God's justice," which transcends particular human laws and which those particular laws emulate when they are at their best. As Gollwitzer puts it, "justice is not whatever is beneficial for people, and it is also not just whatever the people want. We recognize what justice is only by listening to God's Word."[122]

Learning justice under the tutelage of God's Word provides an important critical perspective on the state and its limitations, three of which Gollwitzer elaborates by interrogating the conditions under which it is possible to consider a state just. (a) A state is just when it recognizes that God's claim on human beings supersedes its own claim on them. That is, a just state will not claim for itself "the supreme power of determination over good and evil," and will respect the individual's voice of conscience, rather than compelling people to act against it. (b) A state is just when it recognizes that it is not the most basic institution in human life. Other forms of human relationship are more basic, such as spousal, parental, and familial relationships, as well as friendship and religious communities. A just state respects these relationships rather than trying to subsume them under its own authority. And finally, (c) a state is just when "the power of the state confines and binds the power of those who are powerful."[123] All human beings are sinners in need of God's forgiveness and grace, which means that the powerful are as prone to sin and error as anyone else. The difference is that they have more power at their disposal to execute these sins and errors, and cause greater collateral social damage. The state's

---

121. Ibid., 64.
122. Ibid., 65. For more on the distinction between justice and law, see Paul Lehmann, *The Transfiguration of Politics* (New York: Harper & Row, 1975), 250–59.
123. Gollwitzer, "Was geht den Christen die Politik an?," 66.

responsibility is to set and maintain boundaries to oppose "the despotism of the powerful."

For the state that observes these limitations, which Gollwitzer refers to as a constitutional, democratic, or "just" state (*Rechtsstaat*), Christians have an obligation to help maintain it as such. Rejecting an absolute pacifism, he even envisions the possibility that this would extend to participating in certain kinds of wars or engaging in other uses of "armed defense." But again, such force can only be deployed in support of justice. Gollwitzer gives us this compelling formulation: "Whenever power does not serve justice, but sets justice aside, resistance is a Christian duty."[124] Yes, *whenever*; but also *only* whenever! Christians must resist the use of their own state's power when it is deployed to minimize internal dissent, or to pursue the goals and enforce the values of power rather than justice. Gollwitzer's words ring loudly in our ears still today: "terror does not actually protect against terror. Only justice can do so, even if at first it is uncomfortable and seems less effective. Whoever defends justice and freedom with the tools of injustice can do more harm to our political system" than external enemies could ever do.[125]

Third, "God in Christ is a God of mercy."[126] Gollwitzer elucidates this point as a question of forgiveness. As in his day, we do not often think of forgiveness as a political principle. We are aided today, however, by the historical witness of the Truth and Reconciliation Commission in South Africa as well as the German process of coming to terms with the events of the Third Reich, about which process Gollwitzer speaks here. For Gollwitzer, the political significance of God's mercy is twofold: first, it involves the recognition that we, as members of a particular state with its particular history, need forgiveness; second, it involves the recognition that we, as members of a particular state with its particular history, need to forgive. This forgiving and being forgiven is not only a question of political expediency, that is, of convincing other states to deal favorably with one's own state. It is also a question of individual and communal healing. The people of all nations must continually engage in this process of forgiving and being forgiven, but it is perhaps most pressing today for those of us in the United States, given our nation's long litany of failings both at home and abroad. As Gollwitzer says,

124. Gollwitzer, "What Has the Christian to Do with Politics?," 69.
125. Gollwitzer, "Was geht den Christen die Politik an?," 67.
126. Gollwitzer, "What Has the Christian to Do with Politics?," 70.

those without God afterwards try to forget what they have themselves done, and they try not to forget that for which others have been to blame. Christians must keep it the other way around. Let us forget the atrocities of others, but let us not forget the terrible things that have been done in our name and by the members of our nation. Let us not forget; rather, let us seek forgiveness. For only then can we hope that such things will not be repeated.[127]

These, then, are the principles—or facets of God's identity as revealed in Jesus Christ—that guide Christian political responsibility: peace, justice, and mercy. As we saw previously, Gollwitzer understands Christian political responsibility as mandated by Jesus Christ's command to love God and neighbor. We must not forget Paul's echo of this commandment in his discussion of the theological virtues: "faith, hope, and love abide, these three; and the greatest of these is love" (1 Cor 13:13). It is not a stretch to suggest that the principles Gollwitzer outlines here—peace, justice, and mercy—can be summarized with the concept of "political love" that we discussed above. Although the essay from 1952 in which Gollwitzer articulated these principles does not include it, the decades that followed would see the conviction grow in Gollwitzer's thought that the "direction and orientation" or trajectory demarcated by these principles points inexorably to socialism. But that discussion must await the next chapter.

Conclusion

We have covered a great deal of conceptual ground in this chapter. It began by examining Gollwitzer's articulation of dialectical theology: God cannot be objectified, and we can only encounter God's Thou-objectivity in the event of faith in Jesus Christ. We have traced the consequences of dialectical theology for faithful Christian God-talk. The first consequence is that all theology is contextual theology. It is impossible to make timeless theological statements. Instead, all theological statements arise from encounter with God by particular people in particular sociohistorical locations. We fleshed this out further by discussing dialectical theology's relationship to liberation theology and, more specifically still, Gollwitzer's engagement with black theology. Following from this first consequence is the second—namely, that all theology is political. Precisely because all theological statements

127. Gollwitzer, "Was geht den Christen die Politik an?," 68.

are contextually situated, all theological statements are also politically embedded. It is impossible to escape the political ramifications of our God-talk, even—and, perhaps, especially!—when we try to speak non-politically. It is simply impossible to do so. Either our theology supports the status quo, or it calls that status quo into question. The important thing is to pay attention to which of these things we are doing, and to regulate our political engagement by reflecting on God's identity as the God of peace, justice, and mercy.

Often, those who emphasize the church's political responsibility are accused of "selling out" to politics, of neglecting the importance of careful dogmatic work in order to score cheap political points. This is yet one more strategy employed in defense of the status quo and those who benefit from it—many of whom, sadly, profess to be Christians—to de-fang the gospel and undermine its radical political significance. These accusations have also been leveled against Gollwitzer. But our discussion of Gollwitzer's political theology refutes this claim and substantiates Stieber-Westermann's counter-thesis that "the doctrine of God is the axis of Gollwitzer's work."[128] As we have seen now in some detail, Gollwitzer's commitment to elaborating the church's political responsibility is a direct consequence of his dialectical theological commitments. Indeed, Gollwitzer's articulation of that responsibility and its "direction and line" takes the form of reflection on God's identity as revealed in Jesus Christ: God is the God of peace, justice, and mercy. Consequently, the judgment that Philip Ziegler renders with reference to Dietrich Bonhoeffer holds also for Gollwitzer—he "had a quite specifically *theological* interest in politics."[129]

One of the chief services that Gollwitzer renders to us is to serve as an example of the seamless integration of engagement with the theological tradition, especially in its reformational mode as that took shape in the dialectical theology movement, and socioeconomically progressive politics. For Gollwitzer, theology includes this political work. As Ulrich Dannermann and Matthias Weissinger put it, "social analysis and social criticism are a theme of theological work. Theology can only adequately speak to the real world, to real people, when it

---

128. Stieber-Westermann, *Provokation zum Leben*, 5; see n. 5 for an enumeration of those who level the accusation of "selling out" against Gollwitzer.

129. Philip Ziegler, "Witness to Christ's Dominion: The Political Service of the Church," *Theology* 116, no. 5 (2013): 324. Another way of putting this would be to describe Gollwitzer's theology, like Michael Weinrich does, as concerned with the gospel and oriented in terms of "critical contemporaneity." Michael Weinrich, "Gesellschaftliche Herausforderungen der Theologie: Erinnerungen an Helmut Gollwitzer," *Evangelische Theologie* 59, no. 3 (1999): 169.

tries to plot society . . . on the horizon of the coming kingdom of God."[130] But perhaps Gollwitzer himself puts it best when he draws on a watchword of his dialectical theological heritage to claim that "the wholly other God wants a wholly other society."[131]

---

130. Dannemann and Weissinger, "Helmut Gollwitzer's Beitrag zur Theologie der Gesellschaft," 581.
131. Gollwitzer, "Liberation in History," 421. See further David Congdon's reflections on creaturely being as "unnatural," and especially his comments about "queer creaturehood." Congdon, *God Who Saves*, 230; see 220–32.

4

Gollwitzer's Theological Politics

Thus far, we have examined the interconnection of theology and politics in Gollwitzer's biography, as well as how Gollwitzer's dialectical theological commitments led him to the affirmation that all theology is political. God cannot be objectified; instead, one encounters God's Thou-objectivity in the event of faith in Jesus Christ. This exposes the impropriety of making timeless theological statements and underscores how all theological statements arise from encounter with God by particular people in particular sociohistorical locations. Recognizing the contextual character of all theological statements emphasizes that all theology is political theology. The event of encounter with God's Thou-objectivity occurs in the midst of our socioeconomic and political lives together and demands that those lives assume a decisively different shape. Encounter with God is always a liberating encounter. Gollwitzer's commitment to elaborating the church's political responsibility is, therefore, a direct consequence of his dialectical theological commitments. The present chapter's task is to complete the transition from Gollwitzer's politically oriented theology to his theologically informed politics.

Friedrich-Wilhelm Marquardt orients us to Gollwitzer's theological politics. At stake in Gollwitzer's theological politics is nothing less than the core concern of the Christian gospel. For Gollwitzer, "God is not established in thought," as though God desires from God's people only an abstract, intellectualist faith; rather, "He is established in our lives."[1] The liberating God of the gospel demands not mere intellectual assent, but embodied faithfulness. In this way, Marquardt points out, Gollwitzer affirms on Christian grounds the truth of Karl Marx's second thesis on Feuerbach: "the question whether human thought can attain to objective truth is not a theoretical but a practical question. Man must prove the truth, i.e., the reality and power, the this-sidedness of his thinking in practice."[2] For Gollwitzer, the truth of God unfolds in the practical life of the church as it engages with sociopolitical issues and actualizes liberating change. Indeed, this is how Gollwitzer understands the eschatological character of the New Testament's ethical imperatives—they demand an exemplary life from those who have encountered God in Jesus Christ, and they expect that the community of such people will be the cutting edge of changing the world and birthing a new form of life and society. In other words, "the kingdom of God meets us in imperatives," that is, in the faithful obedience that is called into being by the gospel's gracious commands.[3]

By speaking of Karl Marx and new forms of life, I have signaled the primary track along which Gollwitzer's explication of this faithful obedience—that is, his theological politics—runs, namely, with respect to questions of economic justice. Like Marx, Gollwitzer understood that this is ultimately a question of the contrast between capitalism and socialism. Gollwitzer unabashedly supported democratic socialism, even to the point of arguing that Christians *must* be socialists. Further-

---

1. Friedrich-Wilhelm Marquardt, "Helmut Gollwitzer: Weg und Werk," in *Bibliographie Helmut Goll-witzer*, ed. Christa Haehn, Ausgewählte Werke (München: Chr. Kaiser, 1988), 30.
2. Eugene Kamenka, ed. *The Portable Karl Marx*, Viking Portable Library (New York: Penguin Books, 1983), 155–56.
3. Marquardt, "Weg und Werk," 33. Paul Lehmann distinguishes between the "indicative" and "imperative" aspect in Christian ethics, making the latter subordinate to and dependent upon the former: "the indicative character of the Christian ethos . . . underlies every ethical imperative, underlines the provisional character of such imperatives, and ultimately suspends them. The indicative character of Christian ethics is the consequence of the contextual character of the forgiveness and the freedom with which Christ has set men free to be and to do what they are in the light of what God has done and is doing in him." Paul L. Lehmann, *Ethics in a Christian Context* (New York: Harper & Row, 1963), 161. Gollwitzer speaks of promise and gift rather than of the "indicative," and of the active life for which the promise and gift are given. His position is more paradoxical: "the promise of grace does not aim at passivity but, on the contrary, at activity. . . . Life only becomes life when it is being lived. So completely does the gift of life aim at our activity that it is lost when we refuse to live it. . . . Life is at one and the same time (against Marx) the gift that is received by us in passivity, whose ground lies irrevocably beyond us, *and* (with Marx) at the same time our own activity, our own action. . . . [I]n every moment we are both completely receptive and completely active." Helmut Gollwitzer, *An Introduction to Protestant Theology*, trans. David Cairns (Philadelphia: The Westminster Press, 1982), 168–70. For reflections on the relation between human activity and passivity in Karl Barth's ethics, see Eberhard Jüngel, "Gospel and Law: The Relationship of Dogmatics to Ethics," in *Karl Barth: A Theological Legacy* (Philadelphia: Westminster Press, 1986), 121–26.

more, Gollwitzer's socialism supplied him with a penetratingly critical perspective on the issues of war and revolution. These issues structure this chapter's discussion of Gollwitzer's theological politics. All of this, however, is finally an exercise in concrete political love that testifies to the God whom Christians encounter in the event of faith: a God who loves justice.

Democratic Socialism

Given the confusion that surrounds the concept in the North American context, it is important to clarify at the outset that "socialism" refers not to a political system *per se*, but to an economic system. Consequently, it is possible to join a socialist economic system with a number of different political systems—as history attests. To Gollwitzer's mind, however, democracy is the political system with which socialism has the greatest affinity. He recognized that socialism and democracy must be joined together if either is to truly flourish: "socialism can only be realized through democracy; democracy can only be perfected by socialism."[4] This advocacy for democratic socialism is perhaps Gollwitzer's most distinct contribution, and the one for which he is best known. But this advocacy did not spring fully formed in his mind. His thinking underwent important developments along the way. Therefore, this section will first discuss Gollwitzer's evolution before turning to a more material account of his advocacy for socialism, or more specifically, for the true socialism of the kingdom of God.

Gollwitzer's Development

We saw in chapter 2 that Gollwitzer first encountered socialism as Karl Barth's student. English language reception of Barth has paid insufficient attention to his socialism and its importance for his theology, despite how frequently it bubbles to the surface. For instance, we read in Barth's ethics of creation about how capitalism compromises democracy through a process that Barth describes as "almost unequivocally demonic."[5]

---

4. Helmut Gollwitzer, "Why Am I, as a Christian, a Socialist? Theses," Appendix 2, thesis 1.4, p. 188. For a more extensive analysis of the relation between democracy and capitalism, see Ellen Meiksins Wood, *Democracy against Capitalism: Renewing Historical Materialism*, reprint edition, Radical Thinkers (New York: Verso, 2016).
5. Karl Barth, *Church Dogmatics*, trans. and edited by Geoffrey W. Bromiley and Thomas F. Torrance, 4 volumes in 13 parts (Edinburgh: T&T Clark, 1956–75), 3.4:531; Karl Barth, *Die kirchliche Dogmatik*, 4 volumes in 13 parts (Munich, Zürich: Chr. Kaiser, TVZ, 1932–65), 3.4:610. For more on Barth and

Gollwitzer's first brush with socialist commitment was severely challenged, however, during his time as a prisoner of war in Russia.[6] He encountered there, under Stalin's regime, a sociopolitical order that seemed every bit as authoritarian and destructive to human life as Hitler's Reich. Consequently, Gollwitzer realized that "socialism as such can guarantee neither equality nor liberty nor fraternity," and that Stalinism "revealed [socialism's] limits and dangers which were overlooked during the 'first fine careless rapture' of the socialist idealists." As a result, Gollwitzer could not accept socialism as "an ideal which is an end in itself." He did not think that either capitalism or socialism could solve "the social problem" in any ultimate manner. Each provides only relative solutions, and "every solution will bring with it fresh cases of injustice and opportunities for evil-doing."[7] Indeed, when Gollwitzer returned to West Germany, he advocated not for democratic socialism, but for the sort of democratically oriented reformist capitalism about which many books are still written. As he put it, "the social problem in its material form . . . has its source, not in 'capitalism', that is, industrial production organised under private ownership, but in underdeveloped capitalism, and it cannot be solved by bringing about the downfall of capitalism by means of a revolution, but rather by developing it further and making it more democratic."[8]

socialism, see Martin Rumscheidt, "'Socialists May Be Christians; Christians Must Be Socialists.' Karl Barth Was!," *Toronto Journal of Theology* 17, no. 1 (2001): 107–18.

6. Chung rightly charts three stages in Gollwitzer's engagement with Marxism: the first stage, during and after his imprisonment; the second stage, in the late 1950s and early 1960s, characterized by his *The Christian Faith and the Marxist Criticism of Religion*; and the third stage, from the early 1970s on, epitomized by his *Die kapitalistische Revolution*. Paul S. Chung, *Church and Ethical Responsibility in the Midst of World Economy* (Eugene, OR: Cascade, 2013), 234–35. See also W. Travis McMaken, "The Blame Lies with the Christians: Helmut Gollwitzer's Engagement with Marxist Criticism of Religion," *The Other Journal* 22 (2013): 13–20. For one of Gollwitzer's most concise reflections on Marx and his legacy, see Helmut Gollwitzer, "Thanks to Karl Marx," *Journal of Ecumenical Studies* 22, no. 3 (1985): 589–91.

7. Helmut Gollwitzer, *Unwilling Journey: A Diary from Russia*, trans. E. M. Delacour and Robert Fenn (London: SCM, 1953), 242.

8. Ibid., 239. Dannemann and Weissinger clearly state Gollwitzer's position at this moment in his development, highlighting also his abiding democratic concern: "Gollwitzer advocates a reformed capitalism, i.e., he calls for a democratization of capitalism (strengthening the rights of workers, strengthening the unions)." Ulrich Dannemann and Matthias Weissinger, "Helmut Gollwitzers Beitrag zur Theologie der Gesellschaft," in *Richte unsere Füße auf den Weg des Friedens: Helmut Gollwitzer zum 70. Geburtstag*, ed. Andreas Baudis, Dieter Clausert, Volkhard Schliski and Bernhard Wegener (Munich: Chr. Kaiser, 1979), 582. See also Claudia Lepp, "Helmut Gollwitzer als Dialogpartner der sozialen Bewegungen," in *Umbrüche: der deutsche Protestantismus und die sozialen Bewegungen in der 1960er und 70er Jahren*, ed. Siegfried Hermle, Claudia Lepp, and Harry Oelke (Göttingen: Vandenhoeck & Ruprecht, 2007), 227–28; Helmut Gollwitzer, *Skizzen eines Lebens. Aus verstreuten Selbstzeugnissen gefunden und verbunden von Friedrich-Wilhelm Marquardt, Wolfgang Brinkel und Manfred Weber* (Gütersloh: Christian Kaiser Verlagshaus, 1998), 310. Ironically, this is the position that Eberhard Jüngel would advocate against Gollwitzer's democratic socialism in the 1970s. See their exchange in Wolfgang Teichert, ed. *Müssen Christen Sozialisten sein? Zwischen Glaube und Politik*

Despite this newly critical attitude toward socialism, Gollwitzer nonetheless seized the opportunity to gain deeper understanding of socialist and Marxist thought during his captivity. He did so through conversation with those with whom he came into contact as a prisoner of war at various camps, as well as through reading. He comments at one point: "I am continuing my reading of the Marxist classics in spite of everything else. I shall probably go on doing so till the end of my captivity."[9] This engagement was undoubtedly motivated in no small part by a sense of sharing in the collective guilt of the German people for what had occurred under Hitler. Gollwitzer testifies that during the days of final German collapse on the Eastern Front, his "mind was obsessed with the idea of the German collapse as a gracious divine judgment."[10] The result of this engagement meant that Gollwitzer's newly critical attitude toward socialism did not result in an absolute and unthinking rejection, but was grounded in deep empathy and understanding. As Paul Oestreicher puts it, Gollwitzer "was a man who honestly described the evils of communism which he encountered as a prisoner, yet one who evidently loved communists as fellow human beings and thought of them as brothers."[11]

Given his extensive experience of Soviet Russia and intellectual engagement with socialist and Marxist thought, it is no surprise that people viewed Gollwitzer as an expert on these matters when he returned to West Germany after his years of imprisonment.[12] His critical yet deeply sympathetic stance also made him an important dialogue partner who could bridge the gap between the broader Protestant church and the various socialist groups active in the country. Consequently, he participated in Christian-Marxist dialogues in the 1950s. The fruit of this engagement came to expression in his book, *The Christian Faith and the Marxist Criticism of Religion*. We will hear more from this text below with regard to the criticisms that Gollwitzer levelled against certain kinds of Marxism. For now, however, the impor-

---

(Hamburg: Lutherisches Verlagshaus, 1976). For one of the more prominent contemporary articulations of the need for a reformist capitalism, see Robert B. Reich, *Saving Capitalism: For the Many, Not the Few* (New York: Alfred A. Knopf, 2015).

9. Gollwitzer, *Unwilling Journey*, 179. See also Rolf Stieber-Westermann, *Die Provokation zum Leben: Gott im theologischen Werk Helmut Gollwitzers*, Europäische Hochschulschriften (Frankfurt am Main: Peter Lang, 1993), 25.

10. Gollwitzer, *Unwilling Journey*, 23.

11. Paul Oestreicher, "Helmut Gollwitzer in the European Storms," in *The Demands of Freedom: Papers by a Christian in West Germany* (New York: Harper and Row Publishers, 1965), 8.

12. Andreas Pangritz, "Helmut Gollwitzer als Theologe des Dialogs" (Rheinischen Friedrich-Wilhelms-Universität, Bonn; December 3, 2008), 7.

tant thing is to understand how he responded to Marxist criticism of religion.

Marxist criticism of religion builds on the criticism made by Feuerbach, which Gollwitzer addressed in his *Existence of God* and we discussed in chapter 3. Feuerbach argues that religion represents a society's attempt to understand itself by externalizing its values as the divine as well as other religious symbols and myths. This externalization—or projection, as common parlance has it—in turn facilitates socializing that society's members into those values. Marx's modification of this criticism points out that the process whereby this externalization takes place is not a democratic one. The externalized values are inevitably those of the ruling class. Consequently, religion serves to reinforce the values of the ruling class among the oppressed classes, short-circuiting any impulse to change the material conditions inherent in hierarchical class structures. Indeed, it makes it difficult to imagine any other material conditions and class structures. Marxist criticism of religion targets how "the Christian message" has become "an ideological support of the existing order."[13]

Gollwitzer's analysis of this Marxist criticism enabled him to see the atheism so often associated with Marxism in a new light. At its core, Marxist atheism is a practical, rather than an absolute or ideological, atheism. Marxist criticism of religion is not an abstract (dis)proof of the existence of the divine or transcendent, but a confessional denial of particular gods as those gods are confessed by various religious communities. It is not a neutral logical or theoretical point, but "a fighting doctrine" aimed at supporting the oppressed in the class struggle.[14] Consequently, Christian theology's response to Marxist criticism should be twofold. First, Christian theologians are justified in arguing

---

13. Helmut Gollwitzer, *The Christian Faith and the Marxist Criticism of Religion*, trans. David Cairns (New York: Charles Scribner's Sons, 1970), 151. Elisabeth Schüssler Fiorenza could still say in 1994 that "the threat to Jewish and Christian monotheism consists . . . in the misuse of monotheism for religiously legitimating patriarchal domination. This domination has sanctified the exploitation of women, the poor, and subjected races and religions. The salvific power of the biblical G*d of justice and love . . . [is endangered] by the (ab)use of G*d as an idol for inculcating kyriarchal interests." Elisabeth Schüssler Fiorenza, *Jesus: Miriam's Child, Sophia's Prophet - Critical Issues in Feminist Christology* (New York: Continuum, 1994), 178.

14. Gollwitzer, *Marxist Criticism of Religion*, 102. It could not be otherwise given Marx's second thesis on Feuerbach. Christoph Henning's extensive study of the Marxist tradition and its development recognizes the accuracy of Gollwitzer's reading: "Marx's critique of *servile* Christianity is not necessarily an attack on religion as such. Marx attacks the practice of instrumentalising religion for purposes of political repression—there is a difference." Further: "Marx did not attack the Christian religion in the religious sense . . . ; what he criticised was the fact that it had allowed itself to become the legitimating ideology of the 'Christian State' that was Prussia." Indeed, Henning views theology's "ability to arrest speculative thinking" as an asset for engagement with Marx. Christoph Henning, *Philosophy after Marx: 100 Years of Misreadings and the Normative Turn in Political*

that what this brand of atheism rejects "is not what the Christian affirms."[15] In other words, the God of Abraham, Isaac, and Jacob, the God and Father of Jesus Christ, is rightly understood as an agent of liberation who opposes all structures and relationships by which humans exploit one another. The Christian message is not about reinforcing class structures. However, this reply lacks cogency unless, second, the Christian community recognizes and admits that "the Marxist accusations are a catalogue of actual Christian degenerations."[16] Christianity has, in fact, functioned as a tool of oppression in the way that Marxist criticism identifies, and has thereby betrayed its Lord. Without this confession, and in the absence of political action that demonstrates the church's true repentance and its commitment to solidarity with the oppressed, protestations against Marxist criticism only serve to further prove its point.

The position Gollwitzer articulates mirrors, in some interesting ways, the position that the Marxist tradition takes with reference to religion: just as—from the Marxist side—religion is a secondary phenomenon that is properly addressed not by focusing on it *per se* but by focusing on the revolutionary struggle, so is Marxist atheism—from the Christian side—a secondary phenomenon that is properly addressed not by focusing not on it *per se* but by focusing on the revolutionary struggle. As Roland Boer explicates matters with reference to Lenin:

> Even though a socialist may espouse a materialist worldview in which religion is but a medieval mildew, even though the party may undertake a very public and unhindered program of education against the influence of the church, and even though one hopes that the historical materialist position will persuade all of its truth, the party still does not stipulate atheism as a prerequisite for membership. Even more, no one will be excluded from party membership if he or she holds to religious belief.[17]

What is the result of Gollwitzer's approach? As Henning rightly has it: "this sort of interpretation led to the Christian critique of the church

Philosophy, trans. Max Henninger, Historical Materialism Book Series (Boston: Brill, 2014), 363, 365, 335.

15. Gollwitzer, *Marxist Criticism of Religion*, 168.
16. Ibid., 151. Also: "the Marxists fell into error, but the greater part of the blame lay with the Christians." Ibid., 92. As Gollwitzer puts it already when reflecting on his captivity in Russia: "it is now up to us to show that Christianity is not a class-conscious supporter of the 'reaction', that is, of those powers interested in keeping things as they are; that the Church is able to free itself from the chains of class distinction." Gollwitzer, *Unwilling Journey*, 125.
17. Roland Boer, *Lenin, Religion, and Theology*, New Approaches to Religion and Power (New York: Palgrave Macmillan, 2013), 18. Gollwitzer quips that "Leninism in general is Marxism in a hurry." Gollwitzer, *Marxist Criticism of Religion*, 81.

and the socialist critique of religion coalescing in *social critique*. It was now possible for Christians to be socialists and vice versa."[18]

For Gollwitzer, the proper Christian response to Marxist criticism of religion involves accepting the veracity of that criticism and joining in solidarity with those who wish to address the socioeconomic injustice with which Christianity has been complicit for so long. It should come as no surprise, then, that the 1960s saw Gollwitzer leave behind his impulse toward reforming capitalism to embrace democratic socialism once more. Two important influences coalesced for Gollwitzer in accomplishing this shift—first, his ecumenical work sent him to the 1968 World Council of Churches conference in Uppsala; second, his engagement with the student protests that broke out in Berlin, beginning in 1966 and reaching their apex in 1968. Both of these influences called Gollwitzer's attention to the effects of global capitalism and the structures of neocolonialism that governed the economic relationships between countries of the global North and global South.[19]

These twin influences are on display in Gollwitzer's work, *The Rich Christians and Poor Lazarus*. The tone of this work is very different from that of *The Christian Faith and the Marxist Criticism of Religion*. Whereas, in that earlier work, Gollwitzer accepted that Marxist analysis—that is, analysis concerned with how material conditions and privilege shape society—could helpfully illumine how the church has failed in preserving the Christian message, now we see Gollwitzer himself wielding Marxist analysis. Gollwitzer uses this analysis to articulate how capitalism ultimately undermines democratic forms of government, pushing them inexorably toward authoritarianism. Such a subtle, structural

18. Henning, *Philosophy after Marx*, 370. Dannemann and Weissinger discuss Gollwitzer's engagement with "authentic Marxist concerns." Gollwitzer criticizes "the system of traditional, orthodox Marxism . . . from the perspective of a heterodox Marxism" in order to open up space for a Christian Marxism. Dannemann and Weissinger, "Helmut Gollwitzers Beitrag zur Theologie der Gesellschaft," 588.
19. When investigating "the causes of the repressive policies of the West towards liberation movements in the Third World," Gollwitzer increasingly emphasized Western social structures produced by capitalism and how those structures neglect long-term consequences and are therefore destructive. Dannemann and Weissinger, "Helmut Gollwitzers Beitrag zur Theologie der Gesellschaft," 584. On the role of the student movement, see Helmut Gollwitzer, *The Rich Christians and Poor Lazarus*, trans. David Cairns (New York: Macmillan, 1970), 69–72. Gollwitzer's awakening to this coalescence of capitalism and neocolonialism is simultaneously his return to the roots of dialectical theology. As David Congdon rightly notes, "dialectical theology mobilizes a modern eschatological version of reformational thinking for the sake of developing a responsible missionary theology, one that is not liable to serving colonialist interests. To be sure, Barth would not have recognized the colonial-missionary problem *as* a problem without his socialist convictions. . . . For this reason we must acknowledge the special significance of socialism as an indispensable factor in the formation of dialectical theology." David W. Congdon, *The Mission of Demythologizing: Rudolf Bultmann's Dialectical Theology* (Minneapolis, MN: Fortress Press, 2015), 286–87.

authoritarian undertow is even more dangerous than an explicit authoritarianism because "totalitarian tyrants, . . . however atrocious they may be, prove again and again to be conquerable."[20] Technological development driven by capitalist maximization of profit is what constrains both voters and politicians, taking away their subjectivity to such an extent that it "seems to make democracy impossible."[21] This is perhaps the most insidious way in which the interests of capital short-circuit democratic process. As Gollwitzer rightly notes, "economic power is political power, however much that fact may be disguised in our form of democracy, and to however large an extent the possessors of economic power may leave the business of politics to professional politicians. In this game, every competitor knows where the shoe pinches, the places at which the big interests are touched."[22] The truth of this statement has recently become even clearer to those of us in the United States, as capital increasingly feels free to dispense with the camouflage provided by professional politicians.[23]

Gollwitzer's deployment of Marxist analysis resulted in his conclusion that, as Ulrich Dannemann and Matthias Weissinger put it, "the crisis of Western capitalism is . . . the crisis of Western bourgeois democracy."[24] Capitalism undermines democracy. This is why Gollwitzer could write later in his career that "there are no genuine democracies in any country in our century."[25] To move from a form of democ-

20. Gollwitzer, *Rich Christians*, 72. Gollwitzer's shift to his mature democratic socialism, and his facility with Marxist analysis, comes to full flower in Helmut Gollwitzer, "Die kapitalistische Revolution," in . . . *daß Gerechtigkeit und Friede sich küssen: Aufsätz zur politishen Ethik*, Band 1, ed. Andreas Pangritz, Ausgewählte Werke (München: Chr. Kaiser, 1988), 125–209. See the reflections on Marxist analysis in Gollwitzer, "Why Am I, as a Christian, a Socialist?," thesis 4.9, p. 194.
21. Gollwitzer, *Rich Christians*, 76. The worry about capitalism imperiling democracy is alive and well today even among those who would reform rather than replace capitalism. According to Joseph Stiglitz, "current rules [of global capitalism] are contributing to our growing inequality," which "puts our democracy in peril." Consequently, "we must [reform global capitalism] if we want to preserve our democracy, prevent our rampant inequality from growing worse, and maintain our influence around the world." Joseph E. Stiglitz, *The Price of Inequality: How Today's Divided Society Endangers Our Future* (New York: W. W. Norton and Company, 2012), 145. Unfortunately, Stiglitz not only fails to perceive that it is capitalism's most basic principles that lead to inequality and the imperilment of democracy, but he also promotes the reform of capitalism for the sake of maintaining the United States' neocolonialist hegemony.
22. Gollwitzer, *Rich Christians*, 49–50.
23. The Citizens United v. Federal Election Commission case, which the United States Supreme Court decided in 2010, made it possible for corporate capital to contribute directly to political campaigns. Furthermore, the two most recent GOP presidential candidates have based their campaigns—whether in part (Mitt Romney, 2012) or wholly (Donald Trump, 2016)—on their capitalist acumen.
24. Dannemann and Weissinger, "Helmut Gollwitzers Beitrag zur Theologie der Gesellschaft," 584. Further, "the intensive dialog with the student movement over the 'crisis of capitalism' led Gollwitzer during the 1960s to a new study of Marxism and to his discovery of it as an analytical instrument. He now developed a radical criticism of the capitalist social system." Lepp, "Helmut Gollwitzer als Dialogpartner," 228.

racy that denies its power to true democracy requires socialism because socialism and democracy reinforce and perfect one another. Socialist organization of the economy to serve the interests of all people supports democracy as the exercise of political sovereignty by all people, and democracy perfects socialism insofar as it insulates socialism from the abuses that so easily accrue under totalitarian regimes such as that of Soviet Russia. Gollwitzer makes explicit this connection between socialism and democracy: "democratic socialism is a tautology because democracy without socialism or socialism without the democratic freedom and co-determination of each citizen is a self-contradiction."[26]

Why Socialism?

The preceding account of Gollwitzer's development describes how he came to perceive the fundamental contradiction between capitalism and democracy. But why is it that Gollwitzer opted for socialism as an alternative? Is it simply the case that socialism is the only major challenger to the capitalist imagination in the modern period? There is much truth to this, but it is not a sufficient explanation for Gollwitzer's commitment to democratic socialism. His commitment finally rests upon theological judgments, although such judgments are inclusive of political and other pragmatic considerations. The following subsections discuss some of the key theological factors that support Gollwitzer's democratic socialism: the failure of the traditional Christian ethic of care for the poor organized around charity, the theological problem of spiritual and socioeconomic privilege, and questions of eschatology and the kingdom of God. Finally, we will consider Gollwitzer's claim that a Christian *must* be a socialist.

It is important to give Gollwitzer the chance to explain what he means when he speaks of socialism and socialists before commencing this discussion. Definitions were important to him, as evidenced by the way he distinguished between "Social Democrats" and "dogmatic Marxists" during his time as a prisoner of war.[27] Interestingly, Goll-

25. Gollwitzer, *Protestant Theology*, 204.
26. Helmut Gollwitzer, "Karl Barths Theologie der Freiheit und die Theologie der Befreiung. Für Wolfgang Schweitzer zum 70. Geburtstag," in *Wer ist unser Gott? Beiträge zu einer Befreiungstheologie im Kontext der »ersten« Welt*, ed. Luise Schottroff and Willy Schottroff (Munich: Chr. Kaiser, 1986), 35. Helga Day points out that Gollwitzer's commitment to democratic socialism is a political expression of the Lutheran doctrine of the priesthood of all believers. See Helga Krüger Day, "Christlicher Glaube und gesellschaftliches Handeln: eine Studie der Entwicklung der Theologie Helmut Gollwitzers" (Doctoral dissertation, Union Theological Seminary, 1973), 342.

witzer finds a parallel to Christianity in this need for careful definition insofar as both socialism and Christianity admit of wide variety. Practitioners in either group, therefore, deserve the right to specify in what way they belong to their group. This is especially important because both Christianity and socialism contain elements that the majority of each group would rather not be associated with and for which they cannot in good faith be held accountable. Gollwitzer explains:

> Socialists find themselves today in a situation similar to that of Christians. Those who label themselves as Christians must—given the multiplicity of Christian denominations and groups—immediately add in what sense they label themselves as Christians. And they can stipulate concerning what they will speak about and stress that the burden of the sins of other Christian groups not be placed upon them. Christians (and, in the same way, socialists) will contradict and refute the claim that such sins necessarily follow from the essence of Christianity (or socialism) by means of their different understandings of Christianity (and socialism). The chilling reality of states that call themselves socialist is the same distressing problem for socialists as states that called or still call themselves Christian are for Christians.[28]

In other words, the evils of totalitarian socialism cannot be laid at the door of all socialists just as the evils of the Crusades and Ku Klux Klan cannot be laid at the door of all Christians. And—to extend the analogy—the evils of Islamist fundamentalists cannot be laid at the door of all Muslims. Acceptance of this point is a precondition for any profitable engagement.

Gollwitzer's definition of socialism is deceptively simple: a socialist is someone who "maintains that a better society than the current one is possible and necessary."[29] This has both a positive and a negative aspect, as well as a third determining factor. Negatively, society is currently determined by a capitalist mode of production. This mode of production must be overcome because of the role it plays in "safeguarding . . . inequality." Therefore, the capitalist mode of production must be overcome because it opposes socialism's positive aspect: the better society that it envisions. This vision "takes seriously the original goals of bourgeois society" and is committed to their further realization unfettered by capitalist shackles.[30] As we saw previously, true

---

27. Gollwitzer, *Unwilling Journey*, 10. See also the various distinctions that he makes in Gollwitzer, *Marxist Criticism of Religion*, vi–x.
28. Gollwitzer, "Why Am I, as a Christian, a Socialist?," thesis 2.5, p. 190.
29. Ibid., thesis 1.1, p. 187.

socialism is inextricably linked with true democracy for Gollwitzer. He pulls the positive and negative aspects together well: "socialism means not merely certain social reforms, certain improvements within the capitalist system of production, but rather a society in which all members are assured an equal share in the commonly produced social product, and in which the control of production is in the hands of the producers—a society which is thus as egalitarian as possible, . . . and which is constantly building up a material democracy."[31]

Beyond these negative and positive aspects, the third determining factor is that socialists are convinced that this better society is not only possible but also necessary. Conviction of this necessity arises through a praxis of solidarity with the oppressed, which motivates and orients rational investigation into the root cause of their oppression. Furthermore, Gollwitzer argues that the gospel demands this solidarity. The gospel "assigns me to see and therefore change society from its lowest place which, consequently, is where the disadvantaged of all kinds stand."[32] And one of the things that we see when we view our world from the perspective of the oppressed is the catastrophic failure of the traditional Christian ethic of care for the poor organized around charity.

The Failure of Charity

In pre-industrial societies, there was a much more straightforward relationship between a person's readiness to engage in labor and their material status. Things are vastly more complicated today. The capitalist system dictates that a portion of the population remains un- or under-employed, and it refuses to grant those who are employed an equitable share in the wealth produced by their labor. But in those

30. Ibid., thesis 1.4, p. 188. Terry Eagleton echoes Gollwitzer's point concerning socialism's fidelity to what Gollwitzer calls "bourgeois society" and Eagleton calls "liberal society": "socialism does not simply reject liberal society, . . . it builds on and completes it." Terry Eagleton, *Why Marx Was Right* (New Haven, CT: Yale University Press, 2011), 86. Eagleton's text is an excellent starting point for those who would like to become familiar with Marx and socialism.
31. Helmut Gollwitzer, "Kingdom of God and Socialism in the Theology of Karl Barth," in *Karl Barth and Radical Politics*, ed. George Hunsinger (Philadelphia: Westminster Press, 1976), 100. Harvey Cox corroborates this point: "Full production and democratic control should be the characteristics of an economic system. On both counts our system today is failing. It no longer does what it is intended to do—produce *and* distribute." Harvey Cox, *The Secular City: Secularization and Urbanization in Theological Perspective* (Princeton: Princeton University Press, 2013), 213.
32. Gollwitzer, "Why Am I, as a Christian, a Socialist?," thesis 4.3.b, p. 192–93. Gottfried Orth explains that Gollwitzer took all of reality as his theme and found listening to the marginalized fruitful because they perceive the whole better as a result of dealing at close quarters with the status quo's negative consequences. Gottfried Orth, *Helmut Gollwitzer: zur Solidarität befreit* (Mainz: Matthias-Grünewald Verlag, 1995), 188.

previous societies, it made a certain amount of sense to associate poverty—especially of the abject sort—with laziness, at least in the able-bodied. One seems to find this even in the New Testament, as when we read that "anyone unwilling to work should not eat" (2 Thess 3:10).[33] There is an important counter-current present in scripture, however, when it comes to the impoverishment of those who are systemically marginalized. These figures are often referred to collectively as aliens (i.e., immigrants), orphans, and widows. Provision is made for such people in a number of ways, such as refraining from fully harvesting one's field (e.g., Lev 23:22) and other forms of charity (e.g., Deut 15:11; 1 John 3:17) that are enjoined upon God's people. The prophetic tradition is rife with pronunciations of judgment against those who do not care for the marginalized in these ways (e.g., Mal 3:5). It is no surprise that Christianity developed a firm commitment to caring for the marginalized through acts of charity, even if such commitment was all too frequently betrayed in practice.

John Calvin picks up this thread of the tradition in his discussion of the Christian life. He argues that everything a Christian possesses has been given by God not only for the private good of the individual, but also for the common good of the community. Consequently, "the lawful use of all benefits consists in a liberal and kindly sharing of them with others."[34] This liberality of charity is finally a question of personal decision, however, because Calvin accepts that the possession of disproportionate wealth by individuals is the result of God's providential ordering. He argues that the Eighth Commandment demands that we "strive faithfully to help every man to keep his own possessions."[35] The provision of charity, then, depends on an individual of means deciding to part with a portion of those means to alleviate the misery of the poor. Thomas Aquinas makes this point as well when he writes, "the things that anyone has in superabundance ought to be used to support the poor. . . . However since the needy are many and they cannot all be supplied from the same source, the decision is left to each individual as to how to manage his property."[36]

33. It is possible to interpret this verse differently, however. We can read it as a rejection of ascetic withdrawal in the context of early Christianity's apocalyptic expectation. In other words, the complaint is not that people are layabouts in a general sense, but that they do not feel it is necessary to work in pursuit of the church's mission and for the benefit of the community because Christ's return, and the end of the world as we know it, is just around the corner. My thanks to Scott Jackson, who suggested this alternative reading to me.
34. John Calvin, *Institutes of the Christian Religion*, ed. John T. McNeill, trans. Ford Lewis Battles, 2 vols., Library of Christian Classics (Philadelphia: Westminster Press, 1960), 3.7.5.
35. Ibid., 2.8.45.

In a fascinating twist, Thomas mitigates against the danger of those with means failing to meet the needs of the marginalized. He admits that "a person may legitimately supply his need from the property of someone else" in the case of "an urgent and clear need" where one "is in imminent danger and cannot be helped in any other way."[37] Appropriating someone else's property in such situations is *not* theft. Practically speaking, however, everything depends on the person from whom property has been appropriated in this way, and the social structures that maintain them in their property, recognizing the legitimacy of the need. This underscores further the individualistic limitations of the traditional approach to charity. Insofar as it lacks a strong systemic component aimed at correcting how social structures produce the need for charity, the charity model only serves to ameliorate the worst consequences of those structures.

Gollwitzer discusses this in relationship to the healing story told at the beginning of Acts 3. Peter and John are accosted by a lame beggar while on their way to the temple. Peter responds to the beggar's plea for alms: "I have no silver or gold, but what I have I give you; in the name of Jesus Christ of Nazareth, stand up and walk" (Acts 3:6). The beggar does so. From our location within a capitalist society and conditioned by the traditional conception of charity, we might be tempted to say that Peter did well by giving this beggar a hand-up rather than a hand-out. Peter sent the beggar out to make a living for himself, rather than being a drain upon society. This interpretation overlooks the important middle point, however—through the power of Christ, Peter supernaturally corrected the material conditions (i.e., lameness) that trapped the beggar in his state. Charity cannot do that. It does not even try. As Gollwitzer says, "traditional Christian *caritas* [charity] . . . leaves the world principally unchanged."[38] Traditional Christian charity thus qualitatively fails to address the needs of the oppressed. Or, as he puts it more fulsomely elsewhere: "traditional charity is not enough, because it does not aim at the cause of distress, but only cures the symptoms."[39]

Charity cannot even remove the symptoms, however. In addition to the qualitative failure of charity, Gollwitzer also believes that the real-

36. Thomas Aquinas, *St. Thomas Aquinas on Politics and Ethics: A New Translation, Backgrounds, Interpretations*, trans. Paul E. Sigmund, Norton Critical Editions in the History of Ideas (New York: W. W. Norton and Company, 1988), 72–73.
37. Ibid., 73.
38. Helmut Gollwitzer, "Liberation in History," *Interpretation* 28, no. 4 (1974): 413–14.
39. Gollwitzer, *Rich Christians*, 12.

ities of global capitalism reveal a fundamental quantitative failure as well. "Charity is not enough, because the distress is overwhelming."[40] It is simply impossible for the tradition of charitable giving by individual Christians to keep up with the need created by the capitalist system, which simultaneously limits the surplus wealth available for charitable giving by the majority of the global North's population. Given the overwhelming character of the need, relying upon traditional Christian charity does two things. First, it soothes the individual's conscience by producing an immediate effect and allowing the giver to assume that they have fulfilled their obligation. Second, it reinforces the dynamic at play between those who have privilege and those who do not—e.g., the wealthy and the poor, the global North and global South, etc.—by establishing the former as the superior party, as masters, upon whose good will the inferior must depend. All of this conspires to prevent sober investigation into the cause that produced this overwhelming need in the first place because that investigation would show us that "we ourselves are partly responsible for this condition of distress."[41]

Insofar as traditional Christian practices of charity do not achieve a fundamental change in the socioeconomic structures that produce the need for charity but, rather, serve only to address symptoms, sooth consciences, and provide a sense of moral superiority, traditional Christian practices of charity ultimately legitimize the capitalist system. It is a pressure-release valve that allows the system to address some of its most egregious failures while at the same time distracting people from the fact that it is the system itself that has produced these failures. Nowhere is this truer than in the recent development of philanthrocapitalism.

Philanthrocapitalism is "consumer philanthropy,"[42] such as when the cashier at the grocery store asks if you would like to add a dollar or two to your purchase as a donation for some charitable cause, or when you are induced to purchase one product over another because a portion of the proceeds will be donated to a charitable cause. Under these

---

40. Ibid., 11.
41. Ibid., 12.
42. Mikkel Thorup, "Pro Bono? On Philanthrocapitalism as Ideological Answer to Inequality," *Ephemera: Theory and Politics in Organization* 13, no. 3 (2013): 560. Jung Mo Sung highlights the absurdity here: "They have such a strong faith in the market that when faced with social problems created by the market, they propose more market to solve them. They believe that the problem will be solved when the market comes to be 'all in all.'" Jung Mo Sung, *Desire, Market and Religion*, Reclaiming Liberation Theology (London: SCM Press, 2007), 15. The reference to 1 Corinthians 15:28 is striking. Capitalism advances an implicit secular eschatology no less than does ideological Marxism.

conditions, charity becomes secondary to and derivative of participation in the capitalist system, thereby further legitimizing that system. It also legitimizes the system by supplying a "black-box presentation of charity" as an impersonal system—you put money in, goods and services for the needy come out the other end, and no questions need be asked about the intervening mechanisms. The moral dilemma is restricted to the consumer. Will you behave like a good person and donate, or will you not? But this "says nothing about the system that determines how those necessities are produced and distributed in the first place."[43] To use the example of hunger—why is it the case that there are warehouses full of food waiting to be distributed, and governments that limit the production of foodstuffs in order to stabilize market prices, but the hungry can only receive the food they so desperately need if you—the consumer—pays for it? Philanthrocapitalism camouflages the inconvenient truth that there are a whole host of intermediary figures and entities—indeed, a whole system—that could be held morally responsible, but is not. In other words, it disguises the structures of privilege that constitute the necrotic heart-beat of the capitalist system.

The Problem of Privilege

The capitalist mode of production is constructed upon the assumption that a certain minority of a society's population is superior to the majority. This minority, then, is rightly described as an aristocracy, albeit an "aristocracy of money" rather than the older, feudal "aristocracy of blood."[44] Capitalism's inexorable tendency to undermine democracy derives from this basic aristocratic character. Gollwitzer speaks of this character in terms of "privilege," and he explicates the capitalist mode of production to highlight this feature.

The capitalist mode of production involves three aspects. First comes "the separation of the producer, which means that the means of production is not owned by the producer." Formerly, talk of "the means of production" referred primarily to industrial equipment, but the principle holds true for all the structures and resources necessary for the production of wealth. This situation is analogous to slavery: neither workers nor slavers are owners, but—unlike slaves—workers are

43. Matthew Snow, "Against Charity," *Jacobin* (August 25, 2015), https://www.jacobinmag.com/2015/08/peter-singer-charity-effective-altruism/.
44. Justo L. González, *The Story of Christianity*, revised and updated edition, 2 vols. (New York: HarperOne, 2010), 2:301.

free "to sell their labor in the free market as another commodity."[45] Second, science is integrated with the means of production in the form of technology. This fragments the production process by including vastly more workers within it: those who achieve scientific progress, who translate that progress into technology, who operate the technology, who support, construct, and operate the infrastructure that makes all this possible, and so on. But it also underscores "the cooperative character of the labor process." Third, those who own the means of production appropriate the surplus wealth created by all those who cooperate in its production. According to Gollwitzer, "the use and exchange values of the goods produced are appropriated not by those who produced them but by the owner of their means of production. The latter pays the former a salary that is only a part of the value that they have produced. . . . The remainder of the value generated becomes the property of the owner of the means of production, who can freely dispose of it."[46] In other words, a small minority of those involved in the production of wealth reaps the lion's share of the wealth produced. Because of the Occupy Wall Street movement, it has become common parlance in the United States over the past few years to refer to this disproportionality by contrasting the wealthiest 1 percent of those in our society with the remaining 99 percent. For Gollwitzer, the basic point here is that "the capitalist mode of production . . . is—in principle—not mastered in accordance with the interests of the common good."[47]

This structurally embedded privilege that enables the few to economically and, consequently, politically dominate the many is a problem as far as Gollwitzer is concerned. He explicates this in terms of the traditional touchstone of distributive justice: *suum cuique*—to each his own, or as Gollwitzer paraphrases it, "what I have the right to expect from others, and what others have a right to expect from me."[48] The fundamental problem with capitalism is that it makes a mockery of this principle. "No one in this system receives the *suum cuique*": workers

45. Gollwitzer, "Die kapitalistische Revolution," 144.
46. Ibid., 145. This is exploitation, which "occurs when someone else's labor is utilized without equivalent pay, and where the product of social labor is unequally appropriated." Helmut Gollwitzer, "Auf dem Linken pfad geschmeichelt?," in *Müssen Christen Sozialisten sein? Zwischen Glaube und Politik*, ed. Wolfgang Teichert (Hamburg: Lutherisches Verlagshaus, 1976), 34.
47. Gollwitzer, "Auf dem Linken," 36.
48. Gollwitzer, *Protestant Theology*, 196. I briefly discuss Gollwitzer on *suum cuique* in W. Travis McMaken, "Occupy Wall Street Is Doing the Church's Work: Helmut Gollwitzer and Economic Justice," *Unbound* (January 16, 2013): http://justiceunbound.org/journal/occupy-wall-street-is-doing-the-churchs-work/.

receive less than they should, those who control the means of producing wealth receive more than they should, and a great many people are left out of the system altogether.[49] This fundamental injustice is not only an abstract moral problem for Gollwitzer. It is a *theological* problem. He argues that support of such a system is diametrically opposed to the gospel. Gollwitzer works out this insight in a number of different ways throughout his writings. At their systematic heart, however, is the event of encounter with God, discussed in chapter 3. There we saw that God's nonobjectifiability means God always comes to us from outside of ourselves. At the core of Christian faith is an experience that decenters us and opens us to things outside of ourselves, to the love of God and neighbor. And because that experience comes to us from outside of ourselves, it cannot form the basis of any sense of superiority. Indeed, it is a radically democratic concept: all people are fundamentally equal because all people rely on a God who comes to them from outside of themselves.

Gollwitzer ties this to Martin Luther's doctrine of salvation. Luther emphasizes that faith depends on hearing the divine Word of promise and grace, and he understands the church as those who have heard that Word. Consequently, "no man has any advantages over the other, because all men have to rely on hearing."[50] To put it another way, the doctrine of justification entails the rejection of all religious privileges, or "salvation aristocracies."[51] This insight puts Gollwitzer into company with Anatoly Lunacharsky, a thinker within Lenin's orbit

49. Gollwitzer, *Protestant Theology*, 201. Andrew Cameron, a mid-19th-century labor reform advocate based in Chicago, put it this way: "poverty exists because those who sow do not reap; because the toiler does not receive a just and equitable proportion of the wealth which he produces." Heath W. Carter, *Union Made: Working People and the Rise of Social Christianity in Chicago* (Oxford: Oxford University Press, 2015), 39. This compares favorably with the following passage from Basil the Great of Caesarea, who made this point about the rich and the common good already in the fourth century: "Which things, tell me, are yours? Whence have you brought your goods into life? You are like one occupying a place in a theater, who should prohibit others from entering, treating that as his own which was designed for the common use of all. Such are the rich. Because they preoccupy common goods, they take these goods as their own. If each would take that which is sufficient for his needs, leaving what is superfluous to those in distress, no one would be rich, no one would be poor. . . . The rich man is a thief." As quoted in Andrew Hsiao and Audrea Lim, eds., *The Verso Book of Dissent: Revolutionary Words from Three Millenia of Rebellion and Resistance* (New York: Verso, 2016), 10.
50. Helmut Gollwitzer, "The Real Luther," in *Martinus Luther: 450th Anniversary of the Reformation* (Bad Godesberg: Inter Nationes, 1967), 12. Whereas capitalism treats people as competitors in the pursuit of surplus value, "justification calls us into solidarity with each other." John P. Burgess, "Reconciliation and Justification," in *Sanctified by Grace: A Theology of the Christian Life*, ed. Kent Eilers and Kyle Strobel (London: Bloomsbury, 2014), 99.
51. Max Weber, *From Max Weber: Essays in Sociology*, trans. H. H. Gerth and Wright Mills (New York: Routledge, 2009), 336–37. Chung uses the phrase: "the salvation aristocracies of Puritanism contradict the genuine ethic of brotherliness, which feels responsible before God for the souls of all." Chung, *Church and Ethical Responsibility*, 50–51; see also 39–42 for his discussion of Luther.

who highlighted points of convergence between religion and Marxism, in part through an engagement with the apostle Paul's writings. Lunacharsky discovered that "justification by faith is itself deeply revolutionary, for it destroys the privilege of the rich and powerful."[52] The trajectory of justification, then, runs in direct opposition to the usual trajectory observed in history. Historically speaking, "there is only a small step from the consciousness of religious privilege to political and economic imperialism."[53] In other words, once people come to think of themselves as religiously superior to others, it is easy for them to assume that they ought also to be materially superior as well. By rejecting religious privilege, the gospel also denies the legitimacy of material privilege.

Precisely this dynamic is at play in how the earliest Christian communities responded in faith to their eventful encounter with the God of the gospel, Gollwitzer argues. He looks especially to the description of the early Christian community in Acts 4, where "everything they owned was held in common" (v. 32) so that "there was not a needy person among them" (v. 34), and to their self-understanding as daughters and sons of God and, therefore, as sisters and brothers of one another. Gollwitzer looks also to Galatians 3:28 as something of a summary statement for this new form of life: "In the communal life together there are no privileges. The barbarian, the slave, the woman, count as much as the 'privileged' person in society, and this person surrenders his advantages under the influence of the new spirit."[54] Not only does encounter with the God of the gospel relativize and call into question privilege itself, but that encounter also places demands upon those with privileges. There are two demands in particular—a practical demand and a principled one. Practically speaking, those with privileges must put those privileges to use helping those who can be helped: "what privileges I possess should—in thanks to God, who gave them to me—be used to serve my neighbors."[55]

---

52. Boer, *Lenin, Religion, and Theology*, 83. Marquardt describes Gollwitzer's understanding of justification as "a practical principle" insofar as it is "paradoxically liberating to human praxis." Marquardt, "Weg und Werk," 25. To extend this analysis, justification destroys privilege because it is fundamentally noncompetitive in character. Rather than operating as a zero-sum game such that grace possessed by one person cannot simultaneously be possessed by another, God's grace is sufficient for all.

53. Helmut Gollwitzer, "Why Black Theology?," *Union Seminary Quarterly Review* 31, no. 1 (1975): 41.

54. Gollwitzer, "Liberation in History," 413. Sociocultural and biological differences between these categories persist. These pairings represent socially constructed relationships of power and privilege. Christ removes those oppressive relationships, not the particularity of the people in those relationships.

55. Gollwitzer, "Why Am I, as a Christian, a Socialist?," thesis 4.3.a, p. 192.

Speaking in terms of principle, however, the demand is more exacting. It is not enough simply to use one's privilege to help those who can be helped. "The conversion to which the Christian community is daily called by God's Word also includes the renunciation of their integration in the dominant system of privileges and their active exertion for justice, and so for social structures no longer determined by social privileges."[56] Beyond simply helping those who can be helped through the use of one's privilege, Christians are called to resist the social structures that imbue some with privileges while disadvantaging others.

This privileging and disadvantaging is precisely what the structures of capitalism produce and protect. Consequently, Gollwitzer does not think that the critical question facing Christians is whether they can support socialism, but whether they can support capitalism: "Can Christians approve of and defend the current social system together with its underlying economic order, or must not this be unbearable for Christians?"[57] Historically speaking, Christians *have* supported capitalism despite the unjust privilege that resides at its structural core. Gollwitzer finds it deeply ironic that the majority of Western Christians have no difficulty in accepting the legitimacy of capitalism while, at the same time, vociferously opposing communism.

> As long as they themselves were not oppressed but privileged, the churches have, to a large extent, ignored slavery, the exploitation and pauperization of the masses, the suppression of free expression of opinion, the education of youth to hate, the arbitrariness of police methods (which include torture), prostitution and the degradation of man. All these things, if practiced by communism, are universally denounced in Christian sermons and in the Christian press of the West.[58]

Gollwitzer rightly traces matters to the question of privilege—capitalist nations have left Christian privilege basically intact while communist nations have not. As a result, "the Christian Church's criticism of capitalism has never had the same force and sharpness as its criticism of communism."[59]

Gollwitzer recognizes that capitalism is a system of privilege for the

56. Ibid., thesis 4.6, p. 193. Gollwitzer does not hesitate to treat acts of faithful obedience as ingredient to salvation. They are a direct and necessary consequence of encounter with God. This marks a doctrinal point at which Gollwitzer is decidedly more stereotypically Reformed than Lutheran. See Day, "Christlicher Glaube," 335.
57. Gollwitzer, "Why Am I, as a Christian, a Socialist?," thesis 4.6, p. 193–94.
58. Helmut Gollwitzer, "The Christian in the Search for World Order and Peace," in *Responsible Government in a Revolutionary Age*, ed. Z. K. Matthews (New York: Association Press, 1966), 55.
59. Ibid., 56.

few and disadvantage for the many, and that the gospel proclaimed by Christianity is—on the contrary—concerned with righteousness and peace that aims at love. "Everything that does not serve this end" stands under judgment.[60] This comes out powerfully in Gollwitzer's political sermons. The following passage from a sermon on John 3:31–36 sums things up nicely:

> The central problem today, more clearly recognized by the young people than by our Church traditions, is at the same time the central problem of the New Testament; what are we doing with our privileges? And what is God doing with his privileges? Every one of us, in contrast with someone, probably in contrast with many people, is a privileged person. . . . That is just as true of the whole of society's propertied classes bristling with arms, propertied nations bristling with arms today, and we Christians belong to the rich and satiated third of mankind. By means of religion and soldiers and laws the privileges are defended. The whole system of society is built up on privilege, and is there to defend the privileges of society. . . . Who will free us from our servitude to these privileges? Who will free us for discipleship, for imitation of God? For he is the one who does not hold on to his privileges, who did not remain on the throne of Lordship, but spent himself and gave himself to sinners, to the men of privilege, to free them from enslavement to their privileges. . . . To believe means: following on the way of the Son, who gave up his privileges, to build upon this, that God is true, that this is the true way to life, whatever it may cost us.[61]

Socialism and the Kingdom of God

The gospel demands that Christians put what privileges they have at the service of the oppressed and marginalized while also working to dismantle the socioeconomic structure that creates and reinforces those privileges—namely, capitalism. Alternatively, socialism provides not merely the appearance of democratic political structures but their reality, secured by egalitarian socioeconomic structures. Democratic socialism is, then, the answer to both the qualitative and quantitative failings of traditional charity, as well as the elimination of all socioeconomic privilege. Consequently, democratic socialism embodies in con-

---

60. Gollwitzer, *Rich Christians*, 14.
61. Helmut Gollwitzer, *The Way to Life: Sermons in a Time of World Crisis*, trans. David Cairns (Edinburgh: T&T Clark, 1981), 81–82. Rolf Stieber-Westermann highlights this dynamic in Gollwitzer's thought: "the message of grace does not set the hearer in a harmonious or affirmative relation to their life context, but calls forth a struggle over reality." Stieber-Westermann, *Provokation zum Leben*, 83. For a theopolitical study of Gollwitzer's sermons, see Gottfried Orth, *Vom Abenteuer bürgerlichen Bewusstseins: die Predigten Helmut Gollwitzers, 1938-1976*, Europäische Hochschulschriften (Frankfurt am Main: Peter D. Lang, 1980).

crete social structures the gospel's priorities of justice and peace aimed at love—in this case, a concrete political love: "love in structures."[62] But this raises questions about exactly what relationship obtains between socialism and the kingdom of God, the vision for the world that derives from encounter with the God and Father of Jesus Christ. Can we equate the kingdom of God with socialism, or are matters more complicated?

We can begin to get a handle on this question by returning to Gollwitzer's engagement with Marxism. Our previous discussion of this topic focused on Gollwitzer's response to Marxist criticism of religion, but Gollwitzer also makes his own criticisms of Marxism over the course of this engagement. Gollwitzer distinguished already in his reflections on his captivity in Soviet Russia between "dogmatic Marxism as a politico-philosophical system" and those who employ Marxist analysis without adopting it as an ideology.[63] He gives us a glimpse throughout his narrative at those who are true believers in Marxism, so to speak. These are people for whom "Marxism has become . . . a decisive spiritual experience."[64] In these cases, the line between analysis aimed at identifying material interests embedded in socioeconomic structures and a "metaphysic" or "world-view" is decisively transgressed. Marxism becomes the primary interpretive framework for how these people see and understand the word, and find meaning within it. This meaning-making element is vitally important for Gollwitzer because it discloses that Marxism has, in such cases, become religious: "Marxism becomes a substitute-religion by becoming a substitute source of meaning."[65]

Marxism as a substitute-religion can be a powerful source of meaning, especially for those who are alive enough in their suffering, or to the suffering of their neighbors, to see its source in capitalist structures that have been and are legitimized by religious—and specifically, Christian—institutions. But when compared with true Christianity, rather than with this counterfeit Christianity, Marxism as a substitute religion possesses a serious handicap: Christian hope is "much more radical and

62. Gollwitzer, *Rich Christians*, 16.
63. Gollwitzer, *Unwilling Journey*, 10.
64. Ibid., 136.
65. Gollwitzer, *Marxist Criticism of Religion*, 101. Eagleton rightly explains that Marx was not interested in a "Theory of Everything," a "total philosophy." Eagleton, *Why Marx*, 34. It bears repeating: Gollwitzer only criticized what he called ideological Marxism in this way. He was not concerned about those who use a Marxist perspective for analysis purposes without transforming it into a comprehensive ideology, what Gollwitzer saw as a substitute for religion. Thus, he staunchly affirms that "socialists are not representatives of a soteriology." Gollwitzer, "Why Am I, as a Christian, a Socialist?," thesis 1.7, p. 189; see also thesis 4.9, p. 194.

all-embracing."[66] This should be no surprise. Marxism's hope for the future is a hope without the transcendent. It is a "secularised eschatology," an entirely this-worldly utopian vision whose horizon is bounded by the earthly-historical process.[67] Human beings are left alone in their revolutionary struggle for liberation, and the only validation of meaning left to them is the progress of their struggle. But progress cannot bear this burden; the utopian dawn recedes doggedly into the future, the horizon darkens, and a resigned nihilism descends.

It is in an effort to stave off this nihilist twilight that the greatest danger of dogmatic Marxism arises—namely, the difficulty that it has in maintaining the dignity and value of individual human beings as anything other than means to the end of progress toward the utopian future.[68] And treating humans as a means to an end is the danger that Gollwitzer identified during his years in Russia, which pushed him toward advocating a reforming capitalism in the 1950s. Ironically, this danger brings the Stalinist extreme of dogmatic Marxism into close proximity with the fascist extreme of capitalism—National Socialism. Gollwitzer believes that the Russia he encountered was only held back "by a remnant of the Christian tradition"[69] from going the way of the Third Reich in its treatment of those deemed useless. But even without these extreme forms, the secularized eschatologies of both dogmatic Marxism and capitalism tend toward inhumanity, albeit in different modes. "Perhaps the difference lies in the fact that the West tempts one to be inhuman, while the East forces one to be inhuman. The temptation may be the greater danger" precisely because it is so insidious.[70]

For Gollwitzer, "a this-worldly eschatology can give no foundation for the dignity of man today as a person, and the concept of meaning, because it cannot be understood as grounded in the affirmation of man by an enduring love, must be equated with that of the end and the means to an end."[71] The solution to this quandary, then, is to under-

66. Gollwitzer, *Marxist Criticism of Religion*, 105.
67. Gollwitzer, *Unwilling Journey*, 210. For Gollwitzer's criticism of Marxism, see also "The Church and Marxism in the European Crisis" in Helmut Gollwitzer, *The Demands of Freedom: Papers by a Christian in West Germany*, trans. Robert W. Fenn (New York: Harper and Row Publishers, 1965), 93–108.
68. This runs afoul of Immanuel Kant's moral dictum: "the human being . . . exists as an end in itself, not merely as a means to be used by this or that will at its discretion; instead he must in all his actions, whether directed to himself or also to other rational beings, always be regarded at the same time as an end." Immanuel Kant, *Groundwork of the Metaphysics of Morals*, trans. Mary Gregor, Cambridge Texts in the History of Philosophy (Cambridge: Cambridge University Press, 1997), 37.
69. Gollwitzer, *Unwilling Journey*, 202.
70. Ibid., 178. Taking aim at capitalists, Gollwitzer writes that "Jesus taught them a great lesson: a man is more important than any possessions." Gollwitzer, *Demands of Freedom*, 171.
71. Gollwitzer, *Marxist Criticism of Religion*, 118. As Jürgen Moltmann says, "without hope for the ultimate, hope for the penultimate soon loses its force, or it becomes violent in order to extort the

stand humanity as directed outside of itself by way of a transcendence that disrupts the earthly-historical horizon. This is precisely what the concept of God from Gollwitzer's dialectical theology provides: the God who cannot be objectified nonetheless encounters us in the event of faith within our own earthly-historical reality without ever becoming a fixture within that reality. God's Thou-objectivity remains always nonobjectifiable so that history is opened to a surplus of meaning, and creaturely life is imbued with a surplus of value as an end in itself. The result, as Gollwitzer describes it in a more homiletical mode, is that "I am as important to God as I am to myself, and as He is to Himself."[72]

Conceptually speaking, Gollwitzer describes this different eschatological vision by reflecting on the kingdom of God and its relationship to history. The kingdom of God is a transcendent reality that interrupts the earthly-historical by demonstrating its limits. As such, it is the form of life that God wills for God's creatures. It is the life of love with God and neighbor that Jesus proclaimed and embodied, which includes both a repairing of human failings and an affirmation of the value of creaturely life. And because this affirmation comes to a world and humanity in need of repair, the kingdom of God always aims "at liberation and consummation."[73] Gollwitzer highlights a number of Greek terms from the New Testament—such as *metanoia* (repentance), *dikaiosyne* (justification), and *zoe* (life)—that underscore the kingdom of God's character as "the great revolution of all conditions 'in which humanity is a debased, enslaved, abandoned, contemptible being' (K. Marx)."[74] Gollwitzer does not describe the kingdom of God by quoting from Karl Marx and speaking about revolution merely to be rhetorically provocative. All this is central to his understanding of that kingdom. It is a fundamentally socialist reality insofar as it is oriented toward equality in the absence of all privilege, and it is revolutionary because it radically opposes all imperfect historical societies and their structures of inequality and privilege. The kingdom of God is the "revolutionary, eschatological, and social determination of the present"; it is "the revolution of all revolutions, that is, the eschatological revolution."[75]

---

ultimate from what is penultimate." Jürgen Moltmann, *The Living God and the Fullness of Life*, trans. Margaret Kohl (Louisville, KY: Westminster John Knox Press, 2015), 180.

72. Gollwitzer, *Unwilling Journey*, 43.

73. Helmut Gollwitzer, "Der Wille Gottes und die gesellschaftliche Wirklichkeit," in *Mensch, du bist gefragt: Reflexionen zur Gotteslehre*, ed. Peter Winzeler, Ausgewählte Werke (München: Chr. Kaiser, 1988), thesis 2.1, p. 275.

74. Ibid., thesis 2.2, p. 275.

75. Helmut Gollwitzer, "Die Revolution des Reiches Gottes und die Gesellschaft," in *Umkehr und Rev-*

It is critically important that Gollwitzer understands the kingdom of God's revolution as eschatological rather than historical. The eschatological character of the kingdom prevents it from becoming another deadly utopian vision. Gollwitzer makes a threefold distinction between "absolute utopia," "relative utopia," and "social-revolutionary program[s]."[76] Absolute utopia is a matter of Christian hope and is, consequently, another way of speaking about the kingdom of God. As such, it is a transcendent, eschatological reality whose actualization depends on divine—rather than human—activity. Relative utopia is a vision for the earthly-historical future of society. For Christians, this vision is for life in human society as an analogy to the absolute utopia of the kingdom of God. Because that absolute utopia is a matter of divine rather than human action, the best that we can hope for within the confines of our earthly-historical horizon is to approximate it as much as possible. A social-revolutionary program is the political strategy whereby one works to achieve relative utopia. It is the result of a complex rational negotiation of the concrete sociopolitical and economic possibilities in any given earthly-historical context.

Where, then, does socialism fit into this threefold distinction? Gollwitzer understands socialism in terms of this threefold distinction as well. To begin, "true socialism is the kingdom of God."[77] Consequently, "true socialism" is a way of describing absolute utopia. It is an eschatological socialism that both relativizes and transcendently grounds democratic socialism. In this schema, democratic socialism as a political goal is another way of speaking about relative utopia. It is the earthly-historical goal of increasingly approximating the kingdom of God's true socialism while knowing that such true socialism cannot be accomplished by creaturely action because "the kingdom of God is the always more radical alternative to our implementations."[78] Finally, the particular socialist parties and policy proposals on offer in any particu-

olution: *Aufsätze zu christlichem Glauben und Marxismus*, Band 1, ed. Christian Keller, Ausgewählte Werke (München: Chr. Kaiser, 1988), theses 6.2-3, p. 112. See Dannemann and Weissinger, "Helmut Gollwitzers Beitrag zur Theologie der Gesellschaft," 585–86.

76. Gollwitzer, "Revolution des Reiches Gottes," thesis 7.23, p. 120; see also theses 7.24–25. See Dannemann and Weissinger, "Helmut Gollwitzers Beitrag zur Theologie der Gesellschaft," 586.

77. Gollwitzer, "Kingdom of God and Socialism," 78. Gollwitzer elaborates this with reference to Barth's thought but it holds true in his own as well.

78. Gollwitzer, "Wille Gottes," thesis 3.3.c, p. 277. Further, it makes "a difference whether we perceive an identity between God's kingdom and socialism, or whether we identify our socialism (as idea, movement, and finally achieved condition) with God's kingdom." Gollwitzer, "Kingdom of God and Socialism," 80. The former is legitimate while the latter is illegitimate because it elides the distinction between the kingdom of God as absolute utopia on the one hand, and earthly-historical socialism with its particular parties and policies on the other.

lar sociopolitical moment correspond to the social-revolutionary programs by which we attempt that approximation. And since all that we
can ever attempt or achieve is approximation, Christians find themselves under the conditions of "permanent revolution."[79] Socialism,
then, in this threefold inflection, provides a mode of speech that supplies an intermediate determinacy between abstract talk of "utopia,"
and the detailed material considerations of both the Christian description of the kingdom of God and the particular parties and policy proposals under consideration in particular contexts.

It is important to bring this discussion of socialism and the kingdom
of God to a close by complicating the somewhat schematic picture
that I have developed. Gollwitzer does not understand the kingdom
of God, the utopia of true socialism, as hermetically sealed off from
earthly-historical life. The point is that the kingdom of God is not con-
tained within, subject to, or achievable by way of earthly-historical
processes. The kingdom of God is nonobjectifiable, just as God is nonobjectifiable. But there is also God's Thou-objectivity, God's giving of Godself as a true other in the event of encounter. Just so, we experience
the kingdom of God in the present through embodied proclamation.
As the true socialism of the kingdom of God is proclaimed in word
and deed—in book, sermon, political protest, policy proposals, and so
on—we catch glimpses in the present of that eschatological kingdom.
As Gollwitzer explains: "the kingdom of God is a hidden present reality
where, through the initiating of God's lordship in the lives of people
by the dynamism of the Holy Spirit, they are now already becoming
changed into a new way of life through conversion."[80]

Must Christians be Socialists?

It is fruitful while concluding this discussion of Gollwitzer's democratic
socialism to reflect on one of the most dramatic aspects of his socialist

79. Gollwitzer, "Wille Gottes," thesis 3.3.c, p. 277. The concept of permanent revolution is prominent
within the Marxist tradition. It can be traced back at least as far as Marx's 1850 "Address of the
Central Committee to the Communist League," where Marx discusses the permanence of the revolution as lasting until the worldwide triumph of the proletariat. Kamenka, *Portable Karl Marx*, 249.
Leon Trotsky also made permanent revolution central to his thought. See especially Leon Trotsky, *The Permanent Revolution and Results and Prospects*, trans. Brian Pearce (New York: Pathfinder
Press, 1969). In a manner analogous to Gollwitzer's, John Drury deploys the concept of "perpetual
revolution" to elucidate convergences in the thought of Karl Barth and John Wesley. See John L.
Drury, "Promise and Command: Barth and Wesley on Matthew 5:48," in *Karl Barth in Conversation*,
ed. W. Travis McMaken and David W. Congdon (Eugene, OR: Pickwick, 2014), 3. See also Paul L.
Lehmann, "Karl Barth, Theologian of Permanent Revolution," *Union Seminary Quarterly Review* 28,
no. 1 (1972): 67–81.
80. Gollwitzer, "Wille Gottes," thesis 2.4.b, p. 275.

conviction—namely, his staunch defense of Karl Barth's claim that "a real Christian must become a socialist."[81] This statement demands that we answer two important questions. First, what precisely does the term *socialist* designate when Gollwitzer says that Christians must be socialists? Second, what sort of necessity is operative when Gollwitzer says that Christians *must* be socialists?

We can begin to answer the first question by noting that, for Gollwitzer, socialism characterizes the "direction and orientation" that the gospel supplies for Christian political existence. But the gospel, or the kingdom of God, cannot be identified with democratic socialism in a simplistic way. This is why Gollwitzer is so careful to distinguish between the true socialism of the kingdom of God as absolute utopia, democratic socialism as relative utopia, and particular socialist parties and policies as social-revolutionary programs aimed at the realization of that relative utopia. The true socialism of the kingdom of God can never be reduced to earthly-historical socialism's visions and methods. Christians must be socialists with reference to this true socialism of the kingdom of God insofar as the gospel demands that they proclaim and embody the reality of that kingdom. This is the sense in which the gospel points "toward a solidary, democratic, privilege-free society."[82]

What then of democratic socialism as relative utopia, and particular socialist parties and policies as social-revolutionary programs? Matters are more complicated here. For Gollwitzer, the true socialism of the kingdom of God as absolute utopia establishes the direction and orientation for Christian political existence, and "the decision for socialism"—for democratic socialism as relative utopia, and for particular socialist parties and policies—"develops out of" that direction and orientation.[83] Making the jump, as it were, from the true socialism of the kingdom of God to what we might call *actual* socialism involves using human reason to analyze the political and economic structures of one's society—such as capitalism's anti-democratic character and the failure of traditional Christian approaches to charity. As Christians become "conscious of the incompatibility between the gospel and the capitalist system of privileges," and as "they see that the gospel inevitably and inexorably pushes them to participation in the struggle for a more just and more solidary society," they must "investigate rationally and

---

81. Helmut Gollwitzer, "Must a Christian Be a Socialist?," Appendix 1, 181.
82. Gollwitzer, "Why Am I, as a Christian, a Socialist?," thesis 4.7, p. 194.
83. Ibid., thesis 4.8, p. 194. That the gospel provides "direction and orientation" is central to Gollwitzer's thought. He derives it from Barth. See chapter 3, 87n116.

decide to what extent a social change is now possible and necessary; which strategies, which alliances, and which compromises to choose to favor; and what the structural changes that are now due should look like."[84] Gollwitzer is convinced that such an investigation leads inexorably to recognizing Christianity's trajectory toward democratic socialism as the relative utopia that corresponds to the absolute utopia of the kingdom of God's true socialism.

It also places one within a bounded "channel" of possibilities as far as social-revolutionary programs and policies are concerned.[85] "Capitalism, the authoritarian state, [and] dictatorship" fall outside these boundaries, but within them are a number of possibilities that range from the "only vaguely socialist" to the "strictly socialist." It is up to each Christian to discern which of the options on offer at any particular time provides a realistic chance for concrete improvement of material conditions for the oppressed. However, Gollwitzer privileges the more radically socialist options as opposed to more moderate ones. Those who support more moderate options bear the burden of proof in demonstrating "that they are steps toward the goal" of democratic socialism, or "in any case, detours that are not dead ends." Most important for our present purposes, this discussion highlights that there is no single way to be a socialist, especially when it comes to the question of social-revolutionary programs and policies. Gollwitzer's affirmation that Christians must be socialists, then, is not a demand for monolithic uniformity. As he puts it: "the word socialism has enough determinacy for all its breadth, and it has enough breadth for all its determinacy, to make those statements possible—indeed, necessary!—for Christians."[86]

This raises again the question concerning the sort of necessity that Gollwitzer intends. It is not a coercive necessity, but a logical one that grows out of the twin factors of the direction and orientation given to Christian political existence by the gospel and a rational, clear-sighted analysis of social conditions. Note well: this necessity is a logical consequence of the gospel, rather than the gospel's precondition. Gollwitzer stands squarely within the Augustinian-Protestant tradition in refusing to credit any human action as a precondition for encounter with God in the event of faith. Affirming that Christians *must* be socialists does not contradict this more basic sense in which "Christians 'must' do nothing at all."[87] The sort of necessity involved here is a new kind of

84. Ibid., thesis 4.7, p. 194.
85. Gollwitzer, "Must a Christian Be a Socialist?," 178–79.
86. Ibid., 185.

necessity that is characterized by the freedom bestowed by the gospel. It is an internal necessity that flowers within the Christian, rather than being imposed from the outside. Gollwitzer elaborates this subject with reference to the parable of the prodigal son in Luke 15. The son does not need to serve the father because the father has threatened to cast him out of the house; rather, the necessity by which the son now serves the father is "awakened by love itself and upheld by love." This "must of love" is therefore also a "must of happiness." Thus, the necessity by which Christians must be socialists for Gollwitzer is a logical—or, perhaps better, spiritual—necessity that follows from the gospel. His train of thought flows much like the Apostle Paul's: socialism is the "act of worship that makes sense" (Rom 12:1).[88]

War

It may appear incongruous at first to move from the primarily socioeconomic realm of democratic socialism to a consideration of war, but they are of a piece. Gollwitzer's commitment to democratic socialism meant a rejection of all socioeconomic and political privilege, and military might—both its use and the threat of its use—is the ultimate mechanism for maintaining that privilege. As Ernest Mandel wrote in his classic analysis of *Late Capitalism*, the purpose of bourgeois state power resides "in institutionally protecting and juridically legitimating private property," and it does this by "enforcing the rule of the dominant class by coercion." Paul Chung captures this dynamic succinctly: "economic power [is] backed up by state power."[89] It is natural, then, that the theopolitical analysis that pushed Gollwitzer to embrace democratic socialism also pushed him to criticize the state's use of power to maintain privilege as it reaches its overt zenith in waging war. This section thinks with Gollwitzer about the question of pacifism and the impact of nuclear weapons on traditional just war theory before concluding with broader reflections on the relationship between war and capitalism.

The Question of Pacifism

For Gollwitzer, the question of pacifism was not merely an abstract

---

87. Ibid., 174–75.
88. This is my own translation. It plays on the meaning of λογικὴν.
89. Ernest Mandel, *Late Capitalism*, trans. Joris De Bres (London: Verso, 1978), 494, 475; Chung, *Church and Ethical Responsibility*, 270.

intellectual exercise. It was a personal, existential question. He had to grapple with the prospect that he would be drafted to serve in the armed forces of the Nazi regime, which he believed was deeply malevolent. This was an issue for many Confessing Church pastors and seminarians, but it was not an issue that was widely discussed within the movement. The general feeling was that allegiance to Germany was distinct from allegiance to Hitler and the Nazi regime, and "Confessing [Church] pastors decided that they would fight for Germany, not for Hitler." But this position rests "on the illusion that the consequences of their actions could remain as pure as their intentions."[90]

Gollwitzer saw things more clearly, but he remained conflicted. He recounts a 1939 meeting in Switzerland with Karl Barth and other theological friends where they discussed Barth's assertion that Germany had undertaken an unjust war, which would mean that Christians could not participate in good conscience on the German side of the conflict. Gollwitzer hesitated, and returned to Germany without a clear sense of the path that he should take. As Gollwitzer notes, "conscientious objection had no tradition" in Germany. Hermann Stöhr was executed when he refused to participate in the German war effort even through serving as a medical orderly or in an administrative position. Stöhr's example stayed with Gollwitzer, who nonetheless reported to the German armed forces—the *Wehrmacht*—when drafted. At one level, being drafted ensured that Gollwitzer would be protected from the concentration camps after he was silenced and banished from Berlin. But Gollwitzer did not go with a clear conscience: "I'm not sure what clinched the matter for me, my cowardice or my theological reasons."[91] As recounted in chapter 2, Gollwitzer was initially placed in a machine-gun company but transferred to an ambulance corps, and he made it through the war without using his weapon.

Despite never using his weapon, however, he was reluctant to completely disarm during the collapse of the Eastern Front, where he was eventually taken prisoner. He writes about surrendering his primary sidearm: "Now I was disarmed—not entirely, of course. I had another pistol in my pocket. It is best to have something of the sort for

90. Victoria Barnett, *For the Soul of the People: Protestant Protest against Hitler* (New York: Oxford University Press, 1992), 158.
91. From an interview with Gollwitzer, as quoted in ibid., 160. Eberhard Busch briefly describes the meeting with Barth and lists the following attendees: Ernst Wolf, Gollwitzer, Günther Dehn, Gertrud Staewen, Pierre Maury, and Arthur Frey. Eberhard Busch, *Karl Barth: His Life from Letters and Autobiographical Texts*, trans. John Bowden (Philadelphia: Fortress Press, 1976), 298. See also Gollwitzer's narration: Gollwitzer, *Demands of Freedom*, 124–30.

emergencies." This leads him to reflect on self-defense as a basically selfish consideration that is "fundamentally different" from the values of the Sermon on the Mount, which makes trying to justify self-defense "a false, un-Christlike reaction." He then gives us another window into his thought process in that moment: "I won't throw the pistol away yet, I thought, while I think this over as I walk along. I will postpone the decision: it is pleasant not to have finally decided, to have the alternatives still open, the good and the evil, the Christian and the un-Christian."[92] In telling this story, the older Gollwitzer looks back on the younger with both sympathy and deep criticism. But the episode also reveals something of the delicate balance that remains in Gollwitzer's later thinking about pacifism.

Early in the 1950s, Gollwitzer argued that there is no absolute Christian commitment to pacifism: "In my opinion, God's command does not allow us to be absolute pacifists."[93] Consistent with his reflections above, he does not use self-defense as an argument against such absolute pacifism. Rather, his argument is based on the defense of others. Imagining situations when the rule of justice might be overthrown from without ("from the East") or from within (thinking of Hitler), he declares that "whenever power does not serve justice, but sets justice aside, resistance is a Christian duty."[94] Gollwitzer addressed this issue in the midst of the political debate concerning whether Germany should re-arm. Initially, Gollwitzer took a mediating position, but he finally decided against rearmament. By 1961, he had concluded that the attitude Christians take toward war "in the relations of church and state" is "the test of the understanding of Christian mission,"[95] whereby one can discern whether Christians have understood the gospel. "You can only have the 'Yes' of the gospel and the 'No' to war together today, or else you lose one with the other."[96] What changed?

First, nothing changed. Gollwitzer's call for a defense of justice is not entirely overturned since one can imagine situations where justice must be defended without formal trappings of war. We will examine the question of revolutionary violence shortly, for instance. Second, everything changed. One factor is that Gollwitzer increasingly identified a reactionary drift in the Bonn republic with which he was uncom-

92. Gollwitzer, *Unwilling Journey*, 19.
93. Helmut Gollwitzer, *Forderungen der Freiheit: Aufsätze und Reden zur politischen Ethik* (München: Chr. Kaiser Verlag, 1962), 66.
94. Gollwitzer, *Demands of Freedom*, 69.
95. Ibid., 131.
96. Gollwitzer, *Forderungen der Freiheit*, 347.

fortable.[97] But the lynchpin in Gollwitzer's shift between these two moments was the increasingly real specter of an atomic war that would end human life as we know it.

Just War and Nuclear Weapons

For Gollwitzer, the intellectual and moral issue with nuclear weapons is that they overturn the calculus of traditional just war theory. He suspected that this was not widely enough understood, and worried in the 1960s that the Christian church was witnessing "a relapse into traditional war ethics" despite how nuclear weapons had fundamentally changed the nature of modern warfare.[98] Looking back at this moment fifty years later, it seems that Gollwitzer was correct. The world has gotten used to the presence of nuclear weapons and a majority of Christian leaders in the United States, for instance, seem unconcerned by or at least resigned to this aspect of the *status quo*.

The fundamental issue surrounding nuclear armaments is how they have changed "the traditional function of war, as a political method." Prior to such armaments, it was possible to conceive of war as "a calculable means to an end." Governments, and the Christian church insofar as it concerned itself with making judgments about the justness of a given conflict, could make reasonable evaluative judgments concerning the extent of a conflict, the damage likely to be done, estimates of casualties, and so on. One could weigh a conflict's consequences against the precipitating causes and measure for proportionality. To oversimplify matters, if the injustice that led to the conflict outweighs the injustice produced by the conflict, and if the conflict can be prosecuted in a just manner (for instance, without targeting noncombatants), then the conflict is just. Nuclear war includes the very real possibility that conflict will exceed all such bounds, however, doing irrevocable damage to the environment and even threatening the destruction of all human life. War in a nuclear age "is no longer a means the precise object of which is discernable."[99]

---

97. See the comparison that Gollwitzer makes between West Germany and Israel: Helmut Gollwitzer, "Israel - und Wir," in *Auch das Denken darf dienen: Aufsätze zu Theologie und Geistesgeschichte*, Band 2, ed. Friedrich-Wilhelm Marquardt, Ausgewählte Werke (München: Chr. Kaiser, 1988), 87. Gollwitzer was not the only one with these concerns. "West Germany . . . is a conservative state, where reactionary elements are unquestionably pre-eminent." Jean-Marie Vincent, "West Germany: The Reactionary Democracy," in *The Socialist Register*, ed. Ralph Miliband and John Saville (New York: Monthly Review Press, 1964), 80.
98. Helmut Gollwitzer, "Militär, Staat und Kirche," in *... daß Gerechtigkeit und Friede sich küssen: Aufsätze zur politishen Ethik*, Band 2, ed. Andreas Pangritz, Ausgewählte Werke (München: Chr. Kaiser, 1988), 161.

Gollwitzer saw his own time as a period of transition during which the world grappled with the proper response to these game-changing armaments. This transition means three things. First, any form of warfare today—even when countries with nuclear armaments "deliberately fight a limited war"—constitutes an incalculable risk because these conflicts could come down to a choice "between capitulation and suicide." Second, these armaments may function as deterrents even if the stakes are considerably higher than previously. "A deterrent is a threat to use force," but the use of force threatened today "is no longer calculable, but suicidal."[100] Because of the atomic equilibrium in Gollwitzer's day between the great powers, there could be a certain level of stability in mutual atomic deterrence. However, not all nations possess these weapons, or equal capabilities with them, and this leads to Gollwitzer's third point: the existence of nuclear weapons undermines the sovereignty of those nations that lack them. This produces a covert geopolitical imperialism that complicates the conflicts between smaller states, turning them into proxy wars and "thus keeping the conflicts virulent instead of ending them." Whereas war previously functioned as a political *ultima ratio* for maintaining order, nuclear armament means that this last resort is too risky.[101]

How should Christians respond to this new state of affairs? Gollwitzer reiterates that Christians are not required to maintain an absolute pacifism. "God's law is not against all use of force." As he said previously, there may well be times when force is required to uphold justice. However, matters are clearer when it comes to the waging of war under the conditions of nuclear armament because "there is . . . no possibility of an atomic war being a just war." Consequently, "whoever has recourse to atomic warfare will have God against him." Christians must make themselves heard against such war, breaking through the distortions of the issue produced by politicians and the military-industrial complex. They must work to defuse the propagandistic "us-vs-them" mentality that justifies the build-up of these weapons. Their commitment to peace must extend even to "the sacrifice of national interests to the cause of peace" because, "otherwise, it is no longer possible to be a true Christian in our time."[102]

---

99. Gollwitzer, "Christian in the Search," 47.
100. Ibid., 48.
101. Ibid., 49.
102. Ibid., 51–52. Michael Weinrich highlights Gollwitzer's characterization of the military as a "secular idol." Michael Weinrich, "Gesellschaftliche Herausforderungen der Theologie: Erinnerungen an Helmut Gollwitzer," *Evangelische Theologie* 59, no. 3 (1999): 171.

We live in a world very different from Gollwitzer's. As mentioned above, we have become used to the threat of nuclear annihilation, and experience has suggested that it is possible to conduct conventional warfare against the backdrop of nuclear armament. This comfort level is facilitated by the end of the Cold War and assumptions concerning the superior capabilities of the United States' military. Although other major powers with nuclear weapons continue to exist in the world, the United States military has (so far) only been asked to use its capabilities against non-nuclear enemies. In other words, it has been possible for the United States to wage conventional warfare against non-nuclear nations because of the undisputed superiority of its military's conventional (and nuclear) capabilities. This is a delicate illusion, however, that we can expect to be increasingly challenged. Furthermore, we have seen the emergence of new remotely operated weapons that allow for targeted killing (assassination) on a scale never before possible. These weapons complicate the just war calculus further insofar as they do not require putting American lives in direct danger in the field while raising the likelihood of involving noncombatants, whether through targeting mistakes or collateral damage.[103] At a time when people in the United States seem to be reawakening to awareness of the threat of nuclear war, Gollwitzer's example calls us to think carefully through these issues today and to hold our government accountable for its shortcomings. Perhaps most of all, he calls us to recognize how the violence done in our name is prosecuted in order to maintain "the superiority of particular interests."[104] In other words, we must think about the intersection of war and capitalism.

War and Capitalism

Thus far, we have seen that Gollwitzer resists any absolute pacifism because force must sometimes be employed in the service of justice. We have also encountered Gollwitzer's argument that nuclear weapons

---

103. One major factor contributing to increased reliance on remotely operated weapons systems is that the United States increasingly wages asymmetrical warfare, including waging war against non-state entities (Al-Qaeda, ISIS/ISIL, etc.). This further complicates the just war calculus.

104. Gollwitzer, "Christian in the Search," 50. One thinks, for instance, of the official music video (released on February 21, 2017) for Katy Perry's song, "Chained to the Rhythm" (Capitol Records: February 10, 2017). Set in a theme park named "Oblivia," the video presents the viewer with cotton candy in the shape of mushroom clouds and an attraction named "Bombs Away." The video depicts the eponymous military hardware in a way that is visually evocative of a cross between an intercontinental ballistic missile and the "Fat Man" atomic bomb that the United States used against the Japanese city of Nagasaki in 1945. One periodically sees these bombs falling in the background of the video, suggesting the ever-present danger of nuclear war.

fundamentally change the dynamics of war. Consequently, faithfulness to the God of the gospel demands that Christians oppose warfare even to the point of sacrificing national privilege. Both of these strands develop in Gollwitzer's thought in the 1950s and early 1960s while he supported a reformed capitalism, and before he embraced a thorough-going democratic socialism in the late 1960s. That shift brings together and fulfills these two strands of thought. The first strand culminates in Gollwitzer's position on revolutionary violence, which we will discuss shortly, while the second strand is deepened and enriched by his analysis of how war functions in service of capitalism.

War functions in service of capitalism insofar as it extends capital's empire. Gollwitzer saw this clearly with reference to the United States' war in Vietnam. Writing in 1967, he argued the Vietnam War reveals that capitalism's anti-democratic character and its tendency toward imperialism are two sides of the same coin. Its anti-democratic character appears by revealing that "behind the façade of democracy" in America, there is "an oligarchy of wealth and violence that governs." Furthermore, this oligarchy of capital governs precisely "by exploiting the rest of the world." The interests of capital manufacture the appearance of democracy and then put that simulacrum to work at home and abroad to extend and secure its privileges. For Gollwitzer, the conclusion is clear: "one cannot be a Christian and remain silent about the murder in Vietnam."[105] He also makes a rather prescient comment about the relationship between the United States' foreign and domestic policies: "the brutalization of American foreign policy, if not finally stopped, will lead to the brutalization of American domestic policy."[106] In other words, the inhumanity—starkly revealed in Vietnam—that characterizes American foreign policy as it is bent to the service of capital will inevitably migrate to American domestic policy. Gollwitzer's prediction came true in the intervening fifty years as the United States' embrace of neoliberalism has meant systematically deconstructing its

---

105. Helmut Gollwitzer, "Vietnam 1967," in . . . daß Gerechtigkeit und Friede sich küssen: Aufsätz zur politishen Ethik, Band 2, ed. Andreas Pangritz, Ausgewählte Werke (München: Chr. Kaiser, 1988), 164. Gollwitzer also reflected on the conflicts in Chile, El Salvador, and Nicaragua. This work deserves attention. Many of the key texts can be found in this same volume.
106. Gollwitzer, "Vietnam," 165. There are thought provoking parallels here with the Marvel film, Captain America: The Winter Soldier (2014). This film depicts the United States military-industrial complex turning upon the American people in alliance with underground agents from the former Nazi regime. One of these agents explains that they originally thought they had to force the world to bend to the Nazi order, but then they realized that if they scared people enough, they could get Americans to willingly give up freedom and peace in the pursuit of "security." I am grateful to David Congdon for drawing my attention to this scene.

social safety net, deregulating economic markets, and extending capitalist logic to other spheres such as health care and education.

Mandel extends Gollwitzer's analysis of war's role in service of capitalist imperialism by linking it to the military-industrial complex or "arms economy," which is "one of the hallmarks of late capitalism."[107] Conventional warfare functions to renew the market for arms by expending portions of the existing supply. If you keep sending troops out to shoot bullets, toss grenades, launch missiles, and so on, then you necessarily continue to purchase more of those things. The needs of the battlefield also drive technological advances in armament, which requires replacement of materiel that is not directly expended on the battlefield or in training. Gollwitzer observes that the arms economy achieves consumption levels high enough to produce profits "only through exhaustion by limited wars or the need for replacement as technological development creates obsolescence."[108] Today, we see the same dynamics applied to domestic security forces—that is, to police—through their increasing militarization. The arms economy thereby gains a second market for their products, and also often generates a second profit cycle as equipment rendered obsolete on the battlefield finds its way into the hands of law enforcement. This is yet another fulfillment of Gollwitzer's warning that the inhumanity of America's foreign policy would find its way into domestic policy.

Capitalism demands both the threat and use of military force, and armament reliably produces profit, whether through technological development to maintain superiority or through the demands of resupply as a result of actual conflict and preparedness. Furthermore, military buildup provides capital with important leverage for the imperialist exercise of bending the world to its will. As Mandel summarizes matters, "the growth of the 'permanent arms economy' after the Second World War . . . performed . . . the very concrete function of protecting the vast foreign capital investments of the US, of safeguarding the 'free world' for 'free capital investment' and 'free repatriation of profits,' and of guaranteeing US monopoly capital 'free' access to a series of raw materials."[109] War, then, is how capitalism maintains its power both at home by producing profits, and abroad by imposing its economic will. Gollwitzer is right to say that "military armament"

---

107. Mandel, *Late Capitalism*, 274.
108. Gollwitzer, *Rich Christians*, 51.
109. Mandel, *Late Capitalism*, 308. The Iraq War, officially extending from 2003–2011, clearly illustrates this dynamic.

is how "capitalism . . . maintains itself, against attempts to abolish it for its inhumanity and inefficiency."[110] In addition to Gollwitzer's other arguments against Christian support of war in the contemporary world, Christians must oppose war as part of their faithful advocacy for and pursuit of the true socialism of the kingdom of God.

Revolution

Gollwitzer offers some arresting reflections upon "wearing Hitler's uniform" during his time in the *Wehrmacht*. Regardless of his own reservations about and even opposition to the Nazi regime, his position nonetheless entailed benefitting from the privileges of being a member of an occupying military force. This, in turn, meant that people oppressed by this occupying force rightly viewed him "as Hitler's instrument for their oppression."[111] Christians in the global North—and white Christians in the United States, especially—are in a similar position today. They find themselves always already caught up in an insidious capitalist empire, and they receive a considerable amount of privilege on the basis of wearing that empire's uniform, whether literally or metaphorically. They are also understandably distrusted and disliked by the people that empire has marginalized and oppressed, both at home and abroad. This is why Gollwitzer emphasizes so strongly that Christians "do not become salt and light for humanity until we interpret the gospel theologically and practically such that it hurts our privilege."[112] For Christians to renounce their privilege and put it at the service of others necessarily includes working to dismantle the systems that produce and maintain privilege for some and marginalization for others. It means working to overthrow the existing capitalist empire. As Gollwitzer says, "the Christian faith liberates us, our reason and our will, to fight for socialist world revolution."[113] This section examines Gollwitzer's position on revolution in relationship to

---

110. Gollwitzer, *Rich Christians*, 52. Smedley Butler was a US Marine Corps major general who received the Medal of Honor twice. He said this in 1935 when reflecting on his career: "I spent thirty-three years and four months in active military service and during that period I spent most of my time as a high-class muscle man for Big Business, for Wall Street and the bankers. In short, I was a racketeer, a gangster for capitalism." As quoted in Hsiao and Lim, *Verso Book of Dissent*, 158.
111. Gollwitzer, *Demands of Freedom*, 129–30.
112. Helmut Gollwitzer, "Wo kein Dienst ist, da ist Raub," in *Müssen Christen Sozialisten sein? Zwischen Glaube und Politik*, ed. Wolfgang Teichert (Hamburg: Lutherisches Verlagshaus, 1976), 103. Gollwitzer elaborates: "A class system is always a system of oppression. The church's class-bound character means complicity in and benefiting from a system of oppression." Gollwitzer, "Kingdom of God and Socialism," 111.
113. Gollwitzer, "Auf dem Linken," 36–37.

Christianity and in contrast to political reformism before concluding by reflecting on the issue of revolutionary violence.

Christianity and Revolution

Thinking about Christianity as revolutionary is counterintuitive for many people. Eberhard Jüngel expresses the dominant opinion when he says that the church "in no way pleads for a 'theology of revolution.'"[114] For Jüngel, the church does not want a revolutionary theology and is right not to want such a theology. Gollwitzer admits the church's history suggests that it is anti-revolutionary, serving to safeguard the status quo rather than overturn it. Christianity takes on this reactionary character especially as a result of its integration with the Roman Empire, symbolically represented by the Emperor Constantine's reforms in the early fourth century CE. The usual way of telling this story in the Christianity of the global North is to represent this moment as Christianity's triumph over empire, but Gollwitzer reads it differently. Instead of speaking about "the victory of Christianity over paganism," he thinks it better to speak of "the victory of paganism over Christianity." Rather than the church imposing its values upon the Roman Empire, the Roman Empire succeeded in imposing its values upon the church. It did so insofar as "the ruling-classes co-opted the church . . . and used Christianity to sustain what the gospel declaims." For Gollwitzer, the most obvious example of this misuse of the gospel and cooptation of Christianity was "the retention of the institution of slavery."[115] This institution existed formally in ostensibly Christianized societies until approximately 150 years ago, when the Union's victory against the Confederacy in the American Civil War seemed to sound its death knell. Of course, slavery has not actually been eradicated. It continues to persist in many forms, especially human trafficking and what Michelle Alexander calls *The New Jim Crow* structures of mass incarceration.[116]

This history of Christianity's reactionary captivity does not tell the whole story, however. There have been moments when a deeply revolutionary Christianity emerged. It might be tempting to highlight

---

114. Eberhard Jüngel, "Zukunft und Hoffnung: zur politischen Funktion christlicher Theologie," in *Müssen Christen Sozialisten sein? Zwischen Glaube und Politik*, ed. Wolfgang Teichert (Hamburg: Lutherisches Verlagshaus, 1976), 29.
115. Gollwitzer, "Liberation in History," 419.
116. Michelle Alexander, *The New Jim Crow: Mass Incarceration in the Age of Colorblindness*, revised edition (New York: The New Press, 2012).

those minority movements of Christian resistance to privilege, such as nineteenth-century Christian abolitionism in the United States, but this is unnecessary because there is a much more prominent, mainstream example of revolutionary Christianity. If revolution is "a complete transformation of the power structures" in a given society, then Christianity is revolutionary because of its complicity in "the capitalist revolution," a "revolution of the white, Christianized, Protestant peoples" that has achieved "worldwide victory."[117] Christianity is deeply implicated in a revolution that radically redrew the sociopolitical landscape and birthed a modern economic empire at least as pagan in its basic values as was the Roman Empire because both empires worship at the same altar—that of privilege. Indeed, most Christians in the global North do not think of the development and ascendency of capitalism as a revolution because it leaves their privilege intact, as we saw earlier.[118] They generally benefitted both materially and socially from this revolution, and the violent upheaval that went with it for the most part fell upon other peoples elsewhere—on the other side of the world or the other side of the tracks. History shows that Christians are comfortable with revolution as long as they benefit from it. They reject revolution when it threatens their privilege.

Gollwitzer recognizes that rejecting revolutions that undermine one's privileges while accepting revolutions that maintain them is a betrayal of the gospel. In this sense, the gospel is a progressive revolutionary force. Despite all that came later, "the stance of the New Testament in regard to transformation of this world is not conservative, but revolutionary." This claim may appear contradictory insofar as Jesus "did not organize a socio-political revolutionary movement" and the early Christian community never rose in rebellion against the empire as "a kind of Spartacus movement." Nonetheless, the Christian "*message* was *revolutionary* and aimed at a revolutionary change in history."[119] We see this already in the Gospels' testimony to Jesus's preaching of the kingdom of God. This kingdom is not restricted to an interior relationship between the individual and God; rather, it also and necessarily includes consequences for how we organize our lives together, that is, for politics. Gollwitzer highlights the concept of *metanoia*, which

---

117. Gollwitzer, "Liberation in History," 411; Gollwitzer, "Why Black Theology?," 42. Chung has it right: "Gollwitzer characterizes capitalism as the greatest, the most radical revolution and also the most radical secularization that humanity has ever seen." Chung, *Church and Ethical Responsibility*, 237.
118. See Gollwitzer, "Christian in the Search," 55.
119. Gollwitzer, "Liberation in History," 410. See also Gollwitzer's sermon entitled, "God is the Revolutionary": Gollwitzer, *Way to Life*, 55–59.

133

includes connotations of both "repentance" and "conversion": "Jesus' joining of the heralding of God's kingdom with the call to *metanoia* means that the Kingdom of God consists—not only but also—in a new way of life which should and can be proleptically experienced in the now." In other words, one must live in light of "the coming revolution" even now while "under the condition of the old, not yet revolutionized world."[120]

The gospel demands that Christians live revolutionary lives. But they should neither be revolutionary for revolution's sake, nor revolutionary in just any sense of the term. Instead, they should be lives that promote and enact the revolutionary reconstitution of human society as ever more adequate approximations of the kingdom of God's true socialism. This will necessarily include overturning capitalism and all other structures of privilege. In all this, Gollwitzer hews closely to Jesus's dictum that "the last shall be first, and the first shall be last" (Matt 20:16). But if we stop there, we might leave thinking that this revolution simply means the elevation of the oppressed to a position of privilege and the relegation of the privileged to lives of oppression. In other words, that it means a change in *who* the privileged people are while leaving structures of privilege in place. Matthew's Gospel is more radical still: "whoever wishes to be great among you must be your servant, and whoever wishes to be first among you must be your slave; just as the Son of Man came not to be served but to serve" (Matt 20:26–28).[121] This vision of overturning all sociopolitical and religious privilege is a revolutionary rallying cry if ever there was one. A vision of radically egalitarian servitude takes the place of rejected privilege structures in Jesus's proclamation of the revolution of God's kingdom in word and deed, and all those who proclaim that Jesus is Lord must reject them as well.

Revolution vs. Reform

Christianity at its best is a matter of faithful obedience to a revolutionary message, and Christians are called to live revolutionary lives embodying that message. But does this mean Christians must always reject and work outside of the existing structures of society? Is the revolutionary overthrow of privilege structures absolutely antithetical to their gradual reform? James K. A. Smith gives voice to the many

---

120. Gollwitzer, "Liberation in History," 411.
121. See the parallels in Mark 10 and Luke 13.

Christians who would answer this question with a "Yes." Smith, and those he represents, are eager to distance Christianity from revolution even when they also recognize that the sociopolitical status quo desperately needs correction. He offers the category of "reform," and "the antirevolutionary posture of the Reformed tradition" as a third way between support of the status quo and revolution. The middle option of reformism, then, offers Christians the opportunity to be "liberated from revolutionary hubris, even while we are called to—and caught up in—Christ's renewal of all things."[122]

Gollwitzer contests the notion that revolution and reform are necessarily antithetical. It is true that he emphasizes the revolutionary. For instance, he argues that black theology moves the church beyond "the mild liberal reformism" of a "white social ethics" that "no longer makes sense." Consequently, "it invites white theology finally to become revolutionary and thus truly Christian."[123] But getting the relationship between revolution and reform right in Gollwitzer's thought depends on two basic moves—first, there is Gollwitzer's distinction between absolute and relative utopia, which we discussed previously; and, second, we must make a concomitant distinction between revolutionary goals and revolutionary methods.

The true socialism of the kingdom of God as absolute utopia relativizes every possible sociopolitical order and privilege structure. In this way, faithfulness to the kingdom of God necessitates that Christian political engagement aim at revolution, at the overthrow of all privilege structures. This sets the direction and orientation for faithful Christian political engagement—namely, socialist world-revolution. So, revolution is the *goal* of Christian political faithfulness insofar as the true socialism of the kingdom of God is its goal. Is it also necessary for Christians to employ revolutionary *methods* in pursuit of this revolutionary goal? Because the true socialism of the kingdom of God is an absolute utopia that relativizes every possible sociopolitical order, it cannot be identified with any particular socialist political party or policy proposal. As we discussed previously, the Christian task is to

122. James K. A. Smith, "Editorial: Join the Anti-Revolutionary Party," *Comment Magazine* (August 18, 2016), https://www.cardus.ca/comment/article/4919/editorial-join-the-anti-revolutionary-party/. While Smith's characterization of the Reformed tradition as anti-revolutionary unfortunately holds true for significant portions of that tradition, it is not without revolutionary resources. See, for example, Roland Boer, *Political Grace: The Revolutionary Theology of John Calvin* (Louisville, KY: Westminster John Knox Press, 2009).

123. Gollwitzer, "Why Black Theology?," 50. For further commentary on Gollwitzer, reformism, and revolution, see Dannemann and Weissinger, "Helmut Gollwitzers Beitrag zur Theologie der Gesellschaft," 591–92.

carefully determine, to the best of our ability, what political opportunities exist for making concrete social improvements. The revolutionary goal of the kingdom of God's true socialism provides a criterion against which all methods are measured even while it changes our perception about what is possible in any given situation, freeing us from the blinders imposed by the capitalist system.[124] Nevertheless, these pragmatic judgments concerning method are worked out through rational analysis as part of the political process, especially in democratic societies. Consequently, Christians may well choose reformist strategies or methods in order to pursue revolutionary goals.

Revolution and reform are not antithetical when understood in this manner. It is possible for Christians to act faithfully within existing political structures in order to reform those structures and bring them more closely into alignment with the kingdom of God's revolutionary goal. The reverse is also true, however: it is possible for Christians to act faithfully outside existing political structures by contesting and overturning those structures, and paving the way for new structures that more nearly approximate the true socialism of the kingdom of God. To put it more starkly, Christian political faithfulness may well call for revolutionary methods in pursuit of revolutionary goals. The true socialism of the kingdom of God demands that Christians enact revolution against the injustice of privilege structures and, as Gollwitzer notes, whether this revolution is a peaceful and incremental development or involves "violent upheavals" and "irregular force" will depend on the circumstances.

Revolutionary Violence

Revolutionary violence is a complicated subject to which Gollwitzer devoted a great deal of intellectual energy. It is impossible to do him full justice in such a brief treatment. We can gain a functional picture of his position, however, if we reflect on revolutionary violence as counterviolence, as a function of love, with respect to property, and in terms of responsibility.

---

124. See Gollwitzer, *Protestant Theology*, 192. For some suggestions about what steps might be possible in the North American context today, see Erik Olin Wright, *Redesigning Distribution: Basic Income and Stakeholder Grants as Alternative Cornerstones for a More Egalitarian Capitalism*, The Real Utopias Project (New York: Verso, 2006).

Revolutionary Violence as Counterviolence

Our previous discussion of war and capitalism prepared the ground for this observation. Capitalist empire deploys highly refined, insidious, and efficient forms of violence to maintain its privilege and enforce its will both at home in the global North and abroad in the global South. The violence of empire, very often legally sanctioned by various national and international political organizations, provides the pre-existing context within which any instance of revolutionary violence arises. Indeed, empire necessarily produces counterviolence. Michael Hardt and Antonio Negri make this point well in their analysis of empire. Here, the term "colonialism" describes a particular imperial mode: "the original moment of violence is that of colonialism: the domination and exploitation of the colonized by the colonizer. The second moment [is] the response of the colonized to this original violence. . . . Colonialism by its very operation perpetuates this violence."[125] Indeed, the basic dynamics of the capitalist system are inherently violent and dehumanizing, reducing the human beings that serve the system to disposable parts and condemning them to lives filled with anxiety. As Chung puts it, "capital threatens the workers with death, while guaranteeing the life only of those workers necessary for its own life processes."[126] This ruthlessness holds as much for those who own the means of producing wealth as much as it does anyone else. While the capitalist system itself is remarkably resilient, it is not concerned about any particular industrial giant, corporate executive, or business owner.

Gollwitzer makes this point by expanding the context further. The liberal tradition offers an optimistic picture of history's progress as a movement away from violent barbarity toward ever greater civilization. Such a view is often associated with the famous quote, which goes back at least as far as Martin Luther King Jr. and has again become popular in recent years: "the arc of the moral universe is long, but it bends toward justice."[127] As comforting as this sentiment can be, it is not true. "Human history is the history of violence. . . . [A]ll present societies are sustained by violence, by the threat and use of increasingly perfectionized, terrifying means of violence" including "torture . . . and the horrors of modern military technology."[128] This does not

125. Michael Hardt and Antonio Negri, *Empire* (Cambridge, MA: Harvard University Press, 2000), 131.
126. Chung, *Church and Ethical Responsibility*, 140. It is truly the case that, as an internet meme popular among the American left has put it, everything we feared about communism has come true under capitalism.
127. Martin Luther King Jr., "Out of the Long Night," *The Gospel Messenger* 107, no. 6 (1958): 14.

mean that the struggle for progress is utterly hopeless. While there can be no generic faith in progress, for Gollwitzer, there is still faith in the God whom Christians encounter in eventful Thou-objectivity. Belief in progress counts for nothing; "what counts is fighting for progress without believing in it."[129]

Fighting for progress is a struggle against what is always already an inherently violent sociopolitical and economic order. Martin Luther King Jr. is again a helpful touchstone for the North American context because he understood this point well. In his famous "Letter from Birmingham City Jail," King addresses members of the clergy who had written against the civil rights demonstrations with which King was involved. He writes:

> you deplore the demonstrations that are presenting taking place in Birmingham. But I am sorry that your statement did not express a similar concern for the conditions that brought the demonstrations into being. . . . I would not hesitate to say that it is unfortunate that so-called demonstrations are taking place in Birmingham at this time, but I would say in more emphatic terms that it is even more unfortunate that the white power structure of this city left the Negro community with no other alternative.[130]

Any social disruption or revolutionary violence undertaken by oppressed peoples never occurs in a vacuum. It has precipitating causes, and it cannot be properly understood or evaluated except in relation to those causes. As King said elsewhere, "a riot is the language of the unheard."[131]

Gollwitzer viewed the use of force as problematic in the revolutionary context. Those who would undertake a revolutionary program must recognize "the contradiction between their goal" of "a better, more humane, freer order" and the "method of violence."[132] Furthermore, there is no way of eradicating this contradiction. It remains a sign and a symptom of the world's sinful disorder. And it is this greater disorder that finally makes the use of revolutionary violence possible in exceptional situations where it has become necessary to oppose a

no clear words

---

128. Gollwitzer, "Why Black Theology?," 57.
129. Gollwitzer, "Liberation in History," 419.
130. Martin Luther King Jr., "Letter from Birmingham City Jail," in *A Testament of Hope: The Essential Writings and Speeches of Martin Luther King, Jr.*, ed. James Melvin Washington (New York: HarperOne, 1986), 290.
131. From Mike Wallace's September 27, 1966 interview with Martin Luther King Jr. for CBS Reports: http://www.cbsnews.com/news/mlk-a-riot-is-the-language-of-the-unheard/.
132. Gollwitzer, "Revolution des Reiches Gottes," thesis 8.18, p. 128.

"system which creates and perpetuates injustice and misery." Revolutionary violence is always counterviolence, occurring against the backdrop of violence wielded in the service of capitalist empire. We are unavoidably involved in the perpetuation of violence, whether we like it or not. So "if force *is* to be used, then it can sooner be justified where it is applied to shattering unjust oppressive force than to maintaining it. It is better that the decision to use force should stem from pity for the disenfranchisement and humiliation of men, rather than from obedience to the commands of the powers that be."[133]

Revolutionary Violence as a Function of Love

The contradiction between the goal of revolution and the means of revolutionary violence is not an absolute contradiction when deploying revolutionary violence in the service of love and justice. "Love stands in contrast neither to justice nor to violence. The manufacture of earthly justice is a mode of its realization, and violence is a means of its realization."[134] This stands in continuity with Gollwitzer's reflections on self-defense, which we encountered in our discussion of pacifism above, while also extending those reflections. Self-defense is a selfish and therefore inadequate justification for the use of violence when we consider self-defense as a merely interpersonal issue. However, matters are more complicated when viewing self-defense in the context of violence perpetuated by a system of oppressive socioeconomic and political structures. The line blurs here between selfishly motivated self-defense and defense of the neighbor, motivated by love. Resisting violence against oneself by seeking to overthrow the violent system includes resisting that system's violence against the neighbor. Furthermore, willingly suffering the violence of such systems can serve the system's own interests.[135] Strategies of nonviolent protest, then, are not always the most appropriate or effective. While the pragmatics of particular revolutionary situations may dictate that nonviolent tac-

---

133. Gollwitzer, *Rich Christians*, 61–62. Paul Lehman writes, "there is *systemic violence* and there is a *counterviolence*; and in the dynamics of the relation between power and violence, *counterviolence* is *revolutionary* violence and *systemic* violence is *counterrevolutionary*." Paul L. Lehmann, *The Transfiguration of Politics* (New York: Harper & Row, 1975), 264.

134. Helmut Gollwitzer, "Einige Leitsätze zur christlichen Beteiligung am politischen Leben," in *Forderungen der Umkehr: Beiträge zur Theologie der Gesellschaft* (Munich: Chr. Kaiser, 1976), thesis 5, p. 15. The statement issued by the World Mission Assembly in Bangkok (1972–73) includes the compelling line: "love also involves the right to resistance." As quoted in Jürgen Moltmann, *A Broad Place: An Autobiography* (Minneapolis, MN: Fortress Press, 2009), 175.

135. Schüssler Fiorenza, *Jesus*, 102.

tics will be most effective, Gollwitzer denies that "non-violence in principle" is incumbent upon either Christians or socialists.[136]

Gollwitzer allows for the possibility that there are certain circumstances under which the use of revolutionary violence is justified. But how are we to identify those circumstances? There is a clear analogy here with the question of war. In that context, the just war tradition establishes criteria to help in determining when the use of military violence is justified, and Gollwitzer believes that the same logic applies to revolutionary violence. "If there are few just wars, there are probably just as few just revolutions. . . . But if there are any just wars, then there are also some just revolutions."[137] What then are the criteria of a just revolution? Translating from the just war tradition, Gollwitzer provides six criteria.[138] A just revolution: (a) must aim to overthrow an oppressive power. Furthermore, the decision to undertake a revolutionary program (b) must result from careful consideration of the evil involved, and this analysis must show that there are no other possible means of redress—in other words, the revolution is unavoidable and thus inevitable. This inevitable revolution (c) will not employ means of indiscriminate killing or produce unnecessary suffering. The issue of terrorism, which Gollwitzer calls the "special problem of revolutionary violence," is ingredient here.[139] Gollwitzer engaged extensively with the issue of terrorism in connection with the student protests of the late 1960s, as well as meeting and corresponding with members of the terrorist Baader-Meinhof Gang. He recognized that revolutionary terrorism was produced by the terrorism perpetuated by the state, but he nonetheless rejected terrorism as a justifiable revolutionary tactic. Terrorism necessarily brutalizes and dehumanizes and, therefore, stands in absolute contradiction to the proper revolutionary goals. In

---

136. Helmut Gollwitzer, "Sozialismus und Revolution," in *Umkehr und Revolution: Aufsätze zu christlichem Glauben und Marxismus*, Band 1, ed. Christian Keller, Ausgewählte Werke (München: Chr. Kaiser, 1988), 140.

137. Gollwitzer, *Rich Christians*, 62. Relevant here are Ted Smith's reflections on "divine violence" as a disruptive force that "break[s] the grip of dominant orders to open up a space for genuinely free response, a space in which practical reasoning about public goods can be developed and refined in conversation" precisely by challenging the claims of the state and other institutions to "sovereign violence." Ted A. Smith, *Weird John Brown: Divine Violence and the Limits of Ethics*, Encountering Traditions (Stanford, CA: Stanford University Press, 2015), 13.

138. For the criteria, see Gollwitzer, "Sozialismus und Revolution," 168. I have reordered the criteria to suit the logic of my presentation. See also Lepp, "Helmut Gollwitzer als Dialogpartner," 233. For further engagement with this subject, see Anna Floerke Scheid, *Just Revolution: A Christian Ethic of Political Resistance and Social Transformation* (Lanham, MD: Lexington Books, 2015).

139. Gollwitzer, "Sozialismus und Revolution," 139. For historical context, see Lepp, "Helmut Gollwitzer als Dialogpartner," 236–37. For a more recent theopolitical examination of torture, see George Hunsinger, ed. *Torture Is a Moral Issue: Christians, Jews, Muslims and People of Conscience Speak Out* (Grand Rapids, MI: Eerdmans, 2008).

other words, terrorism is incapable of serving love and establishing justice. A just revolution rejects terrorism because (d) it is not motivated by a desire for revenge.

The two final criteria have special bearing on the contemporary situation in the United States. A revolution is just when: (e) it maintains the rights of the oppressed, and (f) when it is a judgment shared by a community, rather than the conclusion of a single individual. These criteria constitute a particular warning to those of us who represent Christianity's dominant form in the global North—white, bourgeois, cisgender males. They remind us that we cannot speak for the oppressed and make judgments for them. The practical decision for revolution, and the evaluation of whether or not that revolution is justified, must be left to those who suffer most under the injustice of the status quo, who are subjected to the bulk of the system's violence, and who are most dehumanized by the system's values. In the United States today, the Black Lives Matter movement is a prominent example of an oppressed community that is challenging the violence of a system that oppresses them.[140] This movement has been met with the disdain, distrust, or disinterest of the majority of white Americans who would call themselves Christians. But those of us who benefit from the system both socially and materially, or whose oppression by that system takes less obviously violent and dehumanizing forms, are not the moral arbiters of revolution. For privileged Christians, being called to proclaim and embody the true socialism of the kingdom of God means being called to a radical praxis of solidarity with the well and truly oppressed. This solidarity necessarily includes dialogue and even disagreement, but it cannot include paternalism! Anything less than this solidarity fundamentally betrays the gospel.

---

140. The Black Lives Matter movement has no central committee or other formal unifying structure. Reliable orientations to the movement can be found from the following three sources: Black Lives Matter (http://blacklivesmatter.com/guiding-principles/), The Movement for Black Lives (https://policy.m4bl.org/about/), and Campaign Zero (http://www.joincampaignzero.org/#vision). Keeanga-Yamahtta Taylor connects the dots between this movement and the prevailing capitalist order: "Racism in the United States has never been just about abusing Black and Brown people just for the sake of doing so. It has always been a means by which the most powerful white men in the country have justified their rule, made their money, and kept the rest of us at bay. To that end, racism, capitalism, and class rule have always been tangled together. . . . Can there be Black liberation in the United States as the country is currently constituted? No. Capitalism is contingent on the absence of freedom and liberation for Black people and anyone else who does not directly benefit from its economic order." Keeanga-Yamahtta Taylor, *From #BlackLivesMatter to Black Liberation* (Chicago: Haymarket, 2016), 216.

Revolutionary Violence and Property

Upon hearing the words "revolutionary violence," most people will conjure up mental pictures of guillotines, guerrillas, and gulags. It is true that revolutionary violence can encompass these and other forms of violence against people, just as war includes many forms of violence against people. But like war, revolutionary violence can also involve violence against property. Gollwitzer articulated the distinction between violence against people and violence against property in connection with the Berlin student protests in the late 1960s. Some of those protests involved destruction of property.

Gollwitzer tried to help the students think through these events. Violence against property is less serious than violence against people, both legally and morally.[141] In this sense, the students were less morally compromised than the reactionary forces who triggered the "Easter Riots" by trying to assassinate Rudi Dutschke, one of the most prominent student leaders and a friend of Gollwitzer's. However, the violence against property that the students perpetuated was strategically ill-advised. This violence made it much more difficult for the public to recognize the students' "justified demands."[142] Furthermore, violence against property can very easily become violence against people. Gollwitzer mentions students throwing stones in this connection and advises that the worst thing they can do—strategically speaking—is use violence against the police, even if used in self-defense. These cautions are offered in the spirit of avuncular advice and aimed at helping the student protesters be as effective as possible in their particular context. Gollwitzer deeply sympathizes with them. He knows that they act out of deep-seated rebellion against the violence of the world in which they live. This is what most of the older generation cannot understand about the student protests. Because they do not see the violence embedded in the status quo as clearly as do the students, the older generation feels justified in complaining against the violence used by the students and in applauding the violence that the police used against the students. But the students perform a valuable service in dragging this clandestine violence into the light because society as a whole must reject this violence in order to preserve democracy.[143]

141. Helmut Gollwitzer, "Zur Frage der Gewalt hier und heute." In ...daß Gerechtigkeit und Friede sich küssen: Aufsätz zur politishen Ethik, Band 2, ed. Andreas Pangritz, Ausgewählte Werke (München: Chr. Kaiser, 1988), 168. Gollwitzer provides some historical context in the course of his remarks. See also Lepp, "Helmut Gollwitzer als Dialogpartner," 234.
142. Gollwitzer, "Zur Frage der Gewalt," 169.

Revolutionary violence against property is also a pressing issue today in the United States. Instances of such violence have occurred in recent years as part of protests associated with the Occupy Wall Street and Black Lives Matter movements (although those movements consistently advocate nonviolence and disavow instances of violence against property), protests against the Dakota Access Pipeline at Standing Rock Indian Reservation, and other *ad hoc* protests. It may be that violence against property is the most effective kind of counterviolence for drawing into the open the structures of violence that reside at the necrotic heart of the capitalist system. That system uses violence precisely in order to defend property and the privilege entailed by ownership of the means of producing wealth. Consequently, violence against property powerfully symbolizes revolutionary rejection of that system's legitimacy.

The truth of the matter has been demonstrated by police response to these protests. Regardless of whether violence against property actually occurred, our increasingly militarized domestic security forces responded to these protests by enacting a great deal of violence. Any claim that this response was motivated by concern, lest the protests produce violence against people, is belied by the willingness of the police to perpetuate violence against the persons of protestors, and even of journalists documenting the protests. Furthermore, the restraint shown by security forces when Cliven Bundy and his accomplices occupied federal buildings at the Malheur Wildlife Refuge in Oregon further demonstrates that the true concern is to protect property. While restraint in the Bundy case was certainly caused, in part, by other factors—such as Bundy and his accomplices being armed and white—it is nonetheless instructive that the imperial capitalist status quo does not hesitate to unleash violence when its will is thwarted or its privilege threatened, but it can be patient with those forms of protest that do not reject the system as a whole.

Perhaps the most dispiriting feature of these recent events is how they have revealed the extent to which the church still lives in "class-bondage," as Gollwitzer would say. One incident that occurred during the 2014 protests in Ferguson, Missouri stands out in my mind. These protests were sparked by the death of Michael Brown and the decision not to indict Darren Wilson, the officer who shot Brown. The Presbyterian Church (U.S.A.) congregation to which I belong is located

---

143. Ibid., 170.

approximately twenty miles from Ferguson. I will never forget the Sunday morning when I heard one of the pillars of this congregation express his willingness to use deadly force against protestors, should he feel it necessary to do so, in order to protect his property.

All of this is deeply disingenuous, of course. After all, one of the great founding myths of the United States—the Boston Tea Party—is quite literally a textbook example of revolutionary violence against property. The difference, of course, is that this instance of violence against property has become part of the legitimization of the United States' privilege system. One of the most useful privileges of the dominant class is their ability to shape the (hi)stories we tell.

Revolutionary Violence and Responsibility

In concluding this examination of what Gollwitzer has to teach us about revolutionary violence, we must address the question of who bears the responsibility for revolutionary violence when it occurs. The answer to this question that most readily occurs to most people who live within and benefit from the sociopolitical and economic status quo is that only the people who directly perpetuate revolutionary violence are responsible for it. Matters are complicated considerably, however, by recognizing that all revolutionary violence is counterviolence. It does not arise *ex nihilo* (out of nothing), but occurs in response to the violence inherent in the system. While those who perpetuate revolutionary violence remain very much responsible for it, it is also true that the imperial capitalist system as a whole, as well as everyone who lives within and benefits from it, also bears a measure of responsibility. Furthermore, the risk involved in revolutionary violence means that it is always an act of last resort when other options have failed. In other words, revolutionary violence only occurs when oppressors have refused to acknowledge the claims of the oppressed. Everything finally depends on whether and to what extent the powers that be are willing to perpetuate the violence of the system by using force to suppress reformist demands that changes be made to that system. Those who dread the prospect of revolutionary violence—and all true Christians should dread any and all violence: possible and actual; interpersonal and systemic; revolutionary, reactionary, police, and military—must grapple morally with those who hold and defend privilege, rather than with those who struggle to break down the "dividing wall[s]" (Eph 2:14) of that privilege. We must ponder Gollwitzer's statement carefully: "violence brutalizes, even though the oppressed cannot avoid it in their struggle. Limiting violence to a last resort and humanizing the methods of violence as much as possible are in the interest of the revolutionary movement, not only for reasons of expedience, but for retention of the humane freedom-loving character of the movement itself."[144]

Conclusion

Gollwitzer's engagement with the political issues of his day was both deep and extensive. It was also decisively shaped by his commitment to democratic socialism, which depended in turn on his theological commitment to the true socialism of the kingdom of God that flows from the encounter with God's Thou-objectivity in the event of faith. The absolute utopia of this eschatological kingdom of God sets the direction and orientation of Christian political faithfulness, radically calling into question all socioeconomic, political, and religious privilege. It frees Christians to engage in true social analysis and, especially, to learn from socialist and Marxist analysis, in order to identify political steps that are both necessary and possible in any given political moment as they work to nudge society toward ever nearer approximation of God's kingdom. For Gollwitzer, this analysis entailed reckoning with the quantitative and qualitative failures of traditional Christian approaches to charity, as well as with issues pertaining to war and revolutionary violence.

It is difficult to overestimate the importance of social analysis in Gollwitzer's thought and, especially, of the socialist tradition of analysis. This comes out most explicitly in a set of theses that Gollwitzer composed entitled "Theological Study and Socialist Study," in which he briefly recapitulates the pattern of his thought that we have explicated over the last two chapters. In those theses, Gollwitzer defines Christian theology as "rational thinking about the Christian faith in engagement with all contemporary trends and problems" that "occurs in service of the Christian church's task, which is to pass on the gospel to the whole world and witness to it in word and deed." Furthermore, "the core of the gospel is the message that this world and every person is not alone, that they do not live out of themselves" but "are instead borne by the love of God . . . who stands against humanity's plight and promises to overcome it." But what exactly is humanity's plight? Gollwitzer does

144. Gollwitzer, "Why Black Theology?," 57–58.

not deny that this plight (sin) is an internal matter between the individual and God. However, he insists that it is also an external matter that bears upon relationships between people and how we structure those relationships in society. Christians are those whom God has "mobilized to fight against humanity's plight" in both its internal and external aspects.[145] Theology, then, must engage with both the internal and external dimensions, and how those dimensions predispose us—in both explicit and implicit ways—to lives of self-interest rather than love of God and neighbor. In other words, theology must address "the question of the social tendency of the gospel and of today's possibilities for implementing this tendency, which is therefore the question of today's possibilities for implementing socialism."[146] Gollwitzer draws an important conclusion from this: "theological study today is more than a socialist study, but it is also a socialist study." It is impossible to do faithful theological work in the contemporary world without engaging with and in socialist analysis of our society and its structural depth-grammar. We can only hope that institutions of theological education in the United States will recognize Gollwitzer's wisdom on this subject, and the sooner the better.

Theological commitment to the true socialism of the kingdom of God and engagement with socialist analysis of capitalist social structures, which are antithetical to that kingdom, coalesce in Gollwitzer's thought to make the fundamental point that Christians *must take sides* on political issues, and they must take the side *of the oppressed*. Many of those Americans today who think of themselves as Christians feel very uncomfortable when faced with this demand. As Gollwitzer correctly notes, however, taking sides "sounds terrifying only to him who is blind to the fact that the empirical church has actually always taken sides."[147] Christians have, by and large, sided with the status quo. But the gospel's call to repentant conversion—to *metanoia*—"reaches into the politico-social dimension," and "as long as we shrink from revolutionizing [that dimension], we have not really heard" the gospel's call.[148] That is, we have not encountered the God who loves justice, and who is consequently served through the pursuit of political love.

145. Helmut Gollwitzer, "Theologie-Studium und sozialistisches Studium," in *Umkehr und Revolution: Aufsätze zu christlichem Glauben und Marxismus*, Band 2, ed. Christian Keller, Ausgewählte Werke (München: Chr. Kaiser, 1988), 241.
146. Ibid., 242.
147. Gollwitzer, "Why Black Theology?," 50. See Gollwitzer, *Protestant Theology*, 190.
148. Gollwitzer, "Why Black Theology?," 51.

5

———

Church and Confession

This volume's aim has been to bring Helmut Gollwitzer's life and thought to the attention of the church in North America, and especially to white Christians in the United States. Chapter 1's introduction reflected on why we should attend to Gollwitzer today. Capitalism and Christianity, especially Protestantism, in the United States have developed a deeply symbiotic relationship that has become stronger in correlation with the neoliberal turn of the past few decades. But there are also signs that the stigma that has long been attached to socialism is now lifting, and that some Americans are becoming increasingly aware of deeply unjust structures of economic inequality embedded both in our society and around the world. These are precisely the issues that Gollwitzer grappled with fifty years ago, and he did so in deep conversation with traditional theological questions.

Gollwitzer's work at the intersection of theological and political issues was decisively shaped by his biography. He lived through some of the most tumultuous times in recent European history, and he was in the eye of those storms. Chapter two sketched Gollwitzer's life and intellectual influences—from his horizon-broadening *Gymnasium* experience, to his time as Karl Barth's student, to pastoring a radical Confessing Church congregation resulting in being silenced and expelled from Berlin, to being drafted and serving in the German military, to spending five years as a prisoner of war in Soviet Russia, to becoming a leading public intellectual and noted Christian advocate of socialism in West Germany. Gollwitzer's life was full of challenges, but also marked by grace upon grace.

Against the backdrop of this biography, chapter 3 burrowed into the logic of Gollwitzer's political theology. He appropriates and further develops the heritage of dialectical theology's emphasis on God's nonobjectifiability. Although God cannot be treated as generally accessible, like any other object in the world, this does not mean that God lacks objectivity. However, God's objectivity—the true otherness of God's reality—is accessible only through encounter with God in the event of faith. Gollwitzer designates the reality of God's otherness in this event as God's "Thou-objectivity." Because we only encounter God's Thou-objectivity in the event of faith, it follows that there can be no timeless speech of God that somehow holds true, apart from the ever new occurrence of this event. All theology is contextual theology. Furthermore, the event of encounter with God happens to human beings who are always already caught up in the struggle of negotiating life together, that is, in politics. Which means that all theology is political theology. For Gollwitzer, furthermore, it must be *liberating* political theology because encounter with the Thou-objectivity of the transcendent, "wholly other" casts down all hierarchies of privilege, whether religious, social, economic, or political. Christians are called to bear political witness to the God they have encountered—a God of peace, justice, mercy, and ultimately, of love.

Gollwitzer's theological politics is an exercise in thinking through what it means to bear political witness to this God of love, that is, of making the concept of political love concrete. Chapter 4 examined three aspects of Gollwitzer's political engagement. First, it traced the development of Gollwitzer's democratic socialism and examined the logic of his position. Traditional charity is both quantitatively and qualitatively incapable of redressing the fundamental economic injustice that resides at the necrotic heart of capitalism, and the gospel calls Christians to a radical renunciation of the privilege structures that capitalism produces and maintains. The transcendent socialism of the kingdom of God dictates that Christians *must* be socialists, that is, they must pursue the goal of transforming society into an ever nearer approximation of God's kingdom. They do this through the use of reason in discerning which political parties and policy proposals will bring concrete improvement in material conditions for those who are marginalized and oppressed. Second, political love pertains to Gollwitzer's renunciation of atomic war and his conviction that the advent of nuclear weapons falsifies the logic that governs traditional criteria for a just war. Furthermore, war has become a weapon wielded by capitalist empire to enforce its hegemony, which Christians must resist. All this notwithstanding, Gollwitzer does not believe that Christians are bound to a principled or absolute pacifism. There are times when justice and love demand the use of force. Third, justice and love may demand the use of force for revolutionary purposes. Gollwitzer argues that Christianity is not reformist to the exclusion of being revolutionary. Rather, Christianity's goals are always revolutionary, even if it sometimes employs reformist methods. Revolutionary methods—including revolutionary violence—are also legitimate under the right conditions, however, and Gollwitzer develops criteria for identifying a just revolution.

That brings us to the present chapter, which concludes our study of Gollwitzer. Before drawing things to a close, however, we will address an aspect of Gollwitzer's thought that has been present implicitly throughout the study but has not been brought into the open—namely, his doctrine of the church. Gollwitzer's doctrine of the church stands opposed to the contemporary nostalgia for Christendom that one so often finds in treatments of that doctrine. Furthermore, examining Gollwitzer's doctrine of the church provides an opportunity to recapitulate in a new and particularly relevant key much of what we have already discovered. After discussing Gollwitzer's ecclesiology I will offer some final reflections on his significance for the challenges facing the church in North America.

A Dangerous Church

At multiple points throughout this study, we have seen Gollwitzer excoriate the church for its role in supporting and legitimizing society's privilege structures that create and maintain injustice. This is perhaps clearest with reference to his thinking about reform and revolution in Christianity's history, and his persistent reference to the church's bourgeois class-bondage—that is to say, its "complicity in and benefiting from a system of oppression."[1] Gollwitzer is thoroughly dissatisfied with a domesticated church such as this.

His dissatisfaction stretches at least as far back as his time as Martin

---

1. Helmut Gollwitzer, "Kingdom of God and Socialism in the Theology of Karl Barth," in *Karl Barth and Radical Politics*, ed. George Hunsinger (Philadelphia: Westminster Press, 1976), 111.

Niemöller's replacement in Dahlem in the late 1930s, which we discussed in chapter 2. Gollwitzer felt increasing pressure from the Nazi regime as that decade came to a close. This resulted in his silencing and expulsion from Berlin shortly before he was conscripted into the German armed forces. Such was the backdrop for a series of sermons that Gollwitzer preached on the passion narrative in the Gospel of Luke. One of those sermons addresses the story of the women finding Jesus's tomb empty, encountering the angelic messenger, and relaying the story to Jesus's disciples (Luke 24:1–12). Gollwitzer looks into the backstory, pointing out that even before the resurrection event, there seems to have been a church present "to which the first Resurrection message could come."[2] But what held this church together? Loyalty to tradition, to the cause, to friends and comrades? These sorts of ties do bind together numerous earthly-historical communities, Gollwitzer reflects, and even many Christian congregations. "This is all quite good in its way," he admits, "but at bottom it does not mean anything; it has no power." What is more, the social authorities and powers of the day seemed to agree with this assessment insofar as they were not particularly concerned with applying pressure to those who had been associated with Jesus. They "were quite right in thinking that this community, which was held together only by a little loyalty and tradition, was not worth the trouble of a proper persecution."[3]

A church that merely exists as a community in the world, held together by the same dynamics and relationships that hold together the Rotary Club or the Daughters of the American Revolution, is a church in name only. To quote St. Paul, it is "having a form of godliness, but denying the power thereof" (2 Tim 3:5, KJV). What overcomes this ecclesiastical banality is encounter with the church's resurrected Lord, with "the Easter story [that] broke into our world, bringing with it a power, a world-overcoming revolution, which makes everything different in our life, which forces the Church into a totally different direction." This encounter delegitimizes the church's banality and demands that the church become an agent in proclaiming this world-overcoming revolution through word and deed. Instead of leaving the church to its comfortable domestication, "the one thing that matters for the church is that she should be both a danger and a help to the world."[4]

2. Helmut Gollwitzer, The Dying and Living Lord (Philadelphia: Muhlenberg Press, 1960), 92.
3. Ibid., 93.
4. Ibid., 95. Friedrich-Wilhelm Marquardt describes Gollwitzer as a member of "the true church, which sustains a contradiction to all domesticated ecclesiasticism forever. The true church lives not for its own sake. But if she really lives 'for the world,' that usually means in conflict against it."

Gollwitzer's ecclesiology calls for a dangerous church because a church that is not dangerous is no help at all.

Christendom Continued

Unfortunately, contemporary work on the doctrine of the church serves to perpetuate its domestication. The story that Gollwitzer tells—about the church's accommodation to existing social injustice and the structures that create and perpetuate it—continues today and expresses itself in what Dennis Doyle calls "a kind of selective nostalgia for the sense of unity, identity, [and] loyalty" that previously bound together Western culture; nostalgia, that is, for Christendom.[5]

Christendom refers to the state of affairs that obtained in Western society for more than a millennium. It is sometimes traced symbolically to Emperor Constantine's inclusion of the church within the Roman Empire's social structures, for which reason, the term "Constantinianism" is synonymous with Christendom. The basic dynamic at the core of Christendom is the fundamental overlap between civic and religious identity. Under Christendom, one is a Christian just because one is a citizen and it is hard to believe that those who are not Christians are citizens. While such conditions make it possible for the church to seemingly exert a great deal of influence over society, it also domesticates the church insofar as it subtly yet inexorably assimilates the church's values to those of the broader society. At the very least, it leads to interpreting and emphasizing certain of the church's values that align with society's values while neglecting those that contradict society's values. As we had reason to note in chapter 4, Gollwitzer speaks of this event as "the victory of paganism over Christianity," rather than as "the victory of Christianity over paganism."[6] One prime example of this in our own day is how large segments of the church in North America are very concerned with questions of sexual orientation and activity, but pay very little attention to greed, especially as embedded in our society's privilege structures.

Because Western societies have become much more religiously and ethnically diverse, especially since the middle of the twentieth cen-

Friedrich-Wilhelm Marquardt, "Helmut Gollwitzer: Weg und Werk," in *Bibliographie Helmut Gollwitzer*, ed. Christa Haehn, Ausgewählte Werke (München: Chr. Kaiser, 1988), 48.
5. Dennis M. Doyle, *Communion Ecclesiology: Vision and Versions* (Maryknoll, NY: Orbis Books, 2000), 171. Doyle refers especially to nostalgia for Catholicism prior to the Second Vatican Council (1962–65), but the point holds with reference to Christendom as a whole since that council was, in many ways, Catholicism's attempt to reckon with Christendom's dissolution.
6. Helmut Gollwitzer, "Liberation in History," *Interpretation* 28, no. 4 (1974): 419.

151

tury, Christendom can no longer be taken for granted today as it has been in the past. Dissolution of Christendom produces the sort of nostalgia that Doyle identifies, however, especially among the religious and ethnic demographics who benefitted from that previous sociore-ligious order. Thomas Oden's work, discussed in chapter 1, advertises a hankering for Christendom among North American evangelicals, and many of the most surprising political developments of 2016 seem to have been motivated—at least in part—by desire for those halcyon days. Nostalgia for Christendom has also become a central feature in contemporary doctrines of the church, which emphasize the sort of earthly-historical dynamics that Gollwitzer argues ultimately domesti-cate the church.

These ecclesiologies often take their cues from George Lindbeck's "cultural-linguistic" model for understanding how doctrine functions in the Christian community.[7] In this account, Christian talk of God establishes a linguistic world distinct from other linguistic worlds on offer. When this Christian linguistic world is constituted by a set of distinctly Christian practices—especially the sacraments, but often, an idealized, traditional liturgical imagination as a whole—the result is an account of church-as-culture. As Lindbeck says, religious communities "are likely to be practically relevant in the long run" insofar as they "concentrate on their own intratextual outlooks and forms of life," that is, on their own cultures. Because it must carry the weight of Christian identity and significance, there are aspects of this culture that cannot be translated into other cultural-linguistic matrices. Conversion to Christianity means becoming adept at negotiating the church's cultural-linguistic world, according to these ecclesiologies. This is why Lindbeck highlights ancient catechetical practices as particularly relevant; they represent an extended, intensive program aimed at teaching

7. George A. Lindbeck, *The Nature of Doctrine: Religion and Theology in a Postliberal Age* (Louisville, KY: Westminster John Knox Press, 1984), 32–41. For a more extensive treatment, see David W. Congdon, *The God Who Saves: A Dogmatic Sketch* (Eugene, OR: Cascade, 2016), 159–77. James K. A. Smith has lately offered an evangelical-Reformed approach to the church-as-culture model by empha-sizing how traditional Christian liturgy functions to shape imagination, desire, and worldview as a counterpoint to various secular liturgies embedded in Western society. James K. A. Smith, *Desiring the Kingdom: Worship, Worldview, and Cultural Formation*, Cultural Liturgies (Grand Rapids, MI: Baker Academic, 2009). Janice Rees offers a trenchant criticism of Smith's volume that is relevant to the present discussion: "Smith never seems to ask the obvious question: 'what if Christian liturgies de-form people'? What if the patterns of worship experienced in the church do not simply pro-vide a counter-liturgy, but rather act as [a] mirror in which culture and church both mirror the [ideological] de-formations of the present age?" Janice Rees, "Resisting the Kingdom: Women in the Gym, Theological Optimism, and the Liturgical Deformation of Inclusion," *Women in Theology* (October 23, 2013): https://womenintheology.org/2013/10/23/resisting-the-kingdom-women-in-the-gym-theological-optimism-and-the-liturgical-deformation-of-inclusion/.

"the language and practices of [Christianity] to potential adherents," which "has been the primary way of transmitting the faith and winning converts . . . down through the centuries."[8] Furthermore, Lindbeck theologically situates this approach to the doctrine of the church by appealing to the example of Israel in the Old Testament. Indeed, "the Church's story" is "continuous with Israel's" and produces a picture of the church that "is more Jewish than anything else." Whether speaking of the church or Israel, "the people of God consists of cultural-linguistic groupings that can be meaningfully identified by ordinary sociological and historical criteria." The church, like Israel, is "a people."[9]

Here is a sterling example of what Gollwitzer rejects as the domestication of a church that is bound together by earthly-historical considerations. The same dynamic is widespread in ecumenical work on the doctrine of the church, which is characterized by the communion ecclesiology model. This model is prevalent especially among Catholic theologians, although there are notable Protestant articulations as well. Doyle provides a thorough examination of this ecclesiological tradition, going back to Johann Adam Möhler and Friedrich Schleiermacher, and working up through the Second Vatican Council to today. This survey of diverse instances of communion ecclesiology funds Doyle's articulation of "five touchstones" that characterize this model and provide a framework for its further development—communion ecclesiology is *divine* insofar as it has to do with a basic Christian communion with God; it is *mystical* insofar as it encompasses the Body of Christ and Communion of the Saints; it is *sacramental* insofar as it sees the church as a sacrament of communion with God and other Christians; it is *historical* insofar as the church refers to the People of God as their relationship with God is extended through time; and it is *social*

---

8. Lindbeck, *Nature of Doctrine*, 128, 132. John Flett examines this dynamic in Robert Jenson's ecclesiology: John G. Flett, *Apostolicity: The Ecumenical Question in World Christian Perspective*, Missiological Engagements (Downers Grove, IL: IVP Academic, 2016), 115–23. Christine Helmer correctly recognizes that the logic of Lindbeck's position reduces Christianity to a worldview, which means that "conversion is the necessary cause of a dramatic entrance into the Christian worldview." As a result, "God is encased within the notion of a worldview." Christine Helmer, *Theology and the End of Doctrine* (Louisville, KY: Westminster John Knox, 2014), 103–4. As David Congdon rightly notes, dialectical theology rejects such a position: "the eschatological mission of God opposes every worldview, and especially those that claim to be 'Christian.'" David W. Congdon, *The Mission of Demythologizing: Rudolf Bultmann's Dialectical Theology* (Minneapolis, MN: Fortress Press, 2015), 400; see 388–403. See also David W. Congdon, "Demystifying the Program of Demythologizing: Rudolf Bultmann's Theological Hermeneutics," *Harvard Theological Review* 110, no. 1 (2017): esp. 8–11.

9. George A. Lindbeck, "The Church," in *The Church in a Postliberal Age*, ed. James J. Buckley, Radical Traditions: Theology in a Postcritical Key (Grand Rapids, MI: Eerdmans, 2002), 157–58.

insofar as it is a human community that should be characterized by solidarity and commitment to global justice.[10]

Doyle's account of communion ecclesiology is commendable for its subtlety, and his articulation of these five touchstones includes a flexibility that is often missing from particular instances of this ecclesiology. Nonetheless, difficulties arise from the confluence of the church's sacramental and historical natures. The sacramentality of the church includes historical elements such as the liturgical and institutional structures embedded in the tradition, and this historical embeddedness consequently becomes the means by which one accesses the church's divine and mystical dimensions. This comes out especially in the thought of Yves Congar, an important twentieth-century proponent of communion ecclesiology whose thought influenced the Second Vatican Council. For Congar, Christ established the institutional structures of the church, and the Holy Spirit enlivens those structures. Consequently, "the church as a whole"—its liturgy, ordained ministry, and other institutions—"is sacramental in its nature" because the Holy Spirit "establishes [the church] in its truth," rather than "challenging and questioning its institutional character."[11]

As with Lindbeck, Congar's account of the church understands its nature as a distinct community extended through time—with the emphasis on the Holy Spirit-empowered sacramental-institutional character of that community, in this case, rather than on its cultural-lingusitic character. This is a matter of emphasis rather than of real difference, however. In both cases, the church's being resides in the persistence of its earthly-historical form, and the expansion of the church can only be thought in terms of the expansion of that form. This is the logic of Christendom, and Gollwitzer's doctrine of the church

---

10. Doyle, *Communion Ecclesiology*, 175–78.
11. Yves Congar, *I Believe in the Holy Spirit*, trans. David Smith, Milestones in Catholic Theology (New York: Crossroad, 2006), 3:271. See also Yves Congar, *The Word and the Spirit*, trans. David Smith (San Francisco: Harper and Row Publishers, 1986), 28, 33. The Catholic tradition can sometimes speak of the Holy Spirit as the soul of the church, and Congar does as well. This can be problematic, however, and Congar is alive to the danger. He does not intend "an ecclesiological monophysitism" by using such language. Rather, referring to the Spirit as the church's soul makes a "functional" rather than an "ontological" point. Congar, *I Believe in the Holy Spirit*, 1:154. For Congar's positive appropriation of this language, see Yves Congar, *The Mystery of the Church*, trans. A. V. Littledale (London: Geoffrey Chapman, 1960), 21–23, 32–35. Congar allows here that the Holy Spirit is "very close to what we call the soul" (p. 32) in the sense of supplying the Church's animating principle. Reinhard Hütter is more audacious than Congar. He argues that it is fitting to describe the church's "core practices" as "subsist[ing] enhypostatically in the Spirit." Reinhard Hütter, *Suffering Divine Things: Theology as Church Practice* (Grand Rapids, MI: Eerdmans, 2000), 133. This avoids an ecclesiological monophysitism by seeming to embrace an account of the church as the incarnation of the Holy Spirit.

rejects it because it fails to properly distinguish between the revolutionary message of the kingdom of God's true socialism and a specific cultural form of the Christian community. God's transcendent Thou-objectivity in the event of faith means that the Christian community must assume different cultural forms in different times and places as it responds to that encounter. Foreclosing on this diversity by failing to distinguish between the event of faith and the church's earthly-historical forms is a betrayal of that encounter.

Furthermore, the failure of the church-as-culture approach to distinguish between the gospel and the church's earthly-historical forms means that it lacks the resources to resist cooptation from other cultures. At best, such a church can attempt to extend the boundaries of its own culture, but this can result only in objectifying certain earthly-historical values and thereby producing and maintaining new forms of social hierarchy, inequality, and injustice. Feuerbachian and Marxist criticisms loom large here.[12] This churchly counter-culture may well be an improvement upon other actually existing communities if the host culture is informed in some way by Christianity's witness to the God who liberates the oppressed. But church-as-culture remains a pale imitation of the true church and its witness to the in-breaking of the truly transcendent God's world-overcoming revolution, to the true socialism of the kingdom of God that relativizes and judges all earthly-historical communities and their social structures.

Gollwitzer's Political Ecclesiology

Gollwitzer's ecclesiology refuses to objectify a particular earthly-historical form of community, whether cultural-linguistic or sacramental-institutional, as the church's being. Instead, he works out his ecclesiology on the basis of his dialectical theology. In other words, the logic of his doctrine of the church works outward from the event of encounter with God's Thou-objectivity. Consequently, the logic of his ecclesiology

12. Christine Helmer makes this point with reference to "doctrine," which in her analysis encompasses both the cultural-linguistic and sacramental-institutional strands that I have elucidated. "Doctrine reaches its terminus when its own status as social construction is no longer acknowledged and when it takes the place of the transcendent reality to which it is meant to refer." Helmer, *Theology and the End of Doctrine*, 150. Gollwitzer's dialectical ecclesiology rejects this loss of transcendence, which constitutes the fulfillment of Feuerbach's criticism. It is highly significant that Helmer articulates her criticism of postliberal theology, which descends from Lindbeck, with reference to Bruce D. Marshall. Marshall was formerly Lutheran but converted to Catholicism, and thus, represents the personal intersection of what I called the cultural-linguistic and sacramental-institutional. Interestingly, Reinhard Hütter—mentioned in the previous footnote—is also a Lutheran who converted to Catholicism.

155

is analogous to that of his political theology, which we explicated in chapter 3—God cannot be objectified; therefore all theology is contextual; therefore all theology is political. Just so: the church cannot be objectified; therefore, the church is contextual; therefore, the church is political. This is how Gollwitzer's ecclesiology does conceptual justice to the church's nature as both a danger and a help to the world.

The Church Cannot Be Objectified

The church's being and theology's status are inextricably linked. Everything said about talk of God in chapter 3 applies analogously to the being of the church.[13] Just as there can be no pure, objective speech of God that is eternally valid, there is no pure, objective shape of the Christian community that is eternally valid. The particular shapes that Christian communities take in history are fundamentally contingent—part of the entirely human response to encounter with God, rather than instituted by God as permanent fixtures. It is just as much an exercise in natural theology to find God in the church's earthly-historical forms as to find God in nature, human language, reason, and so on. What makes the church "a very special group" is not possession of certain concepts, rituals, or institutions but, rather, that "it is a group called into being, called together, and constituted by a message."[14] Furthermore, "the church is not a fellowship of racial descent" like Israel. This is a decisively different approach than the one taken by Lindbeck who, as we saw above, thinks of the church as a continuation of Israel. Gollwitzer's point is not to disparage Israel as an inferior form of God's people, but simply to explicate the logic of the uniquely Christian character of encounter with the God and Father of Jesus Christ, whom Christians confess is also the God of Abraham, Isaac, and Jacob.[15]

So for Gollwitzer, the church is not the product of an earthly-historical process. Instead, the church is the product of a message. What is

13. Helga Day rightly notes that Gollwitzer's thinking about the church is calibrated to his thinking about God. Helga Krüger Day, "Christlicher Glaube und gesellschaftliches Handeln: eine Studie der Entwicklung der Theologie Helmut Gollwitzers" (Doctoral dissertation: Union Theological Seminary, 1973), 354.

14. Helmut Gollwitzer, *An Introduction to Protestant Theology*, trans. David Cairns (Philadelphia: The Westminster Press, 1982), 23.

15. Ibid., 133. Peter Ochs argues that the postliberalism of Lindbeck and others is the only theological approach available today that avoids supersessionism, that is, the idea that the church displaces Israel as the people of God. Peter Ochs, *Another Reformation: Postliberal Christianity and the Jews* (Grand Rapids, MI: Baker Academic, 2011). Gollwitzer's role as a pioneer of Jewish-Christian dialogue in the middle of the twentieth century should prevent us from writing off his approach without further examination, however.

this message? It is the message of the kingdom of God that invites people to lives characterized by faith and love: "As an invitation to *faith* it says: God, the Creator, cares for you and for all; there is enough for all. As an invitation of *love* it says: You must not, and you do not need to, live at the cost of others! This is not the good life; the good life is the life for others. Let them live at your cost as God in Christ lets us live at his cost!"[16] The church exists as an earthly-historical community insofar as it is gathered together by this message, that is to say, insofar as this message penetrates through people's privilege and produces new forms of life. These new forms of life are a necessary consequence of hearing the gospel message. As John Calvin writes when providing instruction in how to identify a truly Christian community, "wherever we see the Word of God purely preached and *heard*, and the sacraments administered according to Christ's institution, there, it is not to be doubted, a church of God exists."[17]

The life of the church, or the shape that the Christian community takes in history, depends on the conditions under which it must carry out its commission to share this message with its neighbors. Faithfulness to this commission is not a matter of reinforcing existing cultural-linguistic forms or sacramental-institutional structures. Neither is it concerned with "a world view which one has acquired and one defends against other ideologies."[18] Faithfulness is a question of action, and of a very specific mode of action: solidarity. Rather than establishing the church as an alternative community separated from the wider community with its own structures, institutions, and sensibilities, "mission clearly implies living with those to whom one is sent, living *their* life with them, speaking their language, sharing in their problems, speaking to them, not from the outside, bust as one of their own people."[19] As those who have been called together by the gospel message, the church's mission is to break down the sociohistorical barriers—every "dividing wall" (Eph 2:14)—that separate those who have heard that message from those who have not.

This account of the church's mission relativizes all earthly-historical forms that the Christian community has inhabited or will ever inhabit.

---

16. Gollwitzer, *Protestant Theology*, 112.
17. John Calvin, *Institutes of the Christian Religion*, ed. John T. McNeill, trans. Ford Lewis Battles, 2 vols., Library of Christian Classics (Philadelphia: Westminster Press, 1960), 4.1.9. We will see what Gollwitzer makes of baptism and the Lord's Supper shortly.
18. Gollwitzer, *Protestant Theology*, 214. As David Congdon puts it, "faith cannot be turned into a program of civilization and cultural development." Congdon, *Mission of Demythologizing*, 783.
19. Gollwitzer, *Protestant Theology*, 181.

The church's forms are always already called into question by the message that gathers the church together, and—crucially—this message retains the ability to judge all such forms on the basis of encounter with God in the event of faith. Although we saw how Gollwitzer defined the message of the gospel above, that articulation is, nonetheless, a particular instance of contextual-political talk of God. It is an attempt to be faithful to the encounter with God's Thou-objectivity that precedes and exceeds all capacities of thought and language. This encounter with God is what calls the church together, constitutes it, and forms its very being. Consequently, far from being fundamentally cultural-linguistic or sacramental-institutional, "the church is an *event*."[20] The church exists as the event of encounter with God exists, and in this sense, the church does not exist so much as it *occurs*. The church's faithfulness to the gospel's message, its attempt to bring this encounter to speech through word and action, does not constitute its being. This earthly-historical Christian community's mission, its reason for existing, is nothing more or less than to serve this event: not by producing it, but merely by providing occasion for it

> so that from time to time, *ubi et quando visum est Deo* ("where and when God pleases," Augsburg Confession, Art. 5), the church becomes event. . . . [W]hen we speak of the church, we must not look at our organization, not at *the* history of the church, but at these events, both at the beginning and at repeated intervals in the course of church history. The church organizations, however—which we are accustomed, far too easily, to describe as "The Church"—are at best our attempts to serve the event of "the church."[21]

Therefore the Church Is Contextual

The foregoing section already suggested this consequence of conceiving the church as an event of encounter with God. As we noted, Gollwitzer has no truck with viewing the church as a worldview or identifying it with the structures of particular sociohistorical communities. At their best, theological concepts and communal structures function as occasions for the transcendent, free divine act of eventful encounter with humanity. But they can neither extend the duration of that encounter nor be identified with that divine act. In this way, there is a "strict boundary between Creator and creature" even in the event

20. Ibid., 118.
21. Ibid., 118–19.

wherein God overcomes that boundary.[22] However, maintenance of this strict boundary generates a great deal of freedom on the creaturely side with reference to how the community gathered together by this event speaks of God and organizes itself. The community is free to make use of any features of its sociohistorical and intellectual context as it pursues its mission, and this allows for endless recontextualization.

Gollwitzer's doctrine of the church is consistent with the ecclesiological vision that John Flett advances in his discussion of the church's apostolicity. Flett interrogates the tendency to understand the church on a kernel/husk model, where the husk of culture communicates the transcultural kernel of the gospel. This approach runs into significant difficulties when it comes to differentiating between the kernel and husk, however, which triggers the exercise of power in ways that tend to be colonial or neocolonial. That is, churches of the global North make judgments about where to draw this line and then impose those judgments upon churches in the global South. But "such an approach, because the Western church remains the subject, misses the main point. No non-cultural gospel exists."[23] This does not mean that institutions and social structures are unimportant to the church; however, it does mean that such things "are part of the conversion process" whereby the church comes to expression under new contextual conditions. There will necessarily be both continuities and discontinuities with how the church comes to expression in diverse cultural contexts, and discontinuity need not be feared. Flett offers a thought-provoking definition of schism in this regard. Schism occurs not when a new contextual expression of the church is excessively discontinuous; rather, "schism is the petrification of the gospel, its consolidation into a religious culture focused on a range of considerations important in a set time and place, establishing an interpretive lens with which to judge all other positions."[24] In other words, schism occurs as the result of too strong an insistence on continuity, rather than as a result of excessive discontinuity.

For Gollwitzer, the only continuity worth worrying about is that between the church's attempt to live in faithful solidarity with its

---

22. Ibid., 99.
23. Flett, *Apostolicity*, 285. For a thick account of these issues from a self-consciously dialectical theological perspective, see Congdon, *Mission of Demythologizing*, 503–686. For a condensed version, see David W. Congdon, "Emancipatory Intercultural Hermeneutics: Interpreting Theo Sundermeier's *Differenzhermeneutik*," *Mission Studies* 33 (2016): 127–46.
24. Flett, *Apostolicity*, 286.

neighbors and the event of encounter with God that gives the church its being. The Christian community in any particular time and place is not bound to carry out this mission of solidarity in the same way and by making use of the same structures that the community has done in other particular times and places. Indeed, Gollwitzer seems especially predisposed toward new structures of the church's contextual embodiment since the structures of embodiment given to the church by its history have been so thoroughly compromised.[25] Rather than too great a concern about formal continuity, the important thing is that all aspects of the church's life should remain faithful to the event of encounter with God by serving "as a medium for the attack of the gospel on society." Gollwitzer drives the point home: "an essential part of our ever-renewed beginning is the continually renewed attempt to change the organization of the church from a hindrance into a serviceable instrument for the event of 'the church,' for Him who alone can make us the church."[26]

Therefore the Church Is Political

The church's political character has been a feature of this whole discussion of Gollwitzer's doctrine of the church. We began by attending to Gollwitzer's call for a church that is dangerous rather than domesticated, saw that the church's mission is one of lived solidarity with its neighbors, and heard about the need for the church to serve as the staging ground for the gospel's attack against society. Gollwitzer's doctrine of the church is always already on the way to political engagement because the church is already involved in politics. It is involved in politics because it is composed of human beings who must find ways to live together, and because the event of encounter with God impels one into a life characterized by love of God and love of neighbor. As Gollwitzer explains: "we are already involved in politics, and therefore we must go into politics; we have not the choice of taking part in politics or not, but only of *how* to take part." We saw in chapter 4 that Gollwitzer answers the *how* question by appeal to the absolute utopia of the

---

25. Gollwitzer, *Protestant Theology*, 111–12.
26. Ibid., 107, 119. Tom Greggs emphasizes how the church's event-character relativizes the church's forms: "identifying the event of the Spirit as the basis for the existence of the church should prevent us from confusing ecclesial form or cultures of any kind, which can all have the semblance of a church, with the reality of the event of God the Holy Spirit which is the primary condition for the presence of the church as the Spirit makes Christ known to communities of peoples in all their variety in the present." Tom Greggs, "Church and Sacraments," in *Sanctified by Grace: A Theology of the Christian Life*, ed. Kent Eilers and Kyle Strobel (London: Bloomsbury, 2014), 161–62.

kingdom of God's true socialism. Here, however, he alludes to all this by way of the term "togetherness." This constitutes both the aim and the criterion of the church's political engagement. It is a "minimal goal" that "continually presses on . . . to more togetherness, more equality, more solidarity, and toward a life lived less at the cost of others."[27]

Pursuing this goal requires that the church take sides.[28] Taking sides is nothing new for the church, as we have seen Gollwitzer argue before. Just as the church is always already embroiled in the political, so it has always taken sides. The problem is that it has taken—and continues to take—the *wrong* side. Gollwitzer deploys the sacraments in order to highlight both the gospel's attack on existing society and its structures of privilege, and the church's failure to take that attack seriously enough. Both the Lord's Supper and baptism emphasize the solidarity and fellowship that should be characteristic of the Christian community, that is, the church's togetherness: "as there is only *one* baptism which incorporates us in the Body of Christ, so there is only *one* Lord's Supper and *one* Body of Christ."[29] The trouble is that the church today does not appreciate the political ramifications of this theological confession. For Gollwitzer, "the Lord's Supper stands as a judgment over the whole of church history" in which Christians have waged war against and plundered each other. Furthermore, this judgment stands not only against church history but against the church today, especially when considered in global perspective: "the misery of hungry Christians in other parts of the world is a misery within our fellowship" that belies the unity proclaimed and promised in the Lord's Supper. Things only become worse with reference to baptism, which is an embodiment and actualization of the church's missionary being. It is bad enough that Christians treat each other so poorly, Gollwitzer argues, but it is a fundamental rejection of baptism and the church's

---

27. Gollwitzer, *Protestant Theology*, 191–93. The German term is *Miteinander*. See Helmut Gollwitzer, *Befreiung zur Solidarität: Einführung in die evangelische Theologie* (München: Chr. Kaiser Verlag, 1978), 192–93. As Dannemann and Weissinger put it, "given the revolutionary nature of the kingdom of God and the existence of Jesus Christ, the Christian community understands itself as advocate of the permanent revolutionizing of existing social relations of domination. The goal of political ethics is the permanent transcending of oppressive social relations toward their maximum humanization, towards a free, equal, and fraternal society." Ulrich Dannemann and Matthias Weissinger, "Helmut Gollwitzers Beitrag zur Theologie der Gesellschaft," in *Richte unsere Füße auf den Weg des Friedens: Helmut Gollwitzer zum 70. Geburtstag*, ed. Andreas Baudis, Dieter Clausert, Volkhard Schliski and Bernhard Wegener (Munich: Chr. Kaiser, 1979), 593.
28. Gollwitzer, *Protestant Theology*, 190.
29. Helmut Gollwitzer, *The Rich Christians and Poor Lazarus*, trans. David Cairns (New York: Macmillan, 1970), 5.

own being when Christians "rob and destroy non-Christians," "those for whose sake our Lord has dedicated himself and us to service."[30]

When we compare the meaning of baptism and the Lord's Supper with the church's behavior—with its bourgeois class-bondage, especially in the global North—it becomes abundantly clear that the church has always taken sides politically and that it has generally taken the wrong side. The only way to correct this problem is for the church to take the right side—the side of the poor, oppressed, and marginalized across the world. Furthermore, it is not enough for the church to do this in indirect ways. For instance, one might be the member of a trade union where one benefits from the political engagement of union officials. Or one might give support to an economically disadvantaged family in one's town without asking questions about the political structures that help hold them in that position. Gollwitzer argues that this is insufficient and that direct political engagement is necessary, "because the shaping of public affairs, especially legislation and foreign policy, must not be left in the hands of those who are not disturbed by the attack of God."[31] In addition to the political vocations of individual Christians and the various ways they can engage directly with the political process (running for office, community organizing, working for political campaigns, etc.), Gollwitzer argues that the church, as a whole, should function as a "political lobby" or "pressure group."[32] National denominational structures facilitate the church's function as a political lobby at the national level, but worrying only about the national level reintroduces a form of indirect political engagement for many Christians—the denominational headquarters can take care of that so the regional structures and individual congregations need not trouble themselves with this task. This is a mistake. The work of direct

---

30. Ibid., 6. We can particularize this material for the contemporary situation in the United States. For those who would claim to be Christian, to say "America first" is both to betray one's baptism and to "eat and drink judgment" (1 Cor 11:29).

31. Gollwitzer, *Protestant Theology*, 191. Given Gollwitzer's account of the gospel as revolutionary and of the kingdom of God's true socialism, this concept of "the attack of God" depicts God as the revolutionary *par excellence*, attacking all sinful privilege structures at the personal, interpersonal, and sociopolitical levels. This is the revolutionary God whom Christians encounter in the event of faith and who calls them to a new form of life together that is caught up in "the attack of the Kingdom of God, launched against evil, godless life, both in the life of the individual and, because it is a social life, in society." Ibid., 151.

32. Helmut Gollwitzer, *Skizzen eines Lebens. Aus verstreuten Selbstzeugnissen gefunden und verbunden von Friedrich-Wilhelm Marquardt, Wolfgang Brinkel und Manfred Weber* (Gütersloh: Christian Kaiser Verlagshaus, 1998), 327. See Gollwitzer, *Rich Christians*, 28. Gollwitzer's advocacy of direct political action is a departure from Bonhoeffer. Philip Ziegler describes Bonhoeffer's position: "the Church is not a direct political agent, not even on the model of an NGO advocating for humanitarian ideals." Philip G. Ziegler, "Witness to Christ's Dominion: The Political Service of the Church," *Theology* 116, no. 5 (2013): 325.

political engagement, no matter what shape that engagement takes, must occur at every level of the political system if it is to produce enduring change and movement toward ever greater togetherness.

All this amounts to a refusal to understand the church's being as religious. Gollwitzer defines religion as "movements of the human spirit and society which go beyond making our daily living, and which seek for a universal interpretation of human life."[33] The difficulty is that those who live in Western society are increasingly irreligious, giving little thought to human existence beyond the material demands of making a living. Even those who practice a religion are decisively shaped by capitalism's insidious materialism, as the growing corporatization and commodification of North American Christianity amply demonstrates. Furthermore, and as Bonhoeffer perceived near the end of his life, religious categories are no longer necessary for navigating and understanding the world. Dramatic advances in scientific knowledge have given us a "world that has come of age." Proclamation of the gospel under such conditions means articulating a form of Christianity that dispenses with its traditional religious garb—a "religionless Christianity."[34]

Gollwitzer agrees that the church is not a society for the nurture of human religiosity. In a sermon to commemorate the reopening of a church damaged in World War II, he emphasizes that "we have not come in order to cosset our own religious sensibilities and to cultivate our own religious emotional life: reading poetry or listening to music would be useful for that."[35] Instead, the church gathers together to hear the proclamation of the gospel message, to encounter the one

---

33. Gollwitzer, *Protestant Theology*, 82.
34. Dietrich Bonhoeffer, *Letters and Papers from Prison*, trans. Reinhard Krauss, Nancy Lukens, Lisa E. Dahill and Isabel Best, Dietrich Bonhoeffer's Works, vol. 8 (Minneapolis, MN: Fortress Press, 2010), 426, 363.
35. Helmut Gollwitzer, *The Demands of Freedom: Papers by a Christian in West Germany*, trans. Robert W. Fenn (New York: Harper and Row Publishers, 1965), 165. Gollwitzer elaborates on this point elsewhere: "The non-religious man of the present does not require first to be led to religion, transformed into a religious man, in order then to take a second step along this way to come to the Christian faith. Without his putting himself in a religious frame of mind, creating for himself religious experiences, awakening within himself a so-called natural consciousness of God, thus without his being compelled to adopt forms of consciousness which he can no longer recapture, he must be encountered in his life, which has become secular, by the good news from the Lord of the world, who has committed himself in the man Jesus of Nazareth to the world and the secularity of the stable and the gallows." Helmut Gollwitzer, *The Christian Faith and the Marxist Criticism of Religion*, trans. David Cairns (New York: Charles Scribner's Sons, 1970), 155–56. For two thought-provoking articulations of the Christian faith under the conditions of secularity, both of which grew out of dialectical theology in different ways, see Paul M. van Buren, *The Secular Meaning of the Gospel: Based on an Analysis of Its Language* (New York: Macmillan, 1963); Ronald Gregor Smith, *Secular Christianity* (London: Collins, 1966).

who is proclaimed, and to renew that proclamation in its own place and time. Gollwitzer takes Bonhoeffer's insight and offers a concrete proposal concerning the shape that gospel proclamation should take under the conditions of religionless Christianity: "*this* is what Bonhoeffer in my opinion meant by his demand for a non-religious interpretation [of Christian faith]!—to translate . . . Christianity into political terms, to be in quest of love in structures."[36] In other words, the church is not only an *event*—it is a *political* event. And only in its occurrence as such a religionless political event does the church embody true religion by bearing faithful witness to the God who constitutes both the true "beyond" of "human spirit and society," and the "universal interpretation of human life."[37]

Status Confessionis

This volume began by reflecting on why Gollwitzer deserves a hearing among Christians in North America today. Having examined Gollwitzer's life, political theology, and theological politics, I want to conclude by returning to the question of Gollwitzer's timeliness by raising a question in Gollwitzer's spirit—does the church in North America find itself today in a *status confessionis*? To answer simply—Yes, and this *status confessionis* has persisted for decades.

Status confessionis is theological shorthand for a situation in which it becomes imperative for the church to confess its faith clearly because its confession has become internally compromised. Eberhard Jüngel says that *status confessionis* refers to conditions that "make it necessary to designate false teaching unambiguously."[38] The act of confessing identifies and rejects false teaching in a decisive way, thereby highlighting faithful proclamation of the gospel against the backdrop of unfaithful proclamation. Such situations have arisen for doctrinal reasons, traditionally speaking. For instance, the Nicene Creed arose from a *status confessionis*, as did the various confessions from the reformational period. None of these moments are without political dimensions, of course, just as theology is always already either implicitly or explicitly political. It was not until the twentieth century, however, that the explicitly political character of *status confessionis* came to the fore. As Jüngel points out, the Barmen Declaration—issued by the Confessing

36. Gollwitzer, *Rich Christians*, 17.
37. Gollwitzer, *Protestant Theology*, 82.
38. Eberhard Jüngel, *Christ, Justice and Peace: Toward a Theology of the State in Dialogue with the Barmen Declaration*, trans. D. Bruce Hamill and Alan J. Torrance (Edinburgh: T & T Clark, 1992), 55.

Church in 1934 against the German Christians and their support for Hitler—recognizes that a *status confessionis* can also arise with reference to the relationship between church and state. This is confirmed further by the Belhar Confession (1982), which recognized the conditions of apartheid in South Africa as a *status confessionis*. Money is power, so it is a short step from admitting that a *status confessionis* can be political in character to recognizing that it can be *economic* in character as well. The Accra Confession (2004) takes this step with its rejection of "neoliberal economic globalism."[39] But while the Belhar Confession increasingly gains recognition within some sectors of North American Christianity, the Accra Confession remains obscure.

The heresy of the church's spirituality, discussed in chapter 3, makes it difficult for Christians in the United States to recognize that unjust economic conditions require a theological response. This volume has argued that the example of Gollwitzer's life and thought demonstrates the necessity of that response. Economic issues are always also theological issues: economic systems are designed and organized to serve certain ends or goals, and judgments about appropriate ends always depend on a set of values. Jung Mo Sung helpfully explicates "the theology implicit in the current international economic order," addressing such theological topics as eschatology, original sin, and salvation through sacrifice.[40] Serving this economic system constitutes idolatry because this system's goals and values are diametrically opposed to the God whom Christians encounter in the event of faith. Thus, "the established social order and the power-holders are neither righteous nor represent God's will" because "faith in the resurrection of Jesus reveals that salvation stands not for accumulation of wealth, but for the formation of human communities where all people are acknowledged, irrespective of wealth and other social characteristics."[41]

In the face of such an idolatrous—even demonic!—socioeconomic order, an order from which especially white American Christians benefit, the church *must* confess its faith. Failure to do so fundamentally compromises the faithfulness of its speech of God. Paul M. van Buren

39. "The Accra Confession: Covenanting for Justice in the Economy and the Earth," World Alliance of Reformed Churches and North American Covenanting for Justice Working Group (2010): thesis 8, https://www.pcusa.org/site_media/media/uploads/hunger/pdf/accra-confession.pdf. For further analysis of economic *status confessionis* in ecumenical context, see Ulrich Duchrow, *Global Economy: A Confessional Issue for the Churches?*, trans. David Lewis (Geneva: WCC Publications, 1987).
40. Jung Mo Sung, *Desire, Market and Religion*, Reclaiming Liberation Theology (London: SCM Press, 2007), 11; see 10–22. Harvey Cox has renewed this line of inquiry more recently: Harvey Cox, *The Market as God* (Cambridge, MA: Harvard University Press, 2016).
41. Sung, *Desire, Market and Religion*, 24–25.

made this point clearly in the context of American society in the late 1950s. The formal task of confession, like that of theological prolegomena, is to specify who we mean when we use the term "God." That specificity is critically important because "once grant that the 'God' in whom . . . the American people claim to believe is the same God that the church confesses," that this projection of "American" values "is in any way the God and Father of our Lord Jesus Christ, without most serious reservations, and the citadel is surrendered."[42] Unfortunately, the church in the United States has, for the most part, surrendered the citadel without a fight. Even more unfortunately, and as Gollwitzer reminds us, this surrender is not a new phenomenon in the church's history. "There has scarcely been a nonheretical group in all the centuries of church history, nor is there one today"—and this is especially true when one applies the notion of heresy not only to conceptual, but also to the sociopolitical conditions "in which the motivations of individuals have taken objective form."[43] The God of the gospel's attack against human sin involves an attack against the failings of our sociopolitical and economic life together as well as against individual failings.

Gollwitzer reminds us that this surrender, this betrayal of the gospel at the altar of wealth and privilege, is not inevitable. He also helps to arm us for the struggle. In this, he offers something of a mirror image to Karl Marx. One of Marx's most famous contributions is his argument that "the critique of heaven turns into the critique of earth, the critique of religion into the critique of law, and the critique of theology into the critique of politics."[44] But if Marx thus turns theology into politics, Gollwitzer transforms politics into theology. That is, he clarifies for us that there is no such thing as a theologically neutral political position. Either one advocates and undertakes political steps to combat the socioeconomic privilege that oppresses immense swaths of the world's population, or one is a heretic—unfaithful to the God encountered in the event of faith. For this "wholly other God wants a wholly other society"[45] in which all forms of privilege are abolished and social structures ever increasingly approximate the true socialism

42. Paul M. van Buren, *The Austin Dogmatics: 1957–1958*, ed. Ellen T. Charry (Eugene, OR: Cascade, 2012), 4. For contemporary reflection along these lines, see Michael Peppard, "Should Christians Fear Trump's God?," *Commonweal Magazine* (January 24, 2017), https://www.commonweal-magazine.org/blog/should-christians-fear-trumps-god.
43. Gollwitzer, *Protestant Theology*, 115.
44. Eugene Kamenka, ed. *The Portable Karl Marx*, Viking Portable Library (New York: Penguin Books, 1983), 116.
45. Gollwitzer, "Liberation in History," 421.

of the kingdom of God. And why does God want this? Because our God loves justice.

Appendix 1:
Must a Christian Be a Socialist?

Helmut Gollwitzer (1972)

I

"Socialists can be Christians; Christians must be socialists."[1] Adolf Grimme formulated this statement in 1946 as his personal creed and as a basic principle for the relationship between socialism and Christianity.[2] When I merely put it up for discussion in 1971, the fiercest reactions were not from the socialists, but from the Christians. The distance that the intervening 25 years created cannot be more clearly identified. The immediate postwar period, the common experience of hunger, defeat, and the material losses, made a shared bearing of hardships and the burden of rebuilding appear to be the only possible, fair, and promising option. Thus, the word "socialism" received a new luster, freed from the skullduggery of National Socialism. Everyone wanted to get in on it. To admit to being a socialist brought no risk. The demands of socialization penetrated party programs and state constitutions.[3]

---

1. [Ed. Helmut Gollwitzer, "Muß ein Christ Sozialist sein?," *Jenseits vom Nullpunkt? Christsein im westlichen Deutschland*, ed. Rudolf Weckerling (Stuttgart: Kreuz, 1972), 151–70.]
2. I owe the transmission of this sentence to Mrs. Josephine Grimme.
3. [Ed. Gollwitzer refers to the constitutions of the various *Länder* or federal states that comprise Germany.]

Beyond these demands, however, it remained unclear whether a social-ism tinted more by Christianity or by Marxism was meant—except with the communists and with the few other Marxists with whom Marx-ist theory, even though devoid of continued development, had sur-vived the fascist liquidation of German Marxism. Adolf Grimme himself admittedly meant the word in a definite sense, which by all means included the overthrow of private capital's ownership structures. The posthumously published book that he conceived while in prison during the war demonstrates this. In *The Meaning and Absurdity of Christianity*,[4] Grimme continues in an original manner the tradition of religious socialism in which he stood.

Today, however, and among the same demographic who used to be open to it, socialism has become a fear-mongering word that can be used in every instance of anti-reformist propaganda. The following fac-tors coalesce in this: the discrediting of Eastern socialism by its lack of freedom and economic efficiency, the apparent demonstration of the viability of "free market economy" by means of rapid reconstruc-tion and mass prosperity, and finally, the New Left's refusal to share the general conclusion about the unsuitability of the socialist program based on the negative appearance of Eastern socialism and the positive appearance of Western capitalism. Vehement criticism of capitalism and the unflinching goal of a classless society once again gives a shape to the word "socialism" which, admittedly, does not appear immedi-ately attractive to minds that are unaccustomed to it. That Christians must be socialists sounds much more shocking in 1971, therefore, than in 1946. We see this in how forgotten the religious socialists are today in their prophets' graves, that are ornamented everywhere with com-memoration, because Hermann Kutter's *They Must!* (1903)—which was no different than Grimme's statement—was certainly also their slo-gan. We see this in how very much the church and theological acad-emy have come to terms with the restored capitalism of the 1950s and 1960s, so much so that they (including this epoch's literature on social ethics) lack the imagination to think beyond it and are shocked when others do so.

4. Heidelberg, 1969; see my review in EvTh [Ed., the journal *Evangelische Theologie*; trans., *Evangelical* or *Protestant Theology*] 30, 1969, 444ff.

II

Whatever our first response to it might be, the facts of Grimme's statement should be examined calmly. Hardly anyone contests the first part—*"Socialists can be Christians"*—at least in the superficial sense. The socialist parties since the time of Friedrich Engels, including the Leninist parties, have repudiated Eugen Dühring's demand for a religious ban for the socialist movement as "Prussian socialism," and have always affirmed that Christians also can be members of the socialist and communist parties.[5] Of course, in a deeper sense, the still widely prevailing tradition of official Marxism will not concede this statement. Whether we use the word "socialist" to refer to the socialistic militant in the present or to the member of a future socialistic society, anyone who wants to be a socialist in the full sense cannot, at the same time, be a Christian. They must be dead to religion, and religion must be dead to them. While they intend and are able to be socialists and Christians at the same time, they inhabit an inconsistent combination of elements from the future with elements of the past which the party—confident in its enlightening influence—can tolerate so long as the religious elements of the past do not compromise the efficacy of the socialist elements of the future.

The reservations on the side of the church were not less significant. Admittedly, there have always been proponents of the compatibility of Christianity and socialism in the Protestant camp. But this was a minority group which would be silenced by 1933, along with the remaining socialists. And apart from this, the sympathy of the majority of the clergy and church folks for what referred to itself at that time as "national revolution" had dampened it. It still required considerable time even after 1945 before the conviction that Christians can be social democrats attained the self-evidence that it has today. It is still not so widely known in the Catholic camp. Church authorities at one time conceded that the SPD[6] is an option for Catholics, but at other times, they more or less concealed or denied this when the concession generated fears about dangerous consequences for the interests of the

---

5. See H. Gollwitzer, *Die marxistische Religionskritik und der christliche Glaube* (Siebenstern-Taschenbücher, Nr. 33), 37–43. [Ed. Helmut Gollwitzer, *The Christian Faith and the Marxist Criticism of Religion* (New York: Charles Scribner's Sons, 1970), 33–40.]
6. [Ed. SPD stands for the Social Democratic Party of Germany (*Sozialdemokratische Partei Deutschlands*), a party which—over the course of its history—has straddled the line of demarcation between social democracy and democratic socialism. The former is content to work within and reform the capitalist system while the latter aims at replacing that system.]

church hierarchy or of the party that benefited from it. Papal social encyclicals contested the compatibility of socialism and Catholicism before *Populorum progressio* (1967). Pius XII's excommunication of practicing communists showed that the church hierarchy has a lower tolerance level compared with the communist parties, which have never carried out the excommunication of practicing Catholics (even if Catholic members are not allowed to rise to the party's upper echelons). Although at the local level Don Camillo and Peppone[7] can find a human and Christian way of life with each other, this is possible only with the mutual agreement that one cannot be both a priest and a communist.

The first part of Grimme's statement flatly contradicts this agreement, which makes it controversial still today. Admittedly, Grimme initially—in 1946—did not yet have in view the self-evident truth of the compatibility of being a social democrat and being a Christian. But beyond this straightforward political sense, he additionally meant "socialist" in a more radical manner. Grimme stood with his sympathies on the SPD's left wing and did not begrudge Marxism. For him, socialism embraced the abolition of private ownership of the means of production and the goal of a classless society. He was, of course, fully aware that the alliance between being a socialist and being a Christian would change traditional Marxism somewhat. When Marxists become Christians, they do not automatically give up their Marxist conviction if it includes a program of social revolution. But becoming Christian impinges upon their ideological ambition for the removal of all religion—that is, their atheism—and lets their fighting methods be corrected in a humanizing fashion by their being as Christians. That socialists can be Christians implies the compatibility of socialist revolution with Christian faith, and at the same time, breaks Marxism's previous link with obligatory atheism. As long as this previous link existed, and to the extent that it still exists, the link between Marxism and Christianity does not go beyond the category of alliance. And it has already achieved much if both sides will at least take this alliance seriously and maintain it as justified by the convergence of mutual goals. Christians and Marxists have always and again disappointed each other by terminating this alliance the moment it became annoying for its own side, or the moment one side no longer wanted to rely on it. Both sides should be clear about the truth of Roger Garaudy's words: "The

---

7. [Ed. The fictional characters Camillo Tarocci and Giuseppe Bottazzi ("Peppone") are, respectively, the Catholic priest and communist mayor of a small Italian village.]

future of humanity cannot be built against believers, much less with-out them. The future of humanity will not be against the communists, much less can it be built without them."[8] Such words still come out of the recent opposition between the two camps: it is either wage war or ally with one another, and the individual has to choose between them. But that a Christian can be a socialist must not only apply for all kinds of varieties of a Christian or democratic socialism, which have never brought their socialist theory and practice to sufficient determi-nacy. It must also apply for Marxism. The previous link between Marx-ism and obligatory atheism will thereby dissolve, confining Marxism to its political economy and sociorevolutionary program. Ambition for the removal of religion falls away. Whether this is possible without damage to Marxism is the subject of a vibrant discussion within Marx-ism in which the affirmative answer to this question is represented especially by Christian Marxists. Nevertheless, it is also represented by such Marxists who—without being Christians—have become skeptical toward the alleged scientificity of dialectical materialism, toward such an extrapolation to worldview. They see clearly how Marxism is a sub-stitute for religion here through incorporating religious demands that bring with them the risk of dogmatism and fanaticism. And they see the handicap that such traditional Marxism, with its European heritage of atheism, creates for itself when spreading to other continents.

Outside of West Germany, the compatibility of Marxism and Chris-tianity has already become self-evident for many people. The emer-gence of the New Left has also changed the situation within the Federal Republic. In the Latin countries of Europe and Latin America, in Africa, and in Asia, there are not an inconsiderable number of Christians —even pastors and priests—who are members of communist groups. The differences of worldview recede while political praxis unifies. Instead of the former dialogue between Christians and Marxists as representatives of different ideological camps, it is often already the case that, as Günther Nenning[9] rightly observed, "this kind of union of Christianity and Marxism in one person is now becoming normal. Thousands accomplish this as a matter of course, especially young peo-ple and especially in countries with strong Catholic and communist backgrounds, such as France, Italy, Spain, and Latin America. It occurs

8. At the first major Dialogue Conference of the Paul Society in Saltzburg in 1965. See H. Kellner (ed.), *Christentum und Marxismus heute* [Ed., *Christianity and Marxism Today*], 1966, 16. [Ed. Garaudy would be accused of Holocaust denial decades later after publishing a controversial book in 1996. By that time, Gollwitzer had been dead for approximately three years.]
9. *Neues Forum* [Ed., *New Forum*], March 1972, 45.

more than ever in countries with predominantly Protestant backgrounds, especially in Anglo-Saxon countries. Protestant theologians like Paul Tillich carried out the opening of Christianity to socialism long before the Catholic discovery of Marxism. The new dark red wave of socialism, whether it is called the New Left or something else, is full of post-dialogical Christian-Marxists who do not talk but act."

III

Grimme's statement expresses from the socialist side a minimal, pluralistic goal—to unite people with different worldviews for a shared political, socialist goal. Socialists are not required to be Christians any more than they are required to not be Christians. They can be Christians without becoming devalued as socialists. For the Christian side, however, the socialist Christian Grimme gives a maximal formulation: "*Christians must be socialists*," and it is this part of the statement that provokes understandable opposition.

With this "must," Christians as Christians appear to be bound—that is, in the name of God—to a particular political program, even to an "ideology," and to one that does not stem from Christian roots for good measure. And it would not improve matters even if it came from such roots. Christian faith is under an obligation to no philosophy, to no manner of looking at the world, to no social order, and to no program. The root of Christian freedom is infringed upon where such a thing is undertaken. The gospel is perverted into law where this is the content of Christian proclamation so that it has the goal of turning Christians into socialists. The reformational termination of the unity of medieval social order and Christian faith, of Aristotelian philosophy and Christian theology, as well as the Confessing Church's rejection of the German-Christian thesis—"Christians must be Nazis"—are great testimonies to the freedom of the gospel and the freedom of faith. If Grimme's sentence entices one to go back behind the reformational emancipation of reason in its relation to the world through the gospel, then it must be rejected and reduced to the sentence—Just as socialists can be Christians, so also Christians can be socialists.

Christians "must" do nothing at all. No obligation, no compulsion to any prescribed work regulates their relation to God. The prodigal son does not have to head back home in order to acquire the father's love. The father shows him by running to meet him that he has never ceased to love him. His love does not depend on conditions that must be met.

It surrounds the son as the air of freedom: "All that is mine is yours."
Outside, the son had to do all kinds of things to obtain life.[10] Outside,
he was enslaved by conditions, regulations, and ideologies. In the love
of the father, he is a free lord of all things.[11] But "must" he not now
be of service to his father? The must of love is really a new and novel
must. It is not heteronomously imposed, related to the withdrawal of
love with the threat of being thrown out of the father's house. Rather,
it is a must in the recipient of love itself, awakened by love itself and
upheld by love. It is the must of happiness from the new connection
with the father, the union of the will of the son with the will of the
father, through which the son speaks: "Volo omnia, quae vult deus."[12]
Two things demonstrate that this is a new must—it is filled with joy
rather than with fear, and it operates in freedom. "From now on I do
not say that you are servants; for servants don't know what their master does. But to you I have said that you are friends; for everything that
I have heard from my father I have declared to you" (John 15:15).[13] The
Christ-connection between God and humanity makes Jesus's disciples
into accomplices to God's will. And to the one who loves this will and
whose happiness is to be the father's fellow-worker, this fatherly will is
included in one's own will. This is the autonomy of the son, instead of
the heteronomy of the servant.

But what is the will of the father? The lives of his children. My
life and the lives of the fraternity, the lives of others beside me who
are my siblings by a shared father. Life is intended broadly here, as
expressed in our thanks for each gift of life—physical, mental, spiritual,
social, and political life, life in all the relationships in which our existence unfolds. The disciples, to whom the will of the father is declared
through Jesus, will the lives of those whom they know as their siblings,
and will to serve this life. They find themselves with their siblings in
each already organized social relationship. As soon as they begin their
service, they will quickly reveal the extraordinary power of these regulations. Each in their fashion promotes the unfolding of the possibilities of the lives of all their siblings, or they impose very different
judgments over different groups of siblings: promoting the one and

10. [Ed. It is awkward to render in translation, but Gollwitzer continues to highlight the word *must* in this sentence: "Draußen >>mußte<< der Sohn allerlei tun."]
11. [Ed. Gollwitzer closely paraphrases Martin Luther here. Gollwitzer writes, "*ein freier Herr aller Dinge*"; Luther writes, "*ein freier Herr über alle ding.*" Martin Luther, "Von der Freiheit eines Chris-ten Menschen," *D. Martin Luthers Werke. Kritische Gesamtausgabe*, vol. 7, ed. J. K. F. Knaake *et al* (Weimar: H. Böhlau, 1883), 21.]
12. *M. Luther*, WA 14, 609, 26: "I will everything that God wills."
13. [Ed. This biblical quotation is translated from Gollwitzer's German rendering.]

175

discriminating against the other. The disciples encounter the reality of class society. They enter into the service of actively contributing to social regulations (it is out of the question for their discipleship that they refuse this service since their service, in accordance with the will of the father, intends the whole lives of their siblings and not only one part of their life) from the perspective of changing class society. Their regulations precipitate different judgments about the fate of their members' lives. The goal of the disciples' service is a society that gives equality to their unequally endowed members and gives each member the chance for a full unfolding of life: where the strong help the weak, where production stands in the service of all, where the social product is not siphoned off by a privileged minority so that only the modest remainder is at the disposal of the others, a society that ensures appropriate regulation of freedom and of social co-determination for all, the development of social life for the common task and for rich purpose in life for all members of society. The goal is a socialist, classless society. The will of the father leaves the disciples no choice with regard to this formulation of the goal, which, at the same time, provides the criterion for the criticism of every existing society. They must be socialists.

Historical materialism has called for more vigorous attention than other modes of historical interpretation to the fact that not everything is possible at all times. The respective development of productive forces sets the measure and limit of our possibilities. Historical traditions in modes of thought and life are even more tightly restricted by the powerful interests of privileged groups. Triumph over class divisions is not equally possible in each time. The enormous development of productive forces in the last hundred years makes it more possible today than ever before in human history. But there was also, in earlier times, some room to a better or worse extent. The preservation of slavery after the so-called victory of Christianity in the Constantinian period, the subjugation of free peasants in serfdom, and the introduction of slavery in the "new world" were decisions that were conditioned by—but not inevitably caused by—the status of productive forces. If the official church with its theology and proclamation had the totality of the father's will in view, then they would have stepped to the side of those who were the victims of those decisions and who tried to resist them. This formulation of the goal specifies the tendency in which it is possible, under the constraints of each epoch, to extract the utmost for a reduction of social withholding and under-privilege.

It is a question of reason how this is to be realized, in what manner to face the tough class conflict with the privileged percentile, how the improvement of the position of the underprivileged is to be wrested from the privileged, and which regulations, economy, administration, and political distribution of power are expedient for this enjoined tendency. More precisely, it is a question of "technical reason" (Tillich), committed to the freedom of our reasonable discussion and responsibility. Whether total socialization of the means of production or partial, whether Western-style party democracy or soviet democracy, whether central planning or a mixture of planning and freedom for individual initiatives—these and many other questions of concrete societal design are not "from the gospel," but are, rather, to be decided in reasonable consideration of respective historical conditions and possibilities. It is possible and necessary to wrangle about these questions, even among the disciples of Jesus. "The church must stand for social justice in the social sphere. And in choosing between the various socialist possibilities (social liberalism? co-operativism? syndicalism? interest-free economy? moderate or radical Marxism?), it will always choose the movement from which it can expect the greatest measure of economic justice."[14] Karl Barth says in the same work[15] that "Christian political differentiating, adjudicating, choosing, willing, and campaigning has a tendency all along the line toward the shape of the state that, even if it is not realized in them, is more or less honestly and clearly meant and intended in the so-called 'democracies.'" Both

14. K. Barth, *Christengemeinde und Bürgergemeinde*, 1946, Neuausgabe ThSt Nr. 104, 69; rightly concerning this, see F.-W. Marquardt, *Theologie und Sozialismus. Das Beispiel Karl Barths* [Ed., *Theology and Socialism. The Example of Karl Barth*], 1972, 312: "Something other than a socialist measure is out of the question here." [Ed. See Karl Barth, "Christian Community and the Civil Community," *Community, State, and Church: Three Essays* (Glouchester, MA: Peter Smith, 1968), 173. The passage is given here as translated in Clifford Green, "Freedom for Humanity: Karl Barth and the Politics of the New World Order," *For the Sake of the World: Karl Barth and the Future of Ecclesial Theology*, ed. George Hunsinger (Grand Rapids, MI: William B. Eerdmans Publishing Company, 2004), 94. Green's further explanation in note 15 is also helpful: "Barth mentions several quite different approaches to 'socialism' in the passage quoted. *Social liberalism* in Barth's time is about equivalent to 'social democratic' in Europe today, namely, a moderate socialist position consistent with liberal democracy. A *cooperative* is a voluntary nonprofit association of consumers or producers for the benefit of its members. *Syndicalism* is a revolutionary strategy for reorganizing society by overthrowing the state which it regards as intrinsically oppressive and substituting the trade union as the key unit of productive labor and government; the motive is socialist in that production is for use, not profit (*Columbia Encyclopedia*, 1963). *Freigeldwirtschaft* is mistranslated 'free trade' or 'free market economy.' It refers to the economic theories of Silvio Gesell (1862–1930) about an economy in which money would be available without interest (hence 'free money'), and would also depreciate like other capital assets. According to Andreas Pangritz (Aachen [Ed. Now of Bonn]), to whom I am indebted for the following information, Gesell's theories in 1946 were discussed in Swiss anarchist circles and perhaps among the friends of Leonhard Ragaz. Elsewhere in Barth, 'radical socialism' meant Soviet communism."]
15. K. Barth, ibid., 76. [Ed. See Barth, "Christian Community and the Civil Community," 182.]

of Barth's statements, which likewise come from 1946, implement the same differentiation. On the one hand, there is the formulation of a goal—in the social sector, the "highest measure of social justice"; in designing the state, those "designs of the state" that intend "democracy." This defines the "direction and orientation." One cannot be a Christian and, at the same time, move backward from and promote another direction than the "highest measure of social justice" and democracy. On the other hand, there is the task of realization in which the Christian's freedom will have to prove itself as freedom by examining each new respective proposal and program for realization. In that respect, it will not reject at the outset either moderating (because of lust for radicalism) or radicalizing (because of fear in the face of radicalism), nor will it always consider a single program or proposal for realization as correct at all times and in all situations. The selection is given over to reason, but not to arbitrary or even "technical reason" as the supreme authority. To do so would be to supply a guideline that is no higher than the words "responsibility" or "love," and is without any further substantive content. Barth's concern was always to show how these words become filled with substance through the real history of God's love—with a sociopolitical tendency toward the pronounceable content of socialism and democracy.[16]

This freedom of choice entails a boundary and control. It is not a coincidence that Barth named only socialist possibilities in the first of the quotations above, and in fact, those from an only vaguely socialist tendency ("social liberalism") to strictly socialist programs. The tendency to socialism forms a "channel [*Fahrrinne*]" (Thielicke) whose boundaries rule out impossible possibilities. Capitalism, the authoritarian state, dictatorship—a disciple of Jesus cannot "seek" any of this. Disciples can only take existing capitalist, authoritarian, and totalitarian conditions into account for their efforts to overcome them, and they will modify their programs accordingly if they should be successful in this realization. This modification must always keep the strategic goal in mind. That goal gives them the benchmark against which they must justify themselves.

Therefore, not all possibilities within the "channel" are equal. The more radical programs have an advantage on being feasibly justified

---

16. Cf. H. Gollwitzer, *Reicht Gottes und Sozialismus bei Karl Barth*, 1972, ThExh NF, 169. [Ed. An abridged translation appears as "Kingdom of God and Socialism in the Theology of Karl Barth" in George Hunsinger (ed., trans.) *Karl Barth and Radical Politics* (Philadelphia: Westminster Press, 1976), 77–120.]

in the eyes of this benchmark because of their substantive proximity to the formulated goal. Moderate programs must demonstrate that they are steps toward the goal—in any case, detours that are not dead ends—and that compromise with the prevailing conditions occurs in the interest of realizing the goal. Discussion between radicals and moderates saves the radicals from becoming blind to the realities, and consequently, from a dogmatism that bypasses and rapes the people, and it saves the moderates from a resigned assimilation to the status quo that fails to keep the goal in mind.

Examples

Christians and the Christian community cannot support the enslavement of human beings by human beings. Finding themselves in a slavery society, they will, first and foremost, undermine the legal institution of slavery through a new, fraternal attitude (early Christianity)[17] such that they prepare and strive politically for its abolition. They will examine various proposals and must deploy medium-range programs considering how each case of this abolition is generally accepted and the restructuring of the society previously built on slavery takes place. Getting stuck in reforms that somewhat improve the situation of the slaves must be prevented. "Reform or revolution—this is not an alternative for socialists. Reforms instead of revolution—this is a joy for capitalists. Reform and revolution—this is a socialist solution." This formulation from Günther Nennings[18] applies exactly for Christians and is evident in Christianity's attitude toward slavery (whose history from the time of early Christianity has been a history also of Christian failures).

Christians cannot support weapons of mass destruction. "It is a sin to even want to think of humanity—which God so loved, as the gospel of Jesus Christ tells us—as an object of weapons of mass destruction."[19] "There is no conceivable purpose, whether Western or Eastern, that justifies these means."[20] In a world in which we must "live with the

17. Cf. my theses "Die gesellschaftlichen Implikationen des Evangeliums [Ed., The Social Implications of the Gospel]" in: *Christliche Freiheit—im Dienst am Menschen, ein Themaband zum 80. Geburtstag Martin Niemöllers*, edited by K. Herbert, 1972, 141–52. [Ed. This work is reprinted in Helmut Gollwitzer, "Die gesellschaftlichen Implikationen des Evangeliums," *Umkehr und Revolution: Aufsätze zu christlichem Glauben und Marxismus*, Band 2, ed. Christian Keller, Ausgewählte Werke (München: Chr. Kaiser, 1988), 62–74.]
18. *Neues Forum*, April 1972, 39.
19. H. Vogel, *Um die Zukunft des Menschen im atomaren Zeitalter* [Ed., *Concerning the Future of Human Beings in the Atomic Age*], 1960, 20.
20. Ibid., 209.

bomb" (C. Fr. von Weizsäcker), which means with the now irreversible invention of modern weapons of mass destruction, various methods and successive next steps will be given to eliminate the manufacture, storage, political utilization, and eventual application of these "weapons." But at the outset must stand the decision of the "No," and all methods and steps must prove themselves with reference to the goal of abolition.

Christians and the Christian community must be against racial apartheid or they are not a Christian community, according to Galatians 3:28. They will first neutralize this apartheid in their own midst. But they cannot content themselves with existing as an island without racial segregation in a racially segregated population. They must become political and strive for the elimination of apartheid. Which steps are necessary for that in an apartheid society, in which the previously oppressed segments of the population need to develop awareness of their equality, is a matter of discussion and of political contention. There must be strict accountability to the goal[21] concerning whether alleged measures of development are, in reality, measures to hinder equality and to stabilize the systems of racist privilege.

Christians and the Christian community must stand against class society with its privileges of birth, property, and power. "If we really are permitted to live in that absolute freedom where God acquits the sinner through the word of forgiveness, then we are not permitted to be indifferent about the freedom of human existence in political and social conditions. If we believe that God alone is just and establishes justice, then we must blush with shame before heaven because of the glaring injustices in human relationships. In that case it is the content of our Christian responsibility to do our part to gain room for justice in people's life together. If responsibility for the future demands that we oppose conditions that degrade people, then we must work hand in hand with the attempt to make room for a more just order in people's life together."[22] So, Christians must be socialists in view of this goal, which means striving to overcome class society. Moreover, we see under socialism an array of proposals for applying this goal to the political struggle and to the social regulation of living together, for

---

21. [Ed. This cutting German turn of phrase—*streng vorgehaltenen Ziel*—translates particularly poorly into English. The key term here is *vorgehaltenen*, which is used in a number of phrases that render as holding someone at gunpoint (*vorgehalter Pistole* or *vorgehaltener Waffe*) or knifepoint (*vorgehaltenem Messer*). But Gollwitzer here holds political proposals at the point of an aim, end, or goal—*Ziel*. Context supplies the content of this goal as service to the gospel's socialist trajectory.]
22. H. Vogel, ibid., 210f.

establishing modes of production and consumption to eliminate class antagonisms as well as prevent their emergence. Christians must not be socialists in the sense of a particular proposal, whether Marxist or Maoist or Social Democrat or followers of Silvio Gesell or the three-foldness of Rudolf Steiners. Christians have the freedom of reasonable choice, but it is the freedom of responsible choice—and that means a choice that is responsible to the goal. Their knowledge that in this vale of tears they can only ever approximately reach this goal does not release them from their responsibility to choose and decide any more than does their knowledge of human imperfection and the perpetual danger of failure. The particularity of their Christian motivation does not release them from the obligation of working with others who are motivated differently—for example, with atheists—as they fulfill that obligation in all their earthly affairs. As a result of the gospel, responsibility for the path and the fate of the socialist movement today—as the movement which has taken upon itself the goal of liberating the oppressed classes and overcoming class society—falls on nobody as much as on Christians.

IV

Three decades before Grimme's statement, Karl Barth coined one that is similar and characteristically different. In a lecture on "War, Socialism, and Christianity" before the Grütliverein (an assembly in the Swiss Social-Democratic Party) held in Zofingen on February 14, 1915, he said: *"A real Christian must become a socialist (if they want to do with the reformation of Christianity in earnest). A real socialist must be a Christian (if they are concerned with the reformation of socialism)."*[23]

Christianity urgently required a reformation, as did socialism, for the young pastor of the industrial village of Safenwil. The events of the time had made this clear, especially the onset of World War I. His theological teachers in Germany became slaves to the nationalist mania and the Christian churches in Europe said "Yes" to mass slaughter. The socialist parties approved of the war loans, and in all European fatherlands were proud when Karl Bröger—the poet of the working

23. I owe the communication of this statement from the "Sozialistischen Reden [Ed., Socialist Speeches]" (which constitutes the bulk of Karl Barth's papers from Safenwil) to F.-W. Marquardt, who has undertaken the editorship of this part of Barth's unpublished manuscripts with reference to the ongoing Gesamtausgabe from Theologischen Verlag Zürich. [Ed. Karl Barth, *Vorträge und kleinere Arbeiten 1914-1921*, ed. Hans-Anton Drewes. Gesamtausgabe 3 (Zürich: TVZ, 2012). The title page of this volume reads "Im Verbindung mit Friedrich-Wilhelm Marquardt"—"in conjunction with Friedrich-Wilhelm Marquardt."]

class from Nuremberg—sang of the fatherland, "your poorest son was also your most faithful." Barth's expectation was for a double reformation in which Christians would become socialists and socialists would become Christians.

Barth did not speak this clearly in his later work about Christians becoming socialists.[24] He expected the necessary reformation of Christianity from a definitive and unfettered hearing, considering, and bearing witness to the biblical message, and his other work should serve this reformation. So it seemed to many who followed him attentively as if he had transcribed the significance of socialism for the renewal of Christianity. That he spoke only rarely of socialism for a long time—in his later years, incidentally, again more than in his middle period—is bound up with the strain of his theological work as well as with the events of the time, particularly with the history of socialism and, later, also with the Stalinist degeneration of its Eastern form. But he never left any doubt that hearing and bearing witness to the gospel can only occur in the unity of living action, in the unity of witness in word and deed, and that the witness in deed by which the Christian community exhibits its proclamation must always be a political witness as well. He showed the "direction and orientation" that the gospel indicates for this political witness in his conduct as well as in his writings, and that was simply a direction toward socialism and democracy. There could be no renewal of Christianity for him without a decided movement of Christians and the church in this direction. For him, the pursuit of this direction was not commanded only as a consequence of the gospel. Rather, he also expected it to have repercussions for the faith and proclamation of the church. Getting serious with this direction of movement will bring the church out from its restraint by the interests of the middle class, from its class-bondage to the bourgeoisie, from the individualist tradition of its understanding of the gospel, and from the false interiority that allows faith to be socially barren.

This is as relevant today as it was then. All Christian renewal movements will slip beneath the waves where they avoid proving themselves by rigorous work for social renewal. The old salvation-egoism forfeits its being as the self-involved soul of culture when the revolution of the inner person through the message does not entail work for the revolution of society. Being revolutionized by the gospel opposes

24. [Ed. My translation of this sentence is more expansive than usual in order to track the flow of Gollwitzer's argument. The original reads: *Das erstere hat er später nicht mehr in dieser Deutlichkeit gesagt.*]

the mental block, produced by unwillingness to acknowledge one's own class-bondage, that sanctions shying away from attacking the class society. It is not "taken seriously" with the whole will of the Father; it is confined to the individual or the religious sphere. For this reason, it cannot operate comprehensively for us, which is its purpose. Entry into the socialist movement is indispensable for the reformation of Christianity.

As for the socialists, Barth seems to speak more dictatorially than Grimme: socialists "must" be Christians. But this "must" will not, in reality, take the place of Grimme's "can." It will not repeat the old error of linking socialism with a worldview, this time with the Christian worldview rather than with atheistic dialectical materialism. And it will not make Christianity mandatory for socialists and excommunicate the non-Christian socialists from the movement. This "must" has a different quality: the quality of appeal, of advice, of drawing attention. Barth does not apply it to socialists from the outside as a Christian and call them to repentance on account of their atheism, and he does not assert that their atheism is responsible for the poor state of the socialist movement. Rather, he speaks here as one socialist to other socialists. He is concerned with them because of the state of the socialist movement, which is still so necessary for society, just as he previously spoke as a Christian to Christians out of concern about the state of the Christian church, which is still so necessary for society. With his comrades, he asks about what could help the socialist movement and what could renew it. And he answers: We must be Christians.

Perhaps it is not accidental but grounded in the deepest insight that in the first part he says "become" but, in the second part, he says "be." Perhaps (I still don't know the context) he wants to express with this: socialists can become socialists on their own initiative; Christians cannot decide to become Christians. They must be Christians already so that they are Christians—that is, they discover themselves as Christians by discovering what they have become through the action of the divine Word and Spirit. Holding tightly to the difference between the two auxiliary verbs, the second part speaks not so much about a demand made of socialists as of an urgent wish, of socialism's glaring need. If the socialist movement is going to get out of its poor state, if it is going to fulfill the function for which it is so urgently needed by society, if it is not going to again and again fail and degenerate, then the real socialists, those who are located at the reformation of socialism, must come under the influence of God's Word and Spirit so that then the lively bearers of the socialist movement are, at the same time, lively Christians, hearers of the gospel, and disciples of Jesus. Then will a renewed socialism take up the struggle, which has become almost hopeless at the moment through the great failure of the leaders and the masses.

So speaks a socialist who, in hearing the biblical message, has realized how little we humans can protect ourselves from the dangers surrounding us, and how much we need from God's Spirit for protection and equipment especially in the political struggle. Resignation and fanaticism, lust for power and herd-mentality, arrogance and cowardice, miscalculation of the situation through the obfuscation of surrendering reason and the ossification in solidified traditions, through dogmatism and opportunism—all this threatens those who have engaged themselves in so difficult an undertaking as that of overcoming class society. And those who keep aloof from such an undertaking have it easy, gleefully and gloatingly decrying the detriment of such a bold movement. Barth certainly does not mean that Christians are better and smarter than other people. He means instead that where there are lively Christians, their bold movement—which is therefore as vulnerable as the socialist movement—is urgently needed because they bring an instruction and power of preservation and renewal.

Concerning the inner-socialist conversation that the second part entails, he now strikes back instead toward Christians because of how they approach the socialist movement from the outside and count off all sorts of its detriments on their fingers as arguments for why they should stay away from it. In order for it to be renewed, socialism needs people who are themselves real socialists and real Christians. The detriments that place the socialist movement in need of renewal may result from the absence of Christian socialists, of socialist Christians. These detriments, which Christians so self-righteously enumerate from the outside, become the burden of these Christians themselves. But if the socialist movement is urgently necessary in a society situated within the disorder of class antagonisms, then by having missed the socialist movement, Christians have also missed society's needy ones and have not moved into the place in this society in which they were necessary before. Christians will move into this place if they themselves become penitent, instead of calling socialists to repentance. Then they will recognize that the gospel itself makes them responsible for the path and fate of the socialist movement because of the gospel's intrinsic tendency. Their own *metanoia* will therefore be the opportunity for the socialist movement's renewal: the reformation of Christianity and the reformation of socialism are one and the same reformation.

This bold conviction of the young socialist pastor has lost none of its relevance. It is bold because it does not care that Christians who become socialists are, in many cases, admitted into the socialist movement's organizations with no great enthusiasm, and will often have a difficult time for reasons that lie in this movement's tradition and in the tradition of the Christian church. It also does not care that these "real Christians" will probably always be a small minority that often seems powerless enough. This conviction relies on the promise that the little flock of Christians will become effective far beyond its borders as salt and light if it would only risk acting in the world into which it is sent.

V

This discussion of socialism, about the socialist formulation of the goal as well as the empirical socialist movement, was prompted by the two statements from Adolf Grimme and Karl Barth. The question of whether socialism remains a useable word today arises because of socialism's fragmentation and because of the many disappointments that it has suffered and caused. It seems to lack clarity when it is not identified with a particular political program, such as the Third International controlled from Moscow (which both Grimme and Barth confronted with lively criticism). The statements from these two men are no longer correct if the word "socialism" is identified with such a program because this would force Christian freedom under a legal yoke. But looks can be deceiving. The word "socialism" has enough determinacy for all its breadth, and it has enough breadth for all its determinacy, to make those statements possible—indeed, necessary!—for Christians. In the same year that Adolf Grimme formulated his statement, Walter Dirks[25] clarified the determinacy of the word "socialism" in a way that remains valid today such that the interpretation of these two statements can be concluded with his words.

> Socialism is . . . the social, in the sense of the cooperative, raised to a concrete order. There is a definite boundary here between social policy that does not necessarily concern the essence and thus the whole, but rather

25. "Das Wort Sozialismus [Ed., The Word Socialism]," *Frankfurter Hefte* [Ed., *Frankfurt Magazine*], October 1946.

attacks parts and therefore can be unsystematic, and the socialist politics that go all out on social life in its entirety. Sure enough, the awareness that underwrites our politics is that precisely this overall reform is necessary: an actual reconstruction of economic and social life. Those who deny this will justifiably reject the word socialism—because they must reject the subject matter. . . . We recommend it to all Christians who have found out that there is an essential rather than merely quantitative difference between restricted freedom of production and economic planning infused with freedom. Whoever mentally transfers from the one system to the other has a conversion behind them, not a religious but a political one. Whoever has this conversion behind them should confess that this happens through appropriating the word socialism. We believe that Christians who have such conversions behind them cannot continue to be spared this confession. That is why we advocate not only for the subject matter but also for the word.

Appendix 2:
Why Am I, as a Christian,
a Socialist? Theses

Helmut Gollwitzer (1980)

I[1]

What does it mean when people say about themselves:
"I am a socialist"?

1.1. A socialist maintains that a better society than the current one is possible and necessary.

1.2. By "a better society," I mean not only improvements from within the current social order, but also a society whose fundamental structures are changed in comparison to the present society. Socialists collaborate on improvements within the present society, which binds them in active cooperation to all the socially responsible and knowledgeable people of that society. Furthermore, maintaining that funda-

---

1. [Ed. Helmut Gollwitzer, "Warum bin ich als Christ Sozialist? Thesen," *Christ und Sozialist. Blätter der Gemeinschaft für Christentum und Sozialismus* 1.1 (1980): 16–23.]

mental structural changes are possible and necessary is what distinguishes socialists from such people.

1.3. The objective of socialists is a society that is as egalitarian as possible. That is, a society with the greatest possible equality of opportunity, and the greatest possible self-determination (freedom) and co-determination of each member of society—without privileges of birth and property, stated negatively—with the greatest possible minimizing of exploitation, domination, and inequality in the appropriation of the social product.

1.4. The socialist takes seriously the original goals of bourgeois society—"Liberty, Equality, Fraternity"—which are realized by this society in only a limited way because of its safeguarding of privileges and inequality, and often, they will be denied if that seems advisable to keep in place the safeguarding of privileges ("fascism" in all its varieties). Friedrich Naumann (1908): 1. "Socialism is the widest conceivable extension of the liberal approach to all modern relations of domination and dependency." *Godesberger Program* of the Social Democratic Party of Germany: 2. "Socialism can only be realized through democracy; democracy can only be perfected by socialism."

1.5. Socialists have the imaginativeness to envision alternatives to current society, and on that basis, to criticize the current order without extenuation. They emphasize that the current society is not given either by God or by nature, and neither is it the end and goal of all history. Rather, it has become historical and historically surpassable, through both socialism and barbarism.

1.6. Socialists fight for structural change in society, and in this respect, they are revolutionary. The change toward which they move is a long process, and in this respect, they think in an evolutionary fashion. It depends on the circumstances as to whether a political revolution with the use of force is necessary for this change, or whether the transition from the old to the new form will take place gradually, step-by-step and peacefully. And it depends especially on the extent to which the forces interested in preserving the existing system of privilege seek to secure their privilege by the use of force and abolition of democratic rights.

1.7. Socialists are not representatives of a soteriology. They know that social orders cannot make people good or bad and cannot guarantee the happiness of the individual. But they also know that social conditions are deeply engraved upon people's thoughts, feelings, and behavior, and that—as we have lived to see in its most crass form during the time of Nazism—they can make a vast number of people better or worse, and that a system for privileges caused countless people material misery and impoverishment of life.

1.8. Socialists have reasonably come to the conviction that, based on today's scientific and technological development, a structural change that dismantles the previous privileges and leads to a real democracy is conceivable and possible. Furthermore, and given the destructive effects of this scientific and technological development so long as it stands at the service of the system of privileges (i.e., particular interests), such a change is urgently needed if the future is not to decay into barbarism.

II

Today's difficulties for socialists

2.1. The word "socialism" has become ambiguous; it has a positive meaning for some, but it has a negative meaning for many others.

2.2. The negative meaning of the word "socialism" in our country comes from

a. the chilling image—reinforced by anti-socialist and anti-communistic propaganda—offered to the West-German citizen today by the states that call themselves socialist,
b. because the radical change in those states came about by means of bloody civil wars,
c. because the radical change occurred in agrarian, "underdeveloped" countries and, therefore, a paradigm for the transition of a developed industrial country to a new, non-capitalistic society does not yet exist.

2.3. The ambiguity of the word "socialism" also arises because this word means a variety of things:

a. the objective of a new society,
b. the socialist organizations (parties and groups) who are fighting for it,
c. the structural measures that are supposed to lead step-by-step to the goal.

There is a broad consensus about: a) in the vicinity of b), that is, within the socialist organizations. They are in conflict with each other about: c), both concerning the individual measures as well as the necessary strategy.

2.4. The word "socialism" has become almost unusable because of this twofold ambiguity. Those who label themselves as socialists today must immediately add in what sense they are socialists. But they can also reserve the right to debate only about the socialism that they represent.

2.5. In this way, socialists find themselves today in a situation similar to that of Christians. Those who label themselves as Christians must—given the multiplicity of Christian denominations and groups—immediately add in what sense they label themselves as Christians. And they can stipulate concerning what they will speak about and stress that the burden of the sins of other Christian groups not be placed upon them. Christians (and, in the same way, socialists) will contradict and refute the claim that such sins necessarily follow from the essence of Christianity (or socialism) by means of their different understandings of Christianity (and socialism). The chilling reality of states that call themselves socialist is the same distressing problem for socialists as states and parties that called or still call themselves Christian are for Christians.

III

Why do people become socialists?

3.1. People become socialists either because they are powerfully struck by the harmfulness of the current social system itself, or because they identify with those who are affected—whether from moral motivations or from rational insights into the urgency of revolutionary change, or from both.

3.2. People become socialist when they experience or observe this social harmfulness not only as an isolated phenomena, but rather, penetrate through the phenomena in the foreground to their relationship: the relationship they have among themselves, as well as their relationship with the fundamental structures of current society and with the dominant mode of production.

3.3. Such foreground phenomena were, already since early capitalism: unemployment, the great inequality of opportunity and of living conditions, the devastating effects of capitalistic crisis on the existence of innumerable people, the economic causes of international conflicts (wars), the military-industrial complex (the defense industry, arms trafficking), and the enslavement of other peoples (colonialism). Added today is the waste of resources, the inhumanity of cities, the destruction of the countryside, the increase in productivity through increased fragmentation as well as the mechanization of labor (Taylorism) and the monitoring of productivity, the reduction of jobs and devaluing of labor through new technology, the discrepancy between satisfying the needs of consumption and frustrating the needs of life, the commercialization of interpersonal relationships and of sexuality, the breakdown of the family, and the subjugation of citizens under bureaucratic-technocratic devices.

3.4. In addition, at the same time as the material needs of the broad masses in the industrialized nations have been satisfied, the material impoverishment of the majority of the world population has reached a scale unprecedented in history. The question that presents itself is whether the prosperity here and misery there causally form a pair, like two sides of the same coin.

3.5. The relationship of all these appearances becomes visible, according to socialists, when you ask about the laws and consequences of the fundamental mode of production of our time, which is now expanding over the whole globe—namely, the capitalist method.

3.6. The socialist holds that while this mode of production is not the only cause, it is surely the chief cause of the misery of today's world and the dangers of today's future. They see that without knowledge of this chief cause, all analysis of today's problems and all proposed solutions remain on the surface, and therefore, show no way out. They have grounds for the prognosis that human survival, which is endangered today for the first time in history, cannot succeed without overcoming this chief cause.

IV

Why do Christians become socialists?

4.1. Asking why people become socialists today denotes an essentially negative impulse: insight into the extensive harmfulness of today's society, which is grounded in the nature of the capitalist mode of production. According to Jean Ziegler (professor of sociology in Geneva), the indispensable condition in today's international situation for socialists is "to preserve at their inmost depths the sense of horror in order to make it the foundation of daily awareness." For Christians, a crucial positive impulse additionally comes from the gospel.

4.2. The gospel shows us

a. the world as God's beloved creation in which people are placed "to build and to preserve" (Gen 2:15),

b. people as the beloved children of God, whom God—through God's self-giving in God's son, Jesus Christ—wants to save from the effects of their sinful self-destruction, and whom God wants to assemble into a sisterly and brotherly family,

c. that the active love responsible for the physical and spiritual life of the sisterly and brotherly humanity is the fruit of faith, to which we who were previously bound to our egotistical interests become freed by the Spirit of Jesus Christ.

4.3. A new attitude consequently arises toward all the privileges that we possess:

a. What privileges I possess should—in thanks to God, who gave them to me—be used to serve my neighbors. "What is not service, is robbery" (Luther).

b. What I have in social privileges above my creaturely and spiritual privileges should become the rights of all. I will therefore not participate in the struggle of those who want to maintain their privilege but, rather, in the struggle of those who want to dismantle these privileges in favor of the previously disadvantaged. The gospel assigns me to see, and therefore, change society from its lowest place which, consequently, is where the disadvantaged of all kinds stand.

4.4. All historical societies since the agricultural period were privilege-based societies. Their history, systems of law, culture, and religion were determined by the interests of the privileged classes in order to assert their privileges: class warfare from above. The Christian community is intended to be a fellowship that is free of privilege and domination. For this reason. it stands in opposition to the privilege-based society that surrounds it. It belongs to the Christian community's responsibility for the world that it is not only an island within which people live differently, but also a cell that produces an external effect, which participates in dismantling the system of privileges in cooperation with parallel efforts.

4.5. The pervasiveness of the system of privileges results from the relationship between the surrounding society and the Christian community. In the course of their history, the Christian churches have formed various alliances with the systems of privileges and have performed ideological services for them. Through this, they have become complicit in much oppression and injustice ("the class-bondage of the church"). As it applies to today's global world: while class antagonisms are "moderated" within capitalism's countries of origin, there persists the "crass class antagonisms . . . today between the first world, inclusive of labor, and the masses of the third world" (C. Fr. von Weizsäcker, "Fragen zur Weltpolitik" [Ed. "Questions about World Politics"], München 1975, S.42). For that reason, the word of a Latin American bishop applies to us Christians in Germany: "No Germans can say that they are innocent."

4.6. The conversion[2] to which the Christian community is daily called by God's Word also includes the renunciation of their integration in the dominant system of privileges and their active exertion for justice, and so for social structures no longer determined by social privileges. That is why the most important question today is not about the relationship of Christianity and socialism, but is first about the relationship between being a Christian and capitalism: can Christians approve of

2. [Ed. I translate Gollwitzer's use of *Umkehr* as "conversion" rather than as "repentance" or the more abstract "change." Especially within the idiom of North American Christianity, the concept of conversion always includes repentance and a metaphorical change of direction.]

and defend the current social system, together with its underlying economic order, or must not this be unbearable for Christians?

4.7. If Christians are conscious of the incompatibility between the gospel and the capitalist system of privileges, and if they see that the gospel inevitably and inexorably pushes them to participation in the struggle for a more just and more solidary society, then they must investigate rationally and decide to what extent a social change is now possible and necessary; which strategies, which alliances, and which compromises to choose to favor; and what the structural changes that are now due should look like. This happens in rational discussion and in the political decision-making processes. There are no absolute decisions, and therefore, no absolute contrasts in the field of rationality. Instead, the "direction and orientation" (Karl Barth) of our political activity is specified by the gospel: toward a solidary, democratic, privilege-free society.

In this way, the gospel provides Christians' political responsibility with the motive, the goal, and the criterion for choosing the methods and the manner of struggle.

4.8. The gospel specifies this "direction and orientation," and the decision for socialism indeed develops out of it. But the gospel does not specify this decision. It is dependent upon a more reasonable and adequate assessment of the situation, upon information about the situation free from ideological obligation to privileges.

4.9. Socialism is not identical with Marxism. There are many non-Marxist socialists, and there are almost as many Marxist schools of thought as there are Christian theologies. For socialists, Marxism is a theoretical instrument for analyzing the situation and developing strategy. Christians can use this instrument as socialists, regardless of whether it was invented by atheists and is connected with an atheistic worldview through historical circumstances. They use this instrument in accordance with the rule of Christian freedom—"Examine everything; keep hold of what is good (literally: the beautiful)!" (1 Thess 5:21)[3]—and using it in Christian freedom means, therefore, not "believing" in it, not holding it as a rigid doctrine, but using it in free examination and according to suitability.

---

3. [Ed. This biblical quotation is translated from Gollwitzer's German rendering.]

4.10. Movement in this "direction and orientation" and freedom for the practical consequences—to which also belongs the impartial examination of socialist thought—is demanded of us often enough by the Daily Texts[4] such as, for example, those for January 24, 1979: "I know that the Lord directs the cause of the needy" (Ps 140:12). —"Listen, my dear brothers and sisters! Has not God chosen the poor people in this world? But you have done dishonor to the poor" (Jas 2:5–6). —"Now so many are waiting: the blind, the old, / the crippled, the deaf. Who then measures their sorrow? / And we? We want to preserve our lives -, to lose time and eternity." (P. Toaspern)

---

4. [Ed. Gollwitzer refers to the Moravian "Daily Slogans"—*Tageslosungen*—used by my Christians worldwide for devotional purposes. The Moravian Church in North America publishes these texts yearly as *Moravian Daily Texts: A Devotional Guide for Every Day.* The biblical quotations above are translated from Gollwitzer's German rendering.]

Bibliography

"The Accra Confession: Covenanting for Justice in the Economy and the Earth."
World Alliance of Reformed Churches and North American Covenanting for
Justice Working Group, 2010. https://www.pcusa.org/site_media/media/
uploads/hunger/pdf/accra-confession.pdf.

Alexander, Michelle. *The New Jim Crow: Mass Incarceration in the Age of Colorblindness*. Revised ed. New York: The New Press, 2012.

Aquinas, Thomas. *St. Thomas Aquinas on Politics and Ethics: A New Translation, Backgrounds, Interpretations*. Translated by Paul E. Sigmund. Norton Critical Editions in the History of Ideas. New York: W. W. Norton and Company, 1988.

Aristotle. *The Basic Works of Aristotle*. Edited by Richard McKeon. New York: The Modern Library, 2001.

Barnett, Victoria. *For the Soul of the People: Protestant Protest against Hitler*. New York: Oxford University Press, 1992.

Barth, Karl. *Christengemeneinde und Bürgergemeinde*. Theologische Studien, vol. 20. Zollikon-Zürich: Evangelischer Verlag, 1946.

———. "The Christian Community and the Civil Community." In *Community, State, and Church: Three Essays*, 149–89. Gloucester, MA: Peter Smith, 1968.

———. *Church Dogmatics*. Translated and edited by Geoffrey W. Bromiley and Thomas F. Torrance. 4 volumes in 13 parts. Edinburgh: T&T Clark, 1956–75.

———. *The Epistle to the Romans*. Translated by Edwyn C. Hoskyns. Oxford: Oxford University Press, 1968.

———. "The Humanity of God." In *The Humanity of God*. Translated by John Newton Thomas and Thomas Wieser, 37–65. Louisville, KY: Westminster John Knox Press, 1960.

———. "Jesus Christ and the Movement for Social Justice." In *Karl Barth and Rad-*

ical Politics. Edited by George Hunsinger, 19–45. Philadelphia: Westminster Press, 1976.

———. *Die kirchliche Dogmatik*. 4 volumes in 13 parts. Munich, Zürich: Chr. Kaiser, TVZ, 1932–65.

———. "The Word of God and the Task of the Ministry." In *The Word of God and the Word of Man*. Translated by Douglas Horton, 183–217. New York: Harper & Brothers, 1957.

Barth, Karl, and Eduard Thurneysen. *Revolutionary Theology in the Making: Barth-Thurneysen Correspondence, 1914–1925*. Translated by James D. Smart. Richmond, VA: John Knox Press, 1964.

Barth, Markus. "Current Discussions on the Political Character of Karl Barth's Theology." In *Footnotes to a Theology: The Karl Barth Colloquium of 1972*. Edited by Martin Rumscheidt, 77–94. Waterloo, Ont.: Corporation for the Publication of Academic Studies in Religion in Canada, 1974.

Baudelaire, Charles. *Paris Spleen: Little Poems in Prose*. Translated by Keith Waldrop. Middletown, CT: Wesleyan University Press, 2009.

Beevor, Anthony. *The Fall of Berlin, 1945*. New York: Penguin, 2002.

Benjamin, Walter. "Capitalism as Religion." In *Walter Benjamin: Selected Writings, Volume 1 1913–1926*. Edited by Michael W. Jennings, 288–91. Cambridge, MA: Belknap Press, 1996.

Bentley, James. *Between Marx and Christ: The Dialogue in German-Speaking Europe, 1870–1970*. London: Verso Books, 1982.

Bethge, Eberhard. *Dietrich Bonhoeffer: A Biography*, revised edition. Minneapolis, MN: Fortress Press, 2000.

Beutel, Albrecht. *Gerhard Ebeling—Eine Biographie*. Tübingen: Mohr Siebeck, 2012.

Boer, Roland. *Lenin, Religion, and Theology*. New Approaches to Religion and Power. Edited by Joerg Rieger. New York: Palgrave Macmillan, 2013.

———. *Political Grace: The Revolutionary Theology of John Calvin*. Louisville, KY: Westminster John Knox Press, 2009.

Bonhoeffer, Dietrich. *Letters and Papers from Prison*. Translated by Reinhard Krauss, Nancy Lukens, Lisa E. Dahill and Isabel Best. Dietrich Bonhoeffer's Works, volume 8. Minneapolis, MN: Fortress Press, 2010.

Braun, Dietrich. "Helmut Gollwitzer in den Jahren des Kirchenkampfs 1934–1938." In *Coena Domini. Die altlutherische Abendmahlslehre in ihrer Auseinandersetzung mit dem Calvinismus, dargestellt an der lutherischen Frühorthodoxie*, 5–161. München: Chr. Kaiser, 1988.

Braun, Herbert. "Gottes Existenz und meine Geschichtlichkeit im Neuen Testament. Eine Antwort an Helmut Gollwitzer." In *Zeit und Geschichte: Dankesgabe an Rudolf Bultmann zum 80. Geburtstag.* Edited by Erich Dinkler, 399–421. Tübingen: J. C. B. Mohr (Paul Siebeck), 1964.

Brunner, Emil, and Karl Barth. *Natural Theology: Comprising "Nature and Grace" by Professor Dr. Emil Brunner and the Reply "No!" By Dr. Karl Barth.* Translated by Peter Fraenkel. Eugene, OR: Wipf & Stock, 2002.

Buhle, Paul. *Marxism in the United States: Remapping the History of the American Left,* revised edition. Haymarket Series. New York: Verso, 1991.

Burgess, John P. "Reconciliation and Justification." In *Sanctified by Grace: A Theology of the Christian Life.* Edited by Kent Eilers and Kyle Strobel, 91–104. London: Bloomsbury, 2014.

Busch, Eberhard. *Barth.* Abingdon Pillars of Theology. Nashville, TN: Abingdon Press, 2008.

_____. *Karl Barth: His Life from Letters and Autobiographical Texts.* Translated by John Bowden. Philadelphia: Fortress Press, 1976.

Calvin, John. *Commentaries on the Book of Genesis.* Translated by John King. Calvin's Commentaries, vol. 1. Edited by the Calvin Translation Society. Grand Rapids, MI: Baker Book House, 2003.

_____. *Institutes of the Christian Religion,* 2 volumes. Translated by Ford Lewis Battles and edited by John T. McNeill. Library of Christian Classics. Philadelphia: Westminster Press, 1960.

Carr, Raymond. "Barth and Cone in Dialogue on Revelation and Freedom: An Analysis of James Cone's Critical Appropriation of 'Barthian' Theology." Doctoral dissertation, Graduate Theological Union, 2011.

Carter, Heath W. *Union Made: Working People and the Rise of Social Christianity in Chicago.* Oxford: Oxford University Press, 2015.

Carter, J. Kameron. *Race: A Theological Account.* Oxford: Oxford University Press, 2008.

Chung, Paul S. *Church and Ethical Responsibility in the Midst of World Economy.* Eugene, OR: Cascade, 2013.

Cone, James H. *A Black Theology of Liberation,* Twentieth Anniversary edition. Maryknoll, NY: Orbis, 2004.

_____. *The Cross and the Lynching Tree.* Maryknoll, NY: Orbis, 2011.

Congar, Yves. *I Believe in the Holy Spirit.* Translated by David Smith. Milestones in Catholic Theology. New York: Crossroad, 2006.

_____. *The Mystery of the Church.* Translated by A. V. Littledale. London: Geoffrey Chapman, 1960.

_____. *The Word and the Spirit.* Translated by David Smith. San Francisco: Harper & Row, 1986.

Congdon, David W. "Afterword: The Future of Conversing with Barth." In *Karl*

Barth in Conversation. Edited by W. Travis McMaken and David W. Congdon, 255–78. Eugene, OR: Pickwick, 2014.

———. "Demystifying the Program of Demythologizing: Rudolf Bultmann's Theological Hermeneutics." *Harvard Theological Review* 110, no. 1 (2017): 1–23.

———. "Emancipatory Intercultural Hermeneutics: Interpreting Theo Sundermeier's *Differenzhermeneutik.*" *Mission Studies* 33 (2016): 127–46.

———. *The God Who Saves: A Dogmatic Sketch.* Eugene, OR: Cascade, 2016.

———. *The Mission of Demythologizing: Rudolf Bultmann's Dialectical Theology.* Minneapolis, MN: Fortress Press, 2015.

———. *Rudolf Bultmann: A Companion to His Theology.* Cascade Companions. Eugene, OR: Cascade, 2015.

Cox, Harvey. *The Market as God.* Cambridge, MA: Harvard University Press, 2016.

———. *The Secular City: Secularization and Urbanization in Theological Perspective.* Princeton: Princeton University Press, 2013.

Curnow, Rohan M. "Which Preferential Option for the Poor? A History of the Doctrine's Bifurcation." *Modern Theology* 31, no. 1 (2015): 27–59.

Dannemann, Ulrich, and Matthias Weissinger. "Helmut Gollwitzers Beitrag zur Theologie der Gesellschaft." In *Richte unsere Füße auf den Weg des Friedens: Helmut Gollwitzer zum 70. Geburtstag.* Edited by Andreas Baudis, Dieter Clausert, Volkhard Schliski and Bernhard Wegener, 578–96. Munich: Chr. Kaiser, 1979.

Day, Helga Krüger. "Christlicher Glaube und gesellschaftliches Handeln: eine Studie der Entwicklung der Theologie Helmut Gollwitzers." Doctoral dissertation, Union Theological Seminary, 1973.

Doyle, Dennis M. *Communion Ecclesiology: Vision and Versions.* Maryknoll, NY: Orbis, 2000.

Drury, John. "Promise and Command: Barth and Wesley on Matthew 5:48." In *Karl Barth in Conversation.* Edited by W. Travis McMaken and David W. Congdon, 3–20. Eugene, OR: Pickwick, 2014.

Duchrow, Ulrich. *Global Economy: A Confessional Issue for the Churches?* Translated by David Lewis. Geneva: WCC Publications, 1987.

Eagleton, Terry. *Reason, Faith, & Revolution: Reflections on the God Debate.* The Terry Lectures. New Haven, CT: Yale University Press, 2009.

———. *Why Marx Was Right.* New Haven, CT: Yale University Press, 2011.

Ellison, Ralph. *Invisible Man.* New York: Vintage Books, 1995 [1952].

Feuerbach, Ludwig. *The Essence of Christianity.* Translated by George Eliot. New York: Harper & Brothers, 1957.

Flett, John G. *Apostolicity: The Ecumenical Question in World Christian Perspective.* Missiological Engagements. Downers Grove, IL: IVP Academic, 2016.

_____. *The Witness of God: The Trinity, Missio Dei, Karl Barth, and the Nature of Christian Community.* Grand Rapids, MI: Eerdmans, 2010.

Geis, Robert Raphael. *Leiden an der Unerlöstheit der Welt: Briefe, Reden, Aufsätze.* München: Chr. Kaiser Verlag, 1984.

Gilens, Martin, and Benjamin I. Page. "Testing Theories of American Politics: Elites, Interest Groups, and Average Citizens." *Perspectives on Politics* 12, no. 3 (2014): 564–81.

Gloege, Timothy E. W. *Guaranteed Pure: The Moody Bible Institute, Business, and the Making of Modern Evangelicalism.* Chapel Hill, NC: University of North Carolina Press, 2015.

Gollwitzer, Helmut. "Die Abendmahlsfrage als Aufgabe kirchlicher Lehre." In *Theologische Aufsätze: Karl Barth zum 50. Geburtstag.* Edited by Ernst Wolf, 275–98. München: Chr. Kaiser Verlag, 1936.

_____. "Auf dem Linken pfad geschmeichelt?" In *Müssen Christen Sozialisten sein? Zwischen Glaube und Politik.* Edited by Wolfgang Teichert, 31–40. Hamburg: Lutherisches Verlagshaus, 1976.

_____. *Befreiung zur Solidarität: Einführung in die evangelische Theologie.* München: Chr. Kaiser Verlag, 1978.

_____. *Die Christen und die Atomwaffen.* Theologische Existenz heute. Edited by K. G. Steck and G. Eichholz. München: Chr. Kaiser Verlag, 1957.

_____. *The Christian Faith and the Marxist Criticism of Religion.* Translated by David Cairns. New York: Charles Scribner's Sons, 1970.

_____. "The Christian in the Search for World Order and Peace." In *Responsible Government in a Revolutionary Age.* Edited by Z. K. Matthews, 47–66. New York: Association Press, 1966.

_____. *Coena Domini. Die altlutherische Abendmahlslehre in ihrer Auseinandersetzung mit dem Calvinismus, dargestellt an der lutherischen Frühorthodoxie.* München: Chr. Kaiser, 1988.

_____. . . . *daß Gerechtigkeit und Friede sich küssen: Aufsätz zur politishen Ethik*, band 2. Edited by Andreas Pangritz. Ausgewählte Werke. München: Chr. Kaiser, 1988.

_____. *The Demands of Freedom: Papers by a Christian in West Germany.* Translated by Robert W. Fenn. New York: Harper and Row Publishers, 1965.

_____. *The Dying and Living Lord.* Philadelphia: Muhlenberg Press, 1960.

_____. *The Existence of God as Confessed by Faith.* Translated by James W. Leitch. Philadelphia: Westminster Press, 1965.

_____. *Die Existenz Gottes im Bekenntnis des Glaubens.* Beiträge zur evangelischen Theologie, volume 34. München: Chr. Kaiser Verlag, 1963.

_____. *Forderungen der Freiheit: Aufsätze und Reden zur politischen Ethik.* München: Chr. Kaiser Verlag, 1962.

_____. *Forderungen der Umkehr: Beiträge zur Theologie der Gesellschaft.* München: Chr. Kaiser Verlag, 1976.

_____. "Die gesellschaftlichen Implikationen des Evangeliums." In *Umkehr und Revolution: Aufsätze zu christlichem Glauben und Marxismus,* band 2. Edited by Christian Keller, 62–74. Ausgewählte Werke. München: Chr. Kaiser, 1988.

_____. "Introduction." In *Church Dogmatics: A Selection.* Edited by G. W Bromiley, 1–28. New York: Harper Torchbooks, 1961.

_____. *An Introduction to Protestant Theology.* Translated by David Cairns. Philadelphia: The Westminster Press, 1982.

_____. *Israel - und Wir.* Berlin: Lettner Verlag, 1958.

_____. "Israel - und Wir." In *Auch das Denken darf dienen: Aufsätze zu Theologie und Geistesgeschichte,* band 2. Edited by Friedrich-Wilhelm Marquardt, 82–102. Ausgewählte Werke. München: Chr. Kaiser, 1988.

_____. *Die kapitalistische Revolution.* München: Chr. Kaiser Verlag, 1974.

_____. "Die kapitalistische Revolution." In *...daß Gerechtigkeit und Friede sich küssen: Aufsätz zur politishen Ethik,* band 1. Edited by Andreas Pangritz, 125–209. Ausgewählte Werke. München: Chr. Kaiser, 1988.

_____. "Karl Barths Theologie der Freiheit und die Theologie der Befreiung. Für Wolfgang Schweitzer zum 70. Geburtstag." In *Wer ist unser Gott? Beiträge zu einer Befreiungstheologie im Kontext der »ersten« Welt.* Edited by Luise Schottroff and Willy Schottroff, 25–42. Munich: Chr. Kaiser, 1986.

_____. "Kingdom of God and Socialism in the Theology of Karl Barth." In *Karl Barth and Radical Politics.* Edited by George Hunsinger, 77–120. Philadelphia: Westminster Press, 1976.

_____. "Klassenkampf ist keine Illusion. Ein Interview." In *Forderungen der Umkehr: Beiträge zur Theologie der Gesellschaft,* 209–19. München: Chr. Kaiser Verlag, 1976.

_____. *Krummes Holz - aufrechter Gang: zur Frage nach dem Sinn des Lebens.* München: Chr. Kaiser Verlag, 1970.

_____. "Einige Leitsätze zur christlichen Beteiligung am politischen Leben." In *Forderungen der Umkehr: Beiträge zur Theologie der Gesellschaft,* 15–20. Munich: Chr. Kaiser, 1976.

_____. "Liberation in History." *Interpretation* 28, no. 4 (1974): 404–21.

_____. "Lutherisch, reformiert, evangelisch." *Evangelische Theologie* 1 (1934): 307–25.

_____. "Martin Bubers Bedeutung für die protestantische Theologie." In *Leben als Begegnung. Ein Jahrhundert Martin Buber (1878-1978), Vorträge und Aufsätze.*

Edited by Peter von der Osten-Sacken, 63–79. Berlin: Institut Kirche und Judentum, 1982.

_____. "Die marxistische Religionskritik und der christliche Glaube." *Marxismusstudien* 4 (1962): 1–143.

_____. *Militär, Staat und Kirche*. Berliner Reden, volume 4. Berlin: Lettner-Verlag, 1965.

_____. "Militär, Staat und Kirche." In *. . . daß Gerechtigkeit und Friede sich küssen: Aufsätz zur politishen Ethik*, band 2. Edited by Andreas Pangritz, 151–62. Ausgewählte Werke. München: Chr. Kaiser, 1988.

_____. "Muß ein Christ Sozialist sein?" In *Jenseits vom Nullpunkt? Christsein im westlichen Deutschland. Bischof D. Kurt Scharf zum 70. Geburtstag am 21.19.1972.* Edited by Rudolf Weckerling, 151–70. Stuttgart: Kreuz, 1972.

_____. "The Real Luther." In *Martinus Luther: 450th Anniversary of the Reformation*, 7–14. Bad Godesberg: Inter Nationes, 1967.

_____. *Reich Gottes und Sozialismus bei Karl Barth*. Theologische Existenz heute. Edited by Karl Gerhard Steck. Munich: Chr. Kaiser, 1972.

_____. "Die Revolution des Reiches Gottes und die Gesellschaft." In *Umkehr und Revolution: Aufsätze zu christlichem Glauben und Marxismus*, Band 1. Edited by Christian Keller, 102–29. Ausgewählte Werke. München: Chr. Kaiser, 1988.

_____. *The Rich Christians and Poor Lazarus*. Translated by David Cairns. New York: Macmillan, 1970.

_____. "A Sermon About *Kristallnacht*." In *Preaching in Hitler's Shadow: Sermons of Resistance in the Third Reich*. Edited by Dean G. Stroud, 117–26. Grand Rapids, MI: Eerdmans, 2013.

_____. *Skizzen eines Lebens. Aus verstreuten Selbstzeugnissen gefunden und verbunden von Friedrich-Wilhelm Marquardt, Wolfgang Brinkel und Manfred Weber*. Gütersloh: Christian Kaiser Verlagshaus, 1998.

_____. "Sozialismus und Revolution." In *Umkehr und Revolution: Aufsätze zu christlichem Glauben und Marxismus*, band 1. Edited by Christian Keller, 130–40. Ausgewählte Werke. München: Chr. Kaiser, 1988.

_____. "Thanks to Karl Marx." *Journal of Ecumenical Studies* 22, no. 3 (1985): 589–91.

_____. "Theologie-Studium und sozialistisches Studium." In *Umkehr und Revolution: Aufsätze zu christlichem Glauben und Marxismus*, band 2. Edited by Christian Keller, 241–43. Ausgewählte Werke. München: Chr. Kaiser, 1988.

_____. "Theses for Understanding Biblical Speech About God." In *God, Secularization, and History: Essays in Memory of Ronald Gregor Smith*. Edited by Eugene Thomas Long, 125–35. Columbia, SC: University of South Carolina Press, 1974.

_____. *. . . und führen, wohin du nicht willst. Bericht einer Gefangenschaft.* München: Chr. Kaiser, 1959.

_____. *Unwilling Journey: A Diary from Russia.* Translated by E. M. Delacour and Robert Fenn. London: SCM Press, Ltd., 1953.

_____. "Vietnam 1967." In *. . . daß Gerechtigkeit und Friede sich küssen: Aufsätz zur politishen Ethik,* band 2. Edited by Andreas Pangritz, 163–66. Ausgewählte Werke. München: Chr. Kaiser, 1988.

_____. *Vietnam, Israel und die Christenheit.* München: Chr. Kaiser Verlag, 1967.

_____. "Warum bin ich als Christ Sozialist? Thesen." *Christ und Sozialist: Blätter der Gemeinschaft für Christentum und Sozialismus* 1, no. 1 (1980): 16–23.

_____. *The Way to Life: Sermons in a Time of World Crisis.* Translated by David Cairns. Edinburgh: T&T Clark, 1981.

_____. "Die Weltbedeutung des Judentums." In *Forderungen der Freiheit: Aufsätze und Reden zur politischen Ethik.* 268–74. München: Chr. Kaiser Verlag, 1964.

_____. "What Has the Christian to Do with Politics?" In *The Demands of Freedom: Papers by a Christian in West Germany,* 62–73. New York: Harper & Row, 1965.

_____. "Why Black Theology?" *Union Seminary Quarterly Review* 31, no. 1 (1975): 38–58.

_____. "Der Wille Gottes und die gesellschaftliche Wirklichkeit." In *Mensch, du bist gefragt: Reflexionen zur Gotteslehre.* Edited by Peter Winzeler, 274–79. Ausgewählte Werke. München: Chr. Kaiser, 1988.

_____. "Wo kein Dienst ist, da ist Raub." In *Müssen Christen Sozialisten sein? Zwischen Glaube und Politik.* Edited by Wolfgang Teichert, 100–110. Hamburg: Lutherisches Verlagshaus, 1976.

_____. "Zum Problem der Gewalt in der christlichen Ethik." In *. . . daß Gerechtigkeit und Friede sich küssen: Aufsätze zur politischen Ethik,* band 1. Edited by Andreas Pangritz, 100–124. Ausgewählte Werke. München: Chr. Kaiser, 1988.

_____. "Zur Frage der Gewalt hier und heute." In *. . . daß Gerechtigkeit und Friede sich küssen: Aufsätz zur politishen Ethik,* band 2. Edited by Andreas Pangritz, 167–70. Ausgewählte Werke. München: Chr. Kaiser, 1988.

Gollwitzer, Helmut, and Eva Bildt. *Ich will Dir schnell sagen, daß ich lebe, Liebster: Briefe aus dem Krieg 1940-1945.* Edited by Friedrich Künzel and Ruth Pabst. München: C. H. Beck Verlag, 2008.

Gollwitzer, Helmut, and Herbert Braun. "Post Bultmann locutum. Eine Diskussion zwischen Professor D. Helmut Gollwitzer - Berlin und Professor D. Herbert Braun - Mainz am 13. Februar 1964." In *Mensch, du bist gefragt: Reflexionen zur Gotteslehre.* Edited by Peter Winzeler, 42–85. Ausgewählte Werke. München: Chr. Kaiser, 1988.

González, Justo L. *The Story of Christianity*, 2 volumes, revised and updated edition. New York: HarperOne, 2010.

Gorringe, Timothy. *Karl Barth: Against Hegemony*. Christian Theology in Context. Oxford: Oxford University Press, 1999.

Clifford Green, "Freedom for Humanity: Karl Barth and the Politics of the New World Order." In *For the Sake of the World: Karl Barth and the Future of Ecclesial Theology*. Edited by George Hunsinger, 89–108. Grand Rapids, MI: Eerdmans, 2004.

Greene, Alison Collis. *No Depression in Heaven: The Great Depression, the New Deal, and the Transformation of Religion in the Delta*. New York: Oxford University Press, 2016.

Greggs, Tom. "Church and Sacraments." In *Sanctified by Grace: A Theology of the Christian Life*. Edited by Kent Eilers and Kyle Strobel, 157–69. London: Bloomsbury, 2014.

Haehn, Christa, ed. *Bibliographie Helmut Gollwitzer*, Ausgewählte Werke, volume 10. München: Chr. Kaiser, 1988.

Hamm, Berndt. *The Early Luther: Stages in a Reformation Reorientation*. Translated by Martin J. Lohrmann. Grand Rapids, MI: Eerdmans, 2014.

Hammann, Konrad. *Rudolf Bultmann: A Biography*. Translated by Philip E. Davenish. Salem, OR: Polebridge Press, 2013.

Hardt, Michael, and Antonio Negri. *Empire*. Cambridge, MA: Harvard University Press, 2000.

Hart, John W. *Karl Barth Vs. Emil Brunner: The Formation and Dissolution of a Theological Alliance, 1916-1936*. Issues in Systematic Theology. Edited by Paul D. Molnar. New York: Peter Lang, 2001.

Hector, Kevin W. *Theology without Metaphysics: God, Language, and the Spirit of Recognition*. Current Issues in Theology. Edited by Iain Torrance. New York: Cambridge University Press, 2011.

Helmer, Christine. *Theology and the End of Doctrine*. Louisville, KY: Westminster John Knox, 2014.

Henning, Christoph. *Philosophy after Marx: 100 Years of Misreadings and the Normative Turn in Political Philosophy*. Translated by Max Henninger. Historical Materialism Book Series. Boston: Brill, 2014.

Hieb, Nathan D. *Christ Crucified in a Suffering World: The Unity of Atonement and Liberation*. Emerging Scholars. Minneapolis, MN: Fortress Press, 2013.

Hunsinger, George. *The Beatitudes*. Mahwah, NJ: Paulist Press, 2015.

———. *How to Read Karl Barth: The Shape of His Theology*. New York: Oxford University Press, 1991.

———. "Karl Barth and Liberation Theology." *Journal of Religion* 63, no. 3 (1983): 247–63.

_____, ed. *Karl Barth and Radical Politics*. Philadelphia: Westminster Press, 1976.

_____, ed. *Torture Is a Moral Issue: Christians, Jews, Muslims and People of Conscience Speak Out*. Grand Rapids, MI: Eerdmans, 2008.

Hütter, Reinhard. *Suffering Divine Things: Theology as Church Practice*. Grand Rapids, MI: Eerdmans, 2000.

Hsiao, Andrew, and Audrea Lim, eds. *The Verso Book of Dissent: Revolutionary Words from Three Millenia of Rebellion and Resistance*. New York: Verso, 2016.

Jordan, William. "Democrats More Divided on Socialism." YouGov.com (January 28, 2016). https://today.yougov.com/news/2016/01/28/democrats-remain-divided-socialism/.

Jüngel, Eberhard. *Christ, Justice and Peace: Toward a Theology of the State in Dialogue with the Barmen Declaration*. Translated by D. Bruce Hamill and Alan J. Torrance. Edinburgh: T & T Clark, 1992.

_____. *God's Being Is in Becoming: The Trinitarian Being of God in the Theology of Karl Barth. A Paraphrase*. Translated by John Webster. Grand Rapids, MI: Eerdmans, 2001.

_____. "Zukunft und Hoffnung: zur politischen Funktion christlicher Theologie." In *Müssen Christen Sozialisten sein? Zwischen Glaube und Politik*. Edited by Wolfgang Teichert, 11–30. Hamburg: Lutherisches Verlagshaus, 1976.

Kahn, Paul W. *Putting Liberalism in Its Place*. Princeton, NJ: Prinecton University Press, 2005.

Kamenka, Eugene, ed. *The Portable Karl Marx*, Viking Portable Library. New York: Penguin Books, 1983.

Kant, Immanuel. *Groundwork of the Metaphysics of Morals*. Translated by Mary Gregor. Cambridge Texts in the History of Philosophy. Cambridge: Cambridge University Press, 1997.

Kay, James F. *Christus Praesens: A Reconsideration of Rudolf Bultmann's Christology*. Grand Rapids, MI: Eerdmans, 1994.

King, Martin Luther, Jr. "Letter from Birmingham City Jail." In *A Testament of Hope: The Essential Writings and Speeches of Martin Luther King, Jr.* Edited by James Melvin Washington, 289–302. New York: HarperOne, 1986.

_____. "Out of the Long Night." *The Gospel Messenger* 107, no. 6 (February 8 1958): 3–4, 13–15.

Kooi, Akke van der. "Election and the Lived Life. Considerations on Gollwitzer's Reading of Karl Barth in CD II/2 as a Contribution to Actual Discussions on Trinity and Election." *Zeitschrift für dialektische Theologie* Supplement Series, no. 4 (2010): 67–82.

Kruse, Kevin M. *One Nation under God: How Corporate America Invented Christian America*. New York: Basic Books, 2015.

Lehmann, Paul L. *Ethics in a Christian Context*. New York: Harper & Row, 1963.

_____. "Karl Barth, Theologian of Permanent Revolution." *Union Seminary Quarterly Review* 28, no. 1 (1972): 67–81.

_____. *The Transfiguration of Politics.* New York: Harper & Row, 1975.

Lepp, Claudia. "Helmut Gollwitzer als Dialogpartner der sozialen Bewegungen." In *Umbrüche: der deutsche Protestantismus und die sozialen Bewegungen in der 1960er und 70er Jahren.* Edited by Siegfried Hermle, Claudia Lepp, and Harry Oelke, 226–46. Göttingen: Vandenhoeck & Ruprecht, 2007.

Lichtenfeld, Manacnuc Mathias. *Georg Merz— Pastoraltheologe zwischen den Zeiten: Leben und Werk in Weimarer Republik und Kirchenkampf als theologischer Beitrag zur Praxis der Kirche.* Lutherische Kirche, Geschichte und Gestalten. Gütersloh: Gütersloher Verlagshaus, 1997.

Lindbeck, George A. "The Church." In *The Church in a Postliberal Age.* Edited by James J. Buckley, 146–65. Radical Traditions: Theology in a Postcritical Key. Grand Rapids, MI: Eerdmans, 2002.

_____. *The Nature of Doctrine: Religion and Theology in a Postliberal Age.* Louisville, KY: Westminster John Knox Press, 1984.

Losurdo, Domenico. *Liberalism: A Counter-History.* Translated by Gregory Elliott. London: Verso, 2011.

Ludwig, Hartmut. "'Christians Cannot Remain Silent About This Crime': On the Centenary of the Birth of Adolf Freudenberg." *Ecumenical Review* 46, no. 4 (1994): 475–85.

Luther, Martin. *Luther's Works, 25: Lectures on Romans, Glosses and Scholia.* Edited by Jaroslav Pelikan. Saint Louis, MO: Concordia Publishing House, 1972.

_____. "Von der Freiheit eines Christen Menschen," D. Martin Luthers Werke. Kritische Gesamtausgabe, volume 7. Edited by J. K. F. Knaake et al. Weimar: H. Böhlau, 1883.

Mandel, Ernest. *Late Capitalism.* Translated by Joris De Bres. London: Verso, 1978.

Marquardt, Friedrich-Wilhelm. "Helmut Gollwitzer: Weg und Werk." In *Bibliographie Helmut Gollwitzer.* Edited by Christa Haehn, 11–48. Ausgewählte Werke. München: Chr. Kaiser, 1988.

_____. "Hermeneutik des christlichen-jüdischen Verhältnisses. Über Helmut Gollwitzers Arbeit an der 'Judenfrage.'" In *Richte unsere Füße auf den Weg des Friedens: Helmut Gollwitzer zum 70. Geburtstag.* Edited by Andreas Baudis, Dieter Clausert, Volkhard Schliski and Bernhard Wegener, 138–54. München: Chr. Kaiser Verlag, 1979.

_____. "Socialism in the Theology of Karl Barth." In *Karl Barth and Radical Politics.* Edited by George Hunsinger, 47–76. Philadelphia: Westminster Press, 1976.

_____. *Theological Audacities: Selected Essays.* Edited by Andreas Pangritz and Paul S. Chung. Eugene, OR: Pickwick, 2010.

_____. "'Was nicht im Dienst steht, steht im Raub': zum ersten Versuch einer Gollwitzer-Biografie von Gottfried Orth." *Evangelische Theologie* 57, no. 2 (1997): 162–68.

McCann, Dennis P. "Ernst Troeltsch's Essay on 'Socialism.'" *Journal of Religious Ethics* 4, no. 1 (1976): 159–80.

McCormack, Bruce L. "God *Is* His Decision: The Jüngel-Gollwitzer 'Debate' Revisited." In *Theology as Conversation: The Significance of Dialogue in Historical and Contemporary Theology, a Festschrift for Daniel L. Migliore.* Edited by Bruce L. McCormack and Kimlyn J. Bender, 48–66. Grand Rapids, MI: Eerdmans, 2009.

_____. *Karl Barth's Critically Realistic Dialectical Theology: Its Genesis and Development, 1909-1936.* Oxford: Clarendon Press, 1995.

McMaken, W. Travis. "The Blame Lies with the Christians: Helmut Gollwitzer's Engagement with Marxist Criticism of Religion." *The Other Journal* 22 (2013): 13–20.

_____. "Occupy Wall Street Is Doing the Church's Work: Helmut Gollwitzer and Economic Justice." *Unbound* (January 16, 2013). http://justiceunbound.org/journal/occupy-wall-street-is-doing-the-churchs-work/.

_____. "'Shalom, Shalom, Shalom Israel!' Jews and Judaism in Helmut Gollwitzer's Life and Theology." *Studies in Christian-Jewish Relations* 10, no. 1 (2015): 1–22.

_____. *The Sign of the Gospel: Toward an Evangelical Doctrine of Infant Baptism after Karl Barth.* Emerging Scholars. Minneapolis, MN: Fortress Press, 2013.

McMaken, W. Travis, and David W. Congdon, eds. *Karl Barth in Conversation.* Eugene, OR: Pickwick, 2014.

Mead, Julia. "Why Millennials Aren't Afraid of Socialism." *The Nation* (January 10, 2017). https://www.thenation.com/article/why-millennials-arent-afraid-of-the-s-word/.

Merz, Georg. *Der vorreformatorische Luther.* München: Chr. Kaiser, 1926.

Moltmann, Jürgen. *A Broad Place: An Autobiography.* Translated by Margaret Kohl. Minneapolis, MN: Fortress Press, 2009.

_____. *The Living God and the Fullness of Life.* Translated by Margaret Kohl. Louisville, KY: Westminster John Knox Press, 2015.

_____. *Theology of Hope: On the Ground and the Implications of a Christian Eschatology.* Translated by James W. Leitch. Minneapolis, MN: Fortress Press, 1993.

Norton, Michael I., and Dan Ariely. "Building a Better America—One Wealth Quintile at a Time." *Perspectives on Psychological Science* 6, no. 1 (2011): 9–12.

Ochs, Peter. *Another Reformation: Postliberal Christianity and the Jews.* Grand Rapids, MI: Baker Academic, 2011.

Oden, Thomas C. *A Change of Heart: A Personal and Theological Memoir.* Downers Grove, IL: IVP Academic, 2014.

Oestreicher, Paul. "Helmut Gollwitzer in the European Storms." In *The Demands of Freedom: Papers by a Christian in West Germany*, 7–27. New York: Harper and Row Publishers, 1965.

Orth, Gottfried. *Helmut Gollwitzer: zur Solidarität befreit.* Mainz: Matthias-Grünewald Verlag, 1995.

_____. *Vom Abenteuer bürgerlichen Bewusstseins: die Predigten Helmut Gollwitzers, 1938-1976.* Europäische Hochschulschriften. Frankfurt am Main: Peter D. Lang, 1980.

Pangritz, Andreas. "Friedrich-Wilhelm Marquardt – a Theological-Biographical Sketch." *European Judaism* 38, no. 1 (2005): 17–47.

_____. "Helmut Gollwitzer als Theologe des Dialogs." Bonn: Rheinischen Friedrich-Wilhelms-Universität, December 3, 2008.

_____. "Helmut Gollwitzers Theologie des christlich-jüdischen Verhältnisses. Versuch eine kritischen Bilanz." *Evangelische Theologie* 56, no. 4 (1996): 359–76.

Peppard, Michael. "Should Christians Fear Trump's God?" *Commonweal Magazine* (January 24, 2017). https://www.commonwealmagazine.org/blog/should-christians-fear-trumps-god.

Piketty, Thomas. *Capital in the Twenty-First Century.* Translated by Arthur Goldhammer. Cambridge, MA: Belknap Press, 2014.

Piketty, Thomas, Emmanuel Saez, and Gabriel Zucman. "Distributional National Accounts: Methods and Estimates for the United States." Washington, DC: Washington Center for Equitable Growth, December, 2016.

"A Political Rhetoric Test: 'Socialism' Not So Negative, 'Capitalism' Not So Positive." Washington, DC: The Pew Research Center for The People and The Press, May 4, 2010.

Rees, Janice. "Resisting the Kingdom: Women in the Gym, Theological Optimism, and the Liturgical Deformation of Inclusion." *Women in Theology* (October 23, 2013). https://womenintheology.org/2013/10/23/resisting-the-kingdom-women-in-the-gym-theological-optimism-and-the-liturgical-deformation-of-inclusion/.

Reich, Robert B. *Saving Capitalism: For the Many, Not the Few.* New York: Alfred A. Knopf, 2015.

Rieger, Joerg. *Christ & Empire: From Paul to Postcolonial Times.* Minneapolis, MN: Fortress Press, 2007.

_____. *No Rising Tide: Theology, Economics, and the Future.* Minneapolis, MN: Fortress Press, 2009.

Rogers, Jack. *Reading the Bible & the Confessions: The Presbyterian Way.* Louisville, KY: Geneva Press, 1999.

Ruether, Rosemary Radford. *The Radical Kingdom: The Western Experience of Messianic Hope.* New York: Harper & Row, 1970.

Rumscheidt, Martin. "'Socialists May Be Christians; Christians Must Be Socialists.' Karl Barth Was!" *Toronto Journal of Theology* 17, no. 1 (2001): 107–18.

Scheid, Anna Floerke. *Just Revolution: A Christian Ethic of Political Resistance and Social Transformation.* Lanham, MD: Lexington Books, 2015.

Schnübbe, Otto. *Die Existenzbegriff in der Theologie Rudolf Bultmanns. Ein Beitrag zur Interpretation der theologischen Systematic Bultmanns.* Göttingen: Vandenhoeck & Ruprecht, 1959.

Scholder, Klaus. *The Churches and the Third Reich,* 2 volumes. Philadelphia: Fortress Press, 1988.

Schüssler Fiorenza, Elisabeth. *Jesus: Miriam's Child, Sophia's Prophet – Critical Issues in Feminist Christology.* New York: Continuum, 1994.

Smith, James K. A. *Desiring the Kingdom: Worship, Worldview, and Cultural Formation.* Cultural Liturgies. Grand Rapids, MI: Baker Academic, 2009.

_____. "Editorial: Join the Anti-Revolutionary Party." *Comment Magazine* (August 18, 2016). https://www.cardus.ca/comment/article/4919/editorial-join-the-anti-revolutionary-party/.

Smith, Ronald Gregor. *Secular Christianity.* London: Collins, 1966.

Smith, Ted A. *Weird John Brown: Divine Violence and the Limits of Ethics.* Encountering Traditions. Stanford, CA: Stanford University Press, 2015.

Snow, Matthew. "Against Charity." *Jacobin* (August 25, 2015). https://www.jacobinmag.com/2015/08/peter-singer-charity-effective-altruism/.

Soelle, Dorothee. *Political Theology.* Translated by John Shelley. Philadelphia: Fortress Press, 1974.

_____. *The Window of Vulnerability: A Political Spirituality.* Translated by Linda M. Maloney. Minneapolis, MN: Fortress Press, 1990.

Spencer, Archie J. *The Analogy of Faith: The Quest for God's Speakability.* Strategic Initiatives in Evangelical Theology. Downers Grove, IL: IVP Academic, 2015.

Stephens, Randall J. "From Abolitionists to Fundamentalists: The Transformation of the Wesleyan Methodists in the Nineteenth and Twentieth Centuries." *American Nineteenth Century History* 16, no. 2 (2015): 159–91.

Stetzer, Ed. "Politics, Social Media, and More Important Things." ChristianityToday.com (October 10, 2013). http://www.christianitytoday.com/edstetzer/2013/october/politics-social-media-and-more-important-things.html.

Stieber-Westermann, Rolf. *Die Provokation zum Leben: Gott im theologischen Werk*

Helmut Gollwitzers. Europäische Hochschulschriften. Frankfurt am Main: Peter Lang, 1993.

Stiglitz, Joseph E. *The Price of Inequality: How Today's Divided Society Endangers Our Future*. New York: W. W. Norton and Company, 2012.

Sung, Jung Mo. *Desire, Market and Religion*. Reclaiming Liberation Theology. London: SCM Press, 2007.

Surin, Kenneth. "Rewriting the Ontological Script of Liberation: On the Question of Finding a New Kind of Political Subject." In *Theology and the Political: The New Debate*. Edited by Creston Davis, John Milbank, and Slavoj Žižek, 240–66. Durham, NC: Duke University Press, 2005.

Sutton, Matthew Avery. *American Apocalypse: A History of Modern Evangelicalism*. Cambridge, MA: Belknap Press, 2014.

Keeanga-Yamahtta Taylor, *From #BlackLivesMatter to Black Liberation*. Chicago: Haymarket, 2016.

Teichert, Wolfgang, ed. *Müssen Christen Sozialisten sein? Zwischen Glaube und Poltik*. Hamburg: Lutherisches Verlagshaus, 1976.

Thorup, Mikkel. "Pro Bono? On Philanthrocapitalism as Ideological Answer to Inequality." *Ephemera: Theory and Politics in Organization* 13, no. 3 (2013): 555–76.

Thurneysen, Eduard. "Warum nicht Gollwitzer?" *Evangelische Theologie* 22, no. 5 (1962): 271–77.

Tillich, Paul. *The Protestant Era*. Translated by James Luther Adams. Chicago: University of Chicago Press, 1948.

_____. *The Socialist Decision*. Translated by Franklin Sherman. Eugene, OR: Wipf & Stock, 2012.

_____. *Systematic Theology*, 3 volumes. Chicago: University of Chicago Press, 1951–63.

Trotsky, Leon. *The Permanent Revolution and Results and Prospects*. Translated by Brian Pearce. New York: Pathfinder Press, 1969.

van Buren, Paul M. *The Austin Dogmatics: 1957–1958*. Edited by Ellen T. Charry. Eugene, OR: Cascade, 2012.

_____. *The Secular Meaning of the Gospel: Based on an Analysis of Its Language*. New York: Macmillan, 1963.

Vincent, Jean-Marie. "West Germany: The Reactionary Democracy." In *The Socialist Register*. Edited by Ralph Miliband and John Saville, 68–81. New York: Monthly Review Press, 1964.

Wallis, Jim. *America's Original Sin: Racism, White Privilege, and the Bridge to a New America*. Grand Rapids, MI: Brazos Press, 2016.

Weber, Max. *From Max Weber: Essays in Sociology*. Translated by H. H. Gerth and Wright Mills. New York: Routledge, 2009.

Weinrich, Michael. "Gesellschaftliche Herausforderungen der Theologie: Erinnerungen an Helmut Gollwitzer." *Evangelische Theologie* 59, no. 3 (1999): 168–71.

West, Cornel. *Prophesy Deliverance! An Afro-American Revolutionary Christianity*, Anniversary edition. Louisville, KY: Westminster John Knox Press, 2002.

Whitley, Thomas J. "America's Religion Problem." *Marginalia Review of Books* (January 4, 2017). http://marginalia.lareviewofbooks.org/mrblog-americas-religion-problem/.

Wilkes, Andrew. "Doing Political Theology in an Election Season: Howard Thurman on Deception." *Religion Dispatches* (October 3, 2016). http://religiondispatches.org/doing-political-theology-in-an-election-season-howard-thurman-on-deception/.

Wood, Allen W. *The Free Development of Each: Studies on Freedom, Right, and Ethics in Classical German Philosophy*. Oxford: Oxford University Press, 2014.

Wood, Ellen Meiksins. *Democracy against Capitalism: Renewing Historical Materialism*, Reprint edition. Radical Thinkers. New York: Verso, 2016.

_____. *The Origin of Capitalism: A Longer View*. New York: Verso, 2002.

Wright, Erik Olin. *Redesigning Distribution: Basic Income and Stakeholder Grants as Alternative Cornerstones for a More Egalitarian Capitalism*. The Real Utopias Project. New York: Verso, 2006.

Ziegler, Philip G. "Witness to Christ's Dominion: The Political Service of the Church." *Theology* 116, no. 5 (2013): 323–31.

Index of Subjects and Names